T0301395

Government Bond Markets
in the Euro Zone

Government Bond Markets in the Euro Zone

Escuela de Finanzas Aplicadas

Edited by José Manuel Amor

JOHN WILEY & SONS, LTD

Authorised translation from the Spanish language edition published by Analistas Financieros Internacionales.

Published in 2002 by   John Wiley & Sons Ltd,
                              Baffins Lane, Chichester,
                              West Sussex PO19 1UD, England

                              National   01243 779777
                              International (+44) 1243 779777
                              e-mail (for orders and customer service enquiries): cs-books@wiley.co.uk
                              Visit our Home Page on http://www.wiley.co.uk
                                        or http://www.wiley.com

British Library Cataloguing in Publication Data

A catalogue record for this book is available from the British Library

ISBN 978-0-471-49788-2

Contents

List of Currency Abbreviations

ATS	Austrian schilling
BEF	Belgian franc
CAD	Canadian dollar
CHF	Swiss franc
CZK	Czech koruna
DEM	German deutschmark
DKK	Danish krone
EUR	euro
FLM	Finnish Markka
FRF	French franc
GBP	pound sterling
GRD	Greek drachma
ITL	Italian lira
JPY	Japanese yen
LUF	Luxembourg franc
NLG	Dutch florin
USD	United States dollar
ZAR	South African rand

Foreword

Unquestionably, one of the main forces shaping the recent development of financial markets has been the growing trend worldwide towards their liberalisation and integration. The gradual removal of regulatory barriers to the free movement of capital and provision of services, and the application to the financial world of IT and communications advances, have made national borders increasingly a thing of the past.

This is especially true in the heart of the European Union, where the attainment of a genuine Single Financial Market has been one of the fundamental pillars of the community integration process and the advent of the euro a definitive step towards the achievement of fully integrated financial markets.

Turning to the subject that concerns us here, we can say that progress towards a single public debt market in euros has been nothing short of spectacular. Since the start-up of the third stage of EMU, all public debt issues have been conducted in euros, wiping out the old segmentation by national currencies. The resulting greater transparency aids comparison between the domestic markets making up the euro area. At the same time, yield spreads between the securities issued by European Union treasuries have significantly narrowed, thanks to the elimination of exchange-rate risk and the alignment of member-state credit risk, facilitated in turn by the public finance discipline enshrined in the Stability Pact.

In this new setting, competition between issuers is not just about prices, but has extended outwards to the characteristics of debt securities and the operation of national markets. The liquidity, transparency, speed and efficiency of issuance and trading systems, clearing and settlement, regulatory frameworks and so on are more and more highly valued by investors, and consequently by central government issuers.

This changed scenario entails new challenges and opportunities for all the agents operating in financial markets, who must find innovative ways to adapt and advance.

The Spanish Treasury's strategy to address the growing competition brought by the launch of the euro and market globalisation operates simultaneously on several fronts:

- The range of Treasury securities has been widened to take in regular auctions of 30-year *Obligaciones*, covering the longest segment of the curve. Likewise, the Treasury is constantly looking at new debt instruments that may capture investors' interest (for instance, floating-rate or inflation-indexed bonds). In the interim, we are conducting occasional issues of instruments such as callable notes or syndicated loans, tailored to the needs of specific investor groups.

- A series of institutional reforms have been enacted to improve the performance of the Spanish debt market, with particular regard to secondary-market trading. As part of this drive, the market makers' statute has been reformed to reinforce their rights and obligations and allow the entry of non-resident institutions ('remote market makers'). A new category of debt dealer has also been brought into being, with fewer commitments and privileges than the market-maker group. In the blind market, the four interdealer brokers have been merged within a single, electronic trading platform.
- Debt distribution has been perfected not only through the reform of the market-maker statute, opening up a broad sphere of activity to non-resident institutions, but also through the launch of an on-line securities subscription facility. Meanwhile, the Bank of Spain Book-Entry System has signed connection agreements with securities depositories and clearing and settlement systems working out of other European Union countries, which will further the placement of Spanish public debt among non-resident investors.
- The opening of the strips market has widened the range of investor options.
- An exchange programme is under way to withdraw older, illiquid and non-strippable references from the market and replace them with new, strippable lines of guaranteed liquidity.
- Market conventions have been harmonised with those of European partners by adopting the TARGET calendar and amending yield calculation methods.
- The groundwork has been laid for more active, flexible management of the outstanding debt portfolio (through the use of swaps) and treasury operations (allowing sale and purchase transactions in central government debt from the balance of the account held at the Bank of Spain).

The challenge, in short, is to maximise the efficiency of the Spanish debt market and the attractiveness of Treasury securities, while projecting an innovative image as an issuer among participants in the European and global market.

Finally, let me remark on the role to be played by the private sector in the new market environment in complementing and reinforcing public-sector initiative—and, in particular, on the valuable contribution of Analistas Financieros Internacionales in deciding to publish this book, a publication which, by extending our knowledge of national markets within the larger euro setting, not only facilitates the work of participating agents but also advances the cause of market transparency.

If the integration of public debt markets is to be seen, as the Spanish Treasury sees it, not as a threat but as an opportunity, then we must all welcome initiatives like this book which can help to guide the process along.

Gloria Hernández García
Director General of the Treasury and Financial Policy
Spanish Ministry of the Economy

1
The Spanish Government Bond Market

1.1 OVERVIEW OF THE SPANISH PUBLIC DEBT MARKET

1.1.1 Creation of the Book-Entry Market in Public Debt

The creation, in 1987, of the book-entry market in public debt was a key event in the structural change undergone by the Spanish public debt market, now among the most modern and liquid in the euro area alongside its German, French and Italian counterparts. The aim pursued was essentially the replacement of the obsolete bond certificate by a Book-Entry System (BES), as a means to leverage secondary market development and facilitate public-debt marketing to third parties. This, in turn, would allow more efficient management of the high borrowings engendered by the large public deficits accumulated in the 1980s. Since then, the Bank of Spain Book-Entry System has acted as the hub of the market, with the following main functions:

- providing a central register of the securities admitted to trading in the book-entry public debt market
- managing, on behalf of the issuers of eligible securities, the issue, delivery, interest payments, redemption and, in general, all activities relative to the servicing of the securities admitted to market trading
- organising the clearance and settlement of market operations.

The launch of the BES was the first of many changes in the Spanish public debt market, chief among them:

- introduction of the public debt market maker (1991)
- creation of the strips market in public debt (July 1997).

1.1.2 Role of the Treasury in the Spanish Public Debt Market

The role of the Treasury is essentially to meet central government borrowing requirements at the lowest possible cost while maintaining risk within acceptable bounds. Its main objectives are:

1. *Achievement of stable financing flows*, by means of:

   - assured informational transparency via the drawing-up of issuance calendars and communication of the funding strategies to be implemented
   - a stable, publicised issuance schedule with announcement of placement targets for *Bonos del Estado* and *Obligaciones del Estado*, set in collaboration with market makers
   - control of refinancing risk by stepping up medium- and long-term issues
   - smoothing out the maturities curve through exchange policies and the repurchase of outstanding debt.

2. *Reduction of interest costs*, by means of:

- issuance policies targeted on all segments of the curve, to take advantage of funding opportunities as and when they appear
- the repurchase and exchange of debt lines weak in liquidity or with high coupon rates
- interest rate swaps.

3. *Ensuring an adequate level of market liquidity*, by means of:

- a target balance for outstanding issues of approximately 10–15 billion euros, using the technique of line reopening via issue tranches
- exchanging illiquid issues in order to concentrate debt into large-volume benchmarks and thereby boost market liquidity.

4. *Offering investors attractive financial instruments*, in tune with the market and/or tax circumstances prevailing.

1.1.3   Structure of the Outstanding Balance of Government Debt

The structure of the debt position has undergone far-reaching changes since 1987, arising from lower central government borrowing requirements, the policy of lengthening average debt maturity and the need to smooth out the maturities curve to ensure more efficient management of the cost of debt. The result is that, since the start of the 1990s, the balance has been tilting away from short-term assets (*Letras* and Commercial Paper, the latter up to 1993) towards medium- and long-term instruments (*Bonos* and *Obligaciones*). This change was facilitated not only by the steady reduction in the state deficit, but also by the growing depth, breadth and liquidity of the public debt market and nominal and real convergence in interest rates with Spain's euro-zone partners.

At present, the short- versus medium- and long-term split in euro-denominated domestic debt outstanding (previously favourable to money-market assets) stands at 80% for *Bonos* and *Obligaciones* against 20% for *Letras*. And the shift, as shown in Figure 1.1, has intensified over recent years.

Just as short-term assets have reduced their share of the total outstanding, so foreign-currency-denominated issues have receded as a proportion of the government debt portfolio. These assets now make up between 3% and 4% of tradeable debt outstanding (over 11% in 1998, including eurocurrency issues). There is also a stock of eurocurrency-denominated debt and international issues in euros. Finally, outstanding debt as at March 2000 breaks down into 71% for medium- and long-term domestic debt in euros against 17% for *Letras* and 3%–4% for foreign-currency issues (see Figure 1.2).

Longer maturities have also provided a more leisurely redemptions calendar. Specifically, the average life of tradeable government debt in euros is presently 5.35 years, rather shorter than the average of other euro-zone countries.

In conclusion, it is worth noting that the policy of reopening issue lines in tranches targeting an outstanding balance of around 12 billion euros (achieved to date in three debt series) and the exchange operations conducted between 1997 and 1999 (previous exchanges were small-scale only) have delivered a public debt structure that is fairly concentrated in a small number of issues of relatively large size. In fact, the average outstanding amount of medium- and long-term debt in euros stands upwards of 7.30 billion

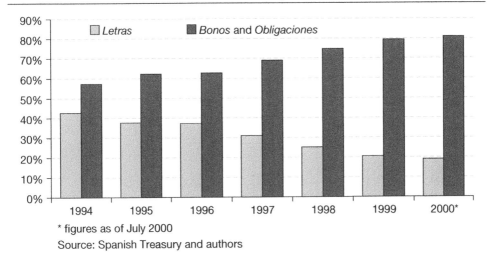

* figures as of July 2000
Source: Spanish Treasury and authors

Figure 1.1   Outstanding balance of Spanish tradeable domestic debt in euros

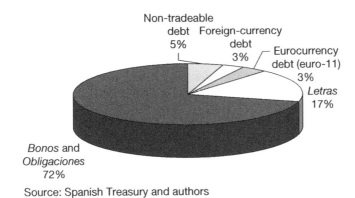

Source: Spanish Treasury and authors

Figure 1.2   Spanish public debt as of July 2000 (in millions of euros)

euros per reference, while 49% of the total in issue, 209.30 billion euros as of 29 March 2000, is bunched in 10 bonds with outstanding amounts exceeding 10 billion euros.

1.2   ASSETS ISSUED BY THE SPANISH TREASURY

1.2.1   *Letras del Tesoro*

Letras del Tesoro are short-term instruments denominated in euros, issued at a discount and represented by entries in the Bank of Spain Book-Entry System. The issuer undertakes to make a single payment on the maturity date, at nominal or reimbursement value, the 'discount' comprising the difference between the latter amount and the price paid by the investor. At the time of writing, the Treasury issues 6-, 12- and 18-month *Letras* via the 'Spanish' auction system, every four weeks in the case of 6-month *Letras* and fortnightly in the case of 12- and 18-month *Letras*.

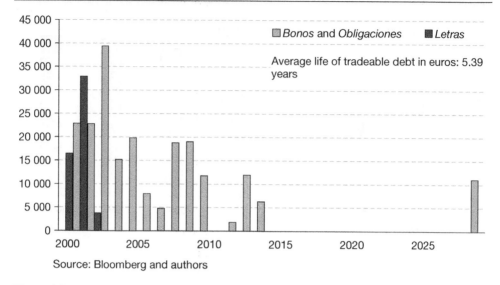

Source: Bloomberg and authors

Figure 1.3 Maturities curve as of July 2000 (domestic issues, in millions of euros)

The price paid at auction, in percentage terms, is calculated according to the following formulae:

For *Letras* maturing in under one calendar year (365 days):

$$PA = \frac{1.000}{\left(1 + R\frac{d}{360}\right)}$$

And for longer-dated *Letras*, the compound capitalisation results from the transformation of the above equation, as follows:

$$PA = \frac{1.000}{(1 + R)^{\frac{d}{360}}}$$

In both cases

PA = acquisition price, to three decimal places
1.000 = minimum or nominal value of bids, in euros
d = days to maturity, on a Current basis
R = gross yield or IRR

The gross yield an investor can obtain from purchasing a *Letra del Tesoro* (at issue or in the secondary market) is calculated as follows:

For *Letras* maturing in less than one calendar year:

$$R = \frac{1.000 - PA}{PA} \times \frac{360}{d} \times 100$$

And for longer maturities, the compound capitalisation results from the transformation of the above equation, as follows:

$$R = \left[\left[\frac{1.000}{PA} \right]^{\frac{360}{d}} - 1 \right] \times 100$$

In both cases

PA = acquisition price (to three decimal places)
d = days to maturity, on a Current basis
R = gross yield or IRR

1.2.2 *Bonos del Estado* and *Obligaciones del Estado*

These are assets denominated in euros represented by entries in the Bank of Spain Book-Entry System, with maturities longer than two years. These instruments pay annual coupons and are only redeemable on maturity (bullet) at their nominal value. The annually payable coupon represents the 'nominal' interest rate of the *Bono* or *Obligación*. In keeping with its policy of operating across the whole debt curve, the Spanish Treasury regularly issues 3- and 5-year *Bonos* and 10-, 15- and 30-year *Obligaciones* via the 'Spanish' auction system.

Persuaded of the positive correspondence between the size of *Bono* and *Obligación* lines and their secondary-market liquidity, the Treasury has opted for a tranche system of issuance, such that the same line or reference is auctioned on at least three occasions. The aim here is to secure an outstanding balance per *Bono* and *Obligación* reference ranging from 10 to 15 billion euros. However, in March 2000 only three series had an outstanding balance of 12 billion euros or more.

The price paid at auction is determined by a formula published in the Official State Gazette (*Boletín Oficial del Estado*, BOE) at the start of each year. The 2000 formula is as follows:

$$PA = (1+R)^{\frac{-d}{base}} \left[\frac{\frac{1}{n} \times I \times \left[1 - (1+R)^{\frac{-Q}{n}} \right]}{(1+R)^{\frac{1}{n}} - 1} + 100\,(1+R)^{\frac{-Q}{n}} \right]$$

where

PA = acquisition price to three decimal places
n = number of coupons payable in a year (1 for annual coupons, 2 for biannual coupons, etc.)
I = annual interest rate of the issue or coupon
R = yield or IRR
Q = total number of coupons payable to maturity
d = number of days, as of the issue date, by which the term of the first coupon payable exceeds ($d > 0$) or falls short of ($d < 0$) its entire accrual period
Base = 365, except when the term of the first coupon payable is shorter than its entire accrual period and the latter is 366 days, or (when the payment and delivery date of securities precedes the date marking the start of accrual) if the number of days between this start date and the date obtained by subtracting one coupon term from it comes out at 366 days. In both these cases, this last number (366) will be the value factored in.

An almost perfect approximation to the price/yield of *Bonos del Estado* and *Obligaciones del Estado* can nonetheless be obtained by using another formula:

$$PA = VR \times (1 + R)^{-\frac{t}{365}} + \sum_{j=1}^{n} C_j \times (1 + R)^{-\frac{t^j}{365}}$$

where

PA = (quoted price + elapsed coupon) is the acquisition price, at auction or in the secondary market, with accrued interest stated on a Current/Current basis

n = number of coupons from the calculation date to the operation's maturity

t = days elapsing from the acquisition date to the date of sale or redemption

C_j = gross amount of each coupon

t^j = days between the value date and maturity of each coupon

VR = reimbursement or redemption value (at par)

The accrued interest *(Cc)* is calculated as follows:

$$Cc = \frac{\text{gross amount of each coupon} \times \text{no. of days since last payment of coupon}}{\text{no. of days of coupon term}}$$

1.3   THE PRIMARY MARKET

1.3.1   Treasury Issuance Procedures

The Spanish Treasury may issue *Letras del Tesoro*, *Bonos del Estado* and *Obligaciones del Estado* using three procedures or instruments:

- *The 'Spanish' or 'modified Dutch' auction*, the method used as standard for the issue of domestic public debt securities denominated in euros. Competitive bidding may be followed by a second, non-competitive round solely in the case of *Bonos* and *Obligaciones*, and provided certain pre-set conditions are met. Only market-maker entities may participate in this second stage.
- *Public offer*, in which the Treasury communicates the issue conditions and receives buy orders from participants (similar to the tap issue format used by the Dutch DSTA).
- *Competitive procedures involving a number of authorised entities*. This is where issue syndication or underwriting comes in, a method used successfully in 1999, and more frequently in 2000, by the Treasury Departments of Austria, Portugal, Finland and Belgium for the first-tranche issues of their new 'on-the-run' series. Participating entities are mandated by the Treasury in the corresponding contracts. The Spanish Treasury is already following this procedure on a regular basis for its international and foreign-currency issues, and for its open EMTN facilities.

Letras, *Bonos* and *Obligaciones* are issued at auctions conducted along 'Spanish' or 'modified Dutch' lines—so termed because they combine specific aspects of the single-price 'Dutch' technique with the competitive 'American' or 'multi-price' format. Though procedures for *Letras* and *Bonos* are practically identical, certain differences do exist (chiefly the announcement of the volumes to be issued and the holding of second, non-competitive rounds restricted to market makers, which only apply in the case of *Bonos* and *Obligaciones*).

1.3.2 Auctions of *Letras del Tesoro, Bonos* and *Obligaciones del Estado*

Publication of Annual Auction Calendars

The Treasury publishes a guidance calendar in the *Boletín Oficial del Estado* (BOE) in the first month of each year, setting out the auction dates for each instrument issued on a regular basis (*Letras, Bonos* and *Obligaciones*). The 2000 calendar was as follows:

- Auctions of 12- and 18-month *Letras* every second Wednesday (or the day before if Wednesday is a public holiday). Six-month *Letras* auctions every fourth Wednesday (or the day before in the case of public holidays).
- Auctions of *Bonos* and *Obligaciones* once a month, on the first working Wednesday or Thursday. Five-year *Bonos* are auctioned on the first Wednesday of each month and 15- and 30-year *Obligaciones* on an alternating basis (one month 5-year *Bonos* and 15-year *Obligaciones*, the next month 5-year *Bonos* and 30-year *Obligaciones*). Auctions of 3-year *Bonos* and 10-year *Obligaciones* take place on the first Thursday of each month.

Further details of the issuance calendar for 2000 are provided in the annexe to this chapter.

Announcement of Placement Targets and Maximum Amounts in Bono *and* Obligación *Auctions*

Two working days prior to the first monthly auction of *Bonos* and *Obligaciones* (T − 2) or three working days prior to the second (T − 3), the Treasury announces its overall placement targets for the securities to be issued in the BOE and other media (Reuters 'TESORO'; Bloomberg 'BOS').

Targets are set in consultation with market makers, thereby helping to stabilise government funding flows, and refer to both the volumes sought and the maximum to be issued in each first auction round. The maximum amount announced is binding, while targeted volume is for guidance purposes only. The Treasury is also obliged, as a general rule, to adhere to a minimum issue volume of 180 million euros for 3- and 5-year *Bonos* and 90 million euros in the case of 10-, 15- and 30-year *Obligaciones*.

Presentation of Bids

Any resident individual or legal entity may bid for and subscribe Treasury securities (*Letras, Bonos* and *Obligaciones*) simply by submitting offers at a Bank of Spain branch. Bids, once made, are regarded as binding and failure to pay in full on the issue date will give rise to liability or loss of the compulsory deposit required as a guarantee, amounting to 2% of the face value bid for. That said, the procedures for bid presentation are not the same for all participants.

- Investors who are not account holders in the Book-Entry System must present their bids through one of three channels:
  1. Directly at any Bank of Spain branch, contingent on their opening of a direct account in the Book-Entry System. The holders of such direct accounts may submit their bids directly up to 13.00 (local time) on the date specified for presentation of bids, i.e. two working days before the auction is resolved (T − 2).
  2. Through a management institution, which will subsequently submit all its bids en bloc (whether on its own or third parties' behalf).

3. Through a placement agency authorised by the General Directorate of the Treasury and Financial Policy (GDTFP).

- Management institutions and account holders in the Book-Entry System must notify their bids to the Bank of Spain between 8.30 and 10.00 (local time) on the auction date. Such notification may be given via their computer terminal connection with the Bank of Spain Settlement Service (BSSS) or called in via the Money Market Telephone Service (MMTS).
- In recognition of their special status, the deadline for market-maker bid presentation is extended by 30 minutes over that set for management institutions and account holders in the Book-Entry System. In other words, they can submit bids up to 10.30 (*local time*) on the auction date (T − 0).

Formulation of Bids

The bids presented by investors participating in *Letra, Bono* and *Obligación* competitive auctions can be of two types:

- Competitive bids: bidders indicate the price and volume of each of their bids. Competitive bids not specifying a price will be considered null and void. Bid prices must be expressed as a percentage of nominal value,

  (a) to three decimal places in the case of *Letras del Tesoro* (the last being 0 or 5)
  (b) to two decimal places in the case of *Bonos del Estado* (the last point from 0 to 9 inclusive)
  (c) to two decimal places in the case of *Obligaciones del Estado* (the last being 0 or 5).

- Non-competitive bids: bidders only specify the quantity sought and thus implicitly accept the weighted average price resulting from the auction. The amount bid in such cases may not exceed 200 000 euros per bidder. This type of bid is not accepted in 6-month *Letra* auctions.

Minimum and Maximum Amounts of Bids for Letras, Bonos *and* Obligaciones del Estado

- Six-month *Letras* are subject to competitive bidding only. The minimum amount allowable is 500 000 euros and thereafter multiples of 100 000 euros.
- In 12- and 18-month *Letra* auctions, both competitive and non-competitive bids must be for a minimum of 1000 euros, then multiples of the same.
- In *Bono* and *Obligación* auctions, competitive bids start at a 5000 euro minimum, then build up in multiples of 1000 euros. Non-competitive bids start at 1000 euros, followed by multiples of the same.
- Non-competitive bids, as a rule, may not exceed an overall 200 000 euros per bidder in auctions of 12- and 18-month *Letras* and *Bonos* and *Obligaciones del Estado*.

Auction Resolution

Once all bids are in, competitive or non-competitive, the Treasury moves to the auction itself. The procedure followed is a mixture of the 'Dutch' or uniform-price system and the 'American' or multiple-price system:

- First, the Treasury sorts all the competitive bids submitted—those specifying price and volume—in descending order of price. Then, the Director General of the Treasury and Financial Policy, on the basis of the proposal of a four-member committee (two representing the Bank of Spain and two from the General Directorate of the Treasury and Financial Policy), decides the nominal amount to be issued.
- The next step is to determine the minimum or stop-out price on which the marginal rate of the auction will be calculated. This price is stated as a percentage of nominal value to three decimal places.
- All non-competitive bids (not specifying price) and competitive bids made at the minimum (stop-out) price or higher are accepted. The possibility is also envisaged of a pro rata allocation of bids submitted at the stop-out price.
- The weighted average price for the auction is next worked out on the basis of the competitive bids accepted. Like the stop-out price, this average is stated as a percentage of nominal value to three decimal places.
- Allocation to successful bidders is carried out as follows: (i) bids made at the stop-out price are allotted at that price; (ii) bids falling between the stop-out price and the weighted average (to three decimal places) are allotted at the price bid; (iii) bids higher than the weighted average price (to three decimal places) and non-competitive bids all pay the weighted average price (derived from the total amount of all competitive bids accepted).

Source: Ezquiaga and Ferrero (1999) and authors

Figure 1.4 Price calculation in the 'Spanish' (modified 'Dutch') auction system

Second Rounds of Bono *and* Obligación *Auctions*

Since 1991, it has been possible for Central Government Debt auctions to go to a second round, restricted solely to market makers in public debt. After a series of minor modifications, the procedure for these auctions stands as follows.

After *Bonos* and *Obligaciones* bids have been resolved at auction (approximately 11.15 (local time) on the auction date, T − 0) and before 12.00 on the second working day ensuing (T + 2), a second round is held. The Treasury may place up to 20% of the nominal amount of each reference allotted in the auction. This 20% may at times be exceeded pursuant to the incentive schemes devised for market makers (see section 1.8 on market makers).

Market-maker bids need not specify a price, since allocation is at the weighted average price of the first, competitive round. Only a given nominal amount is placed per reference, so the maximum market makers can obtain is pro rata with their respective percentage allocations at the previous two auctions. Thus, market makers participating in the second round can only bid up to a predetermined amount.

Publication of Auction and Second-Round Results

The Treasury and the Bank of Spain publish the results of *Letra*, *Bono* and *Obligación* auctions in various media as of 11.15 local time:

- Reuters: TESORO, KSPT, KSPU, BANCN, BCNAO, BANCS and BANCT
- Bloomberg: BOS
- Dow Jones Telerate: page 38 494, pages 20 656–20 657 and 20 660–20 661
- Bridge Information Systems: page 3275.

Results are also printed in the BOE in the form of a Resolution of the General Directorate of the Treasury and Financial Policy.

Payment and Delivery of Letras, Bonos *and* Obligaciones

The payment date for the nominal amounts allotted in *Letra*, *Bono* and *Obligación* auctions depends, as do bid submission procedures, on the status of the subscriber.

- *Investors who are not account holders in the Book-Entry System and entered their bids via a direct account at the Bank of Spain*: this group must credit the account held by the Treasury at the central bank by the difference between the subscription price and the deposit made on account (2% of the nominal amount bid for). Payment will be made on the first working day after the auction resolution date (T + 1) in the case of *Letras*, and two working days after (T + 2) in the case of *Bonos* and *Obligaciones*.
- *Investors who are not account holders in the Book-Entry System and entered their bids through a management institution*: management institutions must credit the amount of subscriptions made for third parties in the Treasury's account. Payment will be two working days after auction resolution (T + 2) for *Letras*, and three days after (T + 3) for *Bonos* and *Obligaciones*.
- *Account holders in the Book-Entry System*: account holders must pay the Treasury for subscriptions made both on their own behalf and on behalf of third parties. Payment will be made two working days after auction resolution (T + 2) for *Letras* and three days after (T + 3) for *Bonos* and *Obligaciones*.

The issue and distribution of the allotted securities takes place two working days after auction resolution in the case of *Letras del Tesoro* (T + 2), and three days after in the case of *Bonos* and *Obligaciones del Estado* (T + 3).

1.3.3 Issuance Characteristics: *Letras*, *Bonos*, and *Obligaciones*

Letras del Tesoro

- *Issue procedure*: 'Spanish' or 'modified Dutch' auction.
- *Auction participants*: any individual or legal entity, resident or otherwise. Investors other than account holders in the Book-Entry System can enter their bids through a

Table 1.1 Example of 6-, 12- and 18-month *Letra* issuance (in millions of euros)

Issue	6-m 6/10/2000	12-m 11/4/2001	18-m 12/10/2001
Nominal bid	1 136	1 382	5 311
Nominal allotted	491	313	1 341
Stop-out price	98 065	95 925	93 650
Marginal interest rate	3.902%	4.224%	4.420%
Average price	98 070	95 939	93 658
Average interest	3.892%	4.209%	4.414%
Allotted at stop-out	351	84	922
First price rejected	98 060	95 920	93 645
Volume at this price	71	75	16
Amount of non-competitive bids	—	86	28

Source: authors

management institution or through a placement agency duly authorised by the General Directorate of the Treasury and Financial Policy.

- *Presentation of bids*: by management institutions and account holders in the Book-Entry System between 8.30 and 10.00 (local time) on the date of the auction (T − 0), by telephone through the MMTS or electronically via the BSSS. Market makers enjoy a half-hour extension to 10.30 on the same day (T − 0). Individuals approaching the Bank of Spain directly must lodge their bids two days (T − 2) beforehand, specifying the management institution which will act as depository of the securities.
- *Minimum amount*: 1000 euros.
- *Competitive bids*: to be stated as a percentage of nominal to three decimal places ending 0 or 5.
- *Minimum amount of competitive bids*: 1000 euros in 12- and 18-month *Letra* auctions, 500 000 euros in 6-month *Letra* auctions.
- *Subsequent bids*: in multiples of 1000 euros in the case of 12- and 18-month *Letras*, and multiples of 100 000 euros in the case of 6-month *Letras*.
- *Minimum amount of non-competitive bids*: 1000 euros, and multiples of the same thereafter in the case of 12- and 18-month *Letras*. Non-competitive bids are not accepted at 6-month Letra auctions.
- *Maximum amount of non-competitive bids*: 200 000 euros in 12- and 18-month *Letra* auctions.
- *Auction results*: published on the auction date as of 11.15 (local time) in the Treasury and Bank of Spain pages of Reuters, Bloomberg, Dow Jones Telerate and Bridge Information Systems.
- *Interest rate basis*: Current/360

Bonos *and* Obligaciones del Estado

- *Issue procedure*: 'Spanish' or 'modified Dutch' auction. The Treasury uses the tranche-issue format to secure the minimum volume needed to guarantee liquidity.
- *Auction participants*: any individual or legal entity, resident or non-resident. Investors other than account holders in the Book-Entry System can enter their bids through a management institution or through a placement agency duly authorised by the General Directorate of the Treasury and Financial Policy.

Table 1.2   Example of 5-year *Bono* and 15-year *Obligación* issues (1/04/00, in millions of euros)

Issue	B-4.95% 2005	O-4.75% 2014
Nominal bid	1 586	718
Nominal allotted	912	381
Stop-out price	97 970	95 400
Marginal interest rate	5.076%	5.563%
Average price	98 015	95 439
Average interest	5.066%	5.559%
Allotted at stop-out	65	177
First price rejected	97 960	95 350
Volume at this price	113	75
Amount of non-competitive bids	14	2

Source: authors

- *Presentation of bids*: Management institutions and account holders in the Book-Entry System, between 8.30 and 10.00 (local time) on the auction date (T − 0) by telephone via MMTS or electronically via the BSSS. Market makers have a half-hour extension to 10.30 on the same day (T − 0). Individuals approaching the Bank of Spain directly must enter their bids two days (T − 2) beforehand, specifying the management institution which will act as depository of their securities.
- *Competitive bids*: to be stated as a percentage of nominal to two decimal places, ending 0–9 in the case of *Bonos del Estado* and 0 or 5 in the case of *Obligaciones del Estado*.
- *Minimum amount of competitive bids*: 5000 euros.
- *Subsequent bids*: multiples of 1000 euros.
- *Minimum amount of non-competitive bids*: 1000 euros, and multiples of the same thereafter.
- *Maximum amount of non-competitive bids*: 200 000 euros.
- *Auction results*: published on the auction date as of 11.15 (local time) in the Treasury and Bank of Spain pages of Reuters, Bloomberg, Dow Jones Telerate and Bridge Information Systems.
- *Interest rate basis*: Current/Current.

1.3.4   Government Debt Exchanges

Exchange operations are a discretionary weapon at the Treasury's disposal for eliminating or reducing the outstanding balance of certain medium- and long-term debt references, by exchanging them for other references (usually on-the-run).

The purpose of debt exchanges is, firstly, to boost market liquidity by raising the outstanding amount of certain issues and to reduce or withdraw insufficiently liquid references; and, secondly, to smooth out the government debt maturities curve as an aid to efficient portfolio management.

Their resolution resembles that of a 'Spanish auction', except that the Treasury releases in advance the price at which it is prepared to issue the new *Bono* or *Obligación*. The remaining steps are exactly as described for ordinary auctions.

Though the Treasury has been using exchanges since 1993, it was not until 1997, 1998 and, most notably, 1999 that the ambitious programme deployed found sufficient echo with investor groups.

1.4 INSTITUTIONAL STRUCTURE OF THE PUBLIC DEBT BOOK-ENTRY MARKET

1.4.1 Participants in the Public Debt Book-Entry Market: an Overview

The Treasury

The functions of the Treasury are as described in section 1.1 of this chapter.

The Bank of Spain

The Bank of Spain is a public corporation with its own legal personality and full powers under public and private law. Since 1994, it has also been empowered to act independently of the government. The Bank of Spain is the governing body of the Public Debt Book-Entry Market and performs the following functions in this regard:

- acting as financial agent for public debt
- provision of public debt treasury services to the Treasury
- management of the Book-Entry System
- supervision of operation and transparency of the public debt market
- laying down the rules governing transactions between members and, together with the Treasury, determining the specific regulations bearing on such entities while overseeing and evaluating their activity
- as of 1990, also functioning as a management institution for resident individuals and legal entities desirous of maintaining their debt holdings in a securities account at the Bank of Spain—the so-called direct accounts.

Account Holders in the Book-Entry System

Account holders operating on their own behalf (henceforth, account holders) are financial institutions authorised to acquire and hold book-entry registered public debt in proprietary accounts in the Book-Entry System. To be eligible for account-holder status, an institution must have shareholders' equity of at least 200 million pesetas and belong to one of the following categories:

- banks
- savings banks
- credit co-operatives
- securities broker–dealers
- finance corporations
- mortgage market regulation funds
- mutual guarantee companies
- reinsurance companies
- securities investment and money-market funds and companies
- insurance companies
- credit institution deposit guarantee funds
- international financial organisations of which Spain is a member
- central banks of countries belonging to the International Monetary Fund.

Since February 1999, eligibility for account-holder status has been extended to non-resident credit institutions and investment services firms.

Other account holders are the Bank of Spain, the Instituto de Crédito Oficial and the Consorcio de Compensación de Seguros.

Management Institutions

Management institutions manage the accounts of those not authorised to operate directly through the Book-Entry System. For this purpose, they maintain a global account in the Book-Entry System which at all times exactly covers the said accounts, known as third-party accounts. Management institutions, with the exception of agency brokers, may also be account holders under their own names in the Book-Entry System. This last status is compulsory when managers themselves wish to stand as counterparty to their customers. Agency brokers, conversely, can only acquire or hold Book-Entry Public Debt on their own behalf through another management institution. The following institutions are eligible for manager status:

- securities broker–dealers and agency brokers
- banks and savings banks, including the Instituto de Crédito Oficial (ICO) and the Confederación Española de Cajas de Ahorros (CECA)
- credit co-operatives.

The functions of management institutions with regard to Book-Entry Public Debt are essentially those of registration, clearance and settlement, and the safekeeping and administration of securities.

Among their registral functions, management institutions must keep records of their balances with third parties permanently updated, specifying holder identity, issue data, nominal balances, purchase terms, legal status and, where appropriate, resale commitments.

As part of their administrative functions, management institutions undertake to notify the Book-Entry System on a daily basis of the global balance held for third parties and to furnish a weekly list of all operations conducted.

There are two types of management institution:

- *Full-capacity management institutions*: authorised to perform all types of operations with their principals, and also account holders under their own name in the Book-Entry System. They are required to have a minimum capital of 750 million pesetas and run a minimum customer balance of 20 billion.
- *Restricted-capacity management institutions*: empowered to stand as counterparty to their clients in spot transactions only. Those without accounts in their own name in the Book-Entry System may transact with third parties on a commission basis only. They must also hold a minimum customer balance of 1 billion pesetas.

Market Makers

Market makers are a select group of financial institutions with special rights and obligations in the primary and secondary markets. Their essential function is to boost the liquidity of the secondary market in Book-Entry Public Debt and to work alongside the General Directorate of the Treasury and Financial Policy in moving government debt securities both within and outside Spain. The pivotal role of these institutions in the Public Debt Book-Entry Market is dealt with in the section on market makers (1.8).

Public Debt Dealers

The status of Kingdom of Spain Public Debt Dealer Institutions (henceforth, dealers) is accorded to book-entry market members meeting certain requirements and accepting certain commitments.

The requirements are as follows:

1. They must have the status of account holder in the Bank of Spain Book-Entry System.
2. They must comply with the technical requirements laid down by the SENAF platform, INFOMEDAS. In particular, they must meet at least one of the following conditions:

   - hold an issuer credit rating equal to or higher than A1, A+ or equivalent, granted by an international ratings agency
   - have shareholders' equity of at least 100 billion euros
   - lodge a 10-billion euro guarantee with the Bank of Spain to cover SENAF platform activities.

Dealers' privileges are as listed below:

1. Dealer experience is a prerequisite for any future market maker, and ranks high among the entry requirements set by the General Directorate of the Treasury and Financial Policy.
2. The General Directorate also privileges dealer status when selecting counterparties for its own operations, such as financial swaps or foreign-currency issues.

Dealers also make the following undertakings or commitments with respect to the secondary market:

1. In order to conserve the status of Kingdom of Spain Debt Dealer, they must have at least a 2% share of total monthly turnover on the INFOMEDAS platform, defined as the sum of spot sale or purchase transactions in *Bonos* and *Obligaciones*. The above calculation may also factor in *Bono* and *Obligación* transactions on other electronic platforms specified by the General Directorate of the Treasury and Financial Policy.
2. They must quote the three references chosen as benchmarks by the General Directorate of the Treasury and Financial Policy at its monthly meetings with market makers on the INFOMEDAS screen over at least 60% of the market session on official trading days, under the following conditions:

Term	Maximum bid/ask spread (bp)	Minimum amount (million euros)
3 years	4	10
5 years	5	10
10 years	7	10

3. They must furnish such information as the General Directorate of the Treasury and Financial Policy may require on the public debt market in general and the dealer's trading activity in particular.
4. Through their interventions, they must contribute to the efficient functioning of the market, and respect all the stipulated trading conditions (in particular, the Chinese wall established between the electronic system and third-party trading).

However, the General Directorate of the Treasury and Financial Policy may relieve dealers of any of these obligations in exceptional market circumstances. To do so, it will need to receive a sufficiently well grounded request from at least three dealers.

Public Debt Interdealer Brokers (the Medas Network)

Interdealer brokers are barred from holding their own positions in public debt. Their role is to match the operations of dealer institutions, posting the best outright prices and closing positions (i.e. a purely brokerage role). The selection and continuance of interdealer brokers are subject to a series of conditions laid down by the Bank of Spain, which oversees their activities.

Four interdealer brokers currently operate in the Spanish market: Gesmosa SA, CIMD SA, Capital Market Interdealer Broker SA and ALL Trading SA.

Over and above traditional telephone brokerage services, these four companies also manage the so-called blind market in public debt (described in detail in section 1.5 on the secondary market in public debt). This works as follows: brokers post debt prices on screens without knowing the identity of the counterparty. Participants can then enter their prices via a broker, or trade against the prices displayed on screen, again via a broker.

In a bid to improve the efficiency of the system, the four brokers have formed a company, INFOMEDAS, to manage a single screen—as opposed to four screens previously—displaying the best prices available for Spanish public debt. Screen information is furnished by market participants through the four broker firms, who act independently to guarantee market competition.

1.4.2 Reform of Trading Parameters: Market Members

New regulations on the Public Debt Book-Entry market now awaiting approval will bring about major changes in the Spanish market's membership structure. The intention, essentially, is to separate the trading side from the settlement side in order to better address the specifics of each.

In the trading sphere, the reform of the Public Debt Book-Entry Market will wipe out institutional distinctions between participating entities. Henceforth, their capacity to operate in the market will depend not on the category assigned them by the market but on their own articles of association, specifying the business activities each may engage in. This reform will create a new category, to be known as market members.

Market members will be those entities empowered to purchase and sell securities in the Public Debt Book-Entry Market, whether on their own or others' account, under the terms laid down in their respective by-laws. Market-member status may be accorded to any entity within the following groups which meets the conditions set:

- securities broker–dealers and agency brokers
- Spanish credit institutions, excepting finance corporations
- credit institutions authorised to operate in another European Union member state
- investment services firms authorised to operate in another European Union member state
- credit institutions and investment services firms authorised to operate in a non-EU member state
- the European Central Bank and the central banks of other EU member states

- other entities whose fixed-income securities may be admitted to trading in the Public Debt Market, provided their articles of association allow membership status.

1.5 THE SECONDARY MARKET

1.5.1 Trading Systems

Secondary-market trading is conducted through various systems (the first two being reserved exclusively for market members):

- *First-tier trading or the 'blind market'*: conducted via intermediaries or blind brokers (Public Debt Interdealer Brokers) and restricted solely to Public Debt Dealers. Trading is performed electronically without counterparty disclosure (hence the name 'blind' market). This is the core of the public debt market, in which participating agents undertake to quote bid and ask prices at only a narrow spread (around 5 basis points in the case of the most heavily traded issues) and thus create sufficient liquidity for the rest of the market. Minimum transaction size is 5 million euros. Trades in this tier are to maturity only, whether in spot or forward transactions. Repo transactions are not permitted. Profits and losses are settled daily by marking to market and the corresponding adjustments made on transaction expiry.
- *Bilateral trading or the second-tier system*: in which participants trade directly or through a broker. This segment channels all remaining trades between account holders. Support is provided by the Bank of Spain Settlement Service (BSSS). All types of operations can be performed, including transactions to maturity (spot or forward) and repos. Operations may be contracted directly or through a broker. In the latter case, the broker matches the transaction and notifies each party of its counterparty—which is known in this case, unlike in the first-tier or blind market. Both parties then inform the BSSS of the terms of the transaction for its subsequent clearance and settlement.
- *Third trading segment*: comprising transactions between management institutions and their clients.
- *EuroMTS*: the launch of the euro and the growing similarity of the public debt instruments traded in European markets, allied with the development of electronic platforms, have ushered in a new trading segment in Spanish government debt securities. The creation of the private electronic trading platform EuroMTS—which grew out of Italy's MTS and its later Dutch, Spanish and Belgian subsidiaries—marks the advent of an interconnected electronic market for the exclusive use of the private financial institutions which now channel around 30% of total turnover in European public debt securities.

1.5.2 Types of Transaction

Book-entry market operations break down into two large groups: simple sale–purchase transactions, spot or forward, and double or repo transactions. In the second group ordinary repos can also be distinguished from blocked or 'Spanish' repos.

- *Simple spot transactions*: settlement takes place within the five working days following the contract date.
- *Simple forward transactions*: settlement takes place after the fifth working day following the transaction. Usually, this date coincides with the expiry date of standard futures contracts (the third Wednesday in March, June, September and December). The terms of

transactions must be notified to the Bank of Spain and may not be modified thereafter. In recent years, this kind of transaction has waned in importance compared to futures trading, coinciding with the development of the MEFF Renta Fija futures market. This is chiefly because the Spanish official futures market provides a more appropriate setting for the standardisation and counterparty security that are such vital factors in operations of this kind, which imply a significant credit risk.

This category of operations includes a type of transaction that has a special and important tie-in with the dissemination of Treasury security issues. These are transactions conducted in the 'grey' or 'when issued' market. In this market, trading in Treasury securities generally begins two working weeks before the corresponding auction date—as of the moment the main characteristics of the issue are announced or confirmed. 'Grey market' trading can be via the 'blind' network or the second-tier system.

In double transactions (blocked and ordinary repos), contracting parties simultaneously agree two simple transactions, a buy and a sell: one spot and the second forward, or both forward. The buyer in the first transaction will be the seller in the second and vice versa. These are firm transactions, with the sale and repurchase price previously agreed in the case of fixed-date operations, and the sale price and associated yield in the case of sight transactions. This repo arrangement allows the holder of the assets to collect coupon payments as they mature. Double transactions can be divided into:

- *Ordinary repos*: the buyer can transact freely with the securities acquired, regardless of the return date contracted, since it is not the same asset that must be surrendered, but only a similar one.
- *Blocked repos*: these differ from ordinary repos in that the securities cannot be transacted freely and, therefore, repo transactions can only take place up to the date set for their return.

The last type of operation covered here is the stripping and reconstitution of *Bonos* and *Obligaciones del Estado*. Strip transactions involve the *Bonos* and *Obligaciones* designated as 'strippable'. Stripping occurs when a strippable bond is withdrawn from the Book-Entry System and replaced by new securities with an implicit yield, arising from the cash flow generated by its coupons and principal (SC or stripped coupon and SP or stripped principal, sharing all the features of a zero-coupon bond). Reconstitution is the same operation in reverse, such that all the SCs and SPs representing the cash flows of a strippable asset are withdrawn from the Book-Entry System and replaced in turn by the bond itself.

1.5.3   The Strips Market in Government Debt

The strips market in Book-Entry Debt, specifically *Bonos* and *Obligaciones del Estado*, was formally launched in 1997, and the first strippable securities were issued by the Treasury in July of the same year. However, stripping as such, and the trading of the resulting strips, did not get under way until January 1998.

The stripping and reconstitution of strippable bonds is the exclusive province of market makers, who must also make certain undertakings, subject to annual review. Public debt market members who are not market makers and agents other than market members can only acquire strips by buying them from market makers. By the same token, they can only replace stripped securities with strippable bonds by selling the former and buying the latter, and may under no circumstances reconstitute.

The stripping and reconstitution orders processed by market makers must involve a minimum nominal amount of 500 000 euros, with any additional sums in multiples of 100 000 euros.

Both stripping and reconstitution activity and the outstanding balance of stripped public debt have expanded apace since the start of trading in January 1998. Specifically, the outstanding amount of stripped debt exceeded 17.5 billion euros in March 2000, more than 16% of total strippable debt.

1.5.4   The Public Debt Derivatives Markets

The first derivatives market in Spain, OM Ibérica, came into being in 1989, then three years later made way for MEFF Renta Fija, the official market for public debt futures and options. The Barcelona-based market channels the trading, clearing and settlement of all futures and options contracts on Treasury securities. MEFF is an electronic market in which members feed buy and sell orders into a central processing unit which stores, matches and executes them. In 1999, the fixed- and variable-income wings MEFF Renta Fija and MEFF Renta Variable merged into MEFF Holding, which now centralises the trading, clearance and settlement of all futures and options contracts on fixed-income and equity assets.

Members of the public debt derivative markets belong to one of the following categories:

- *settling members*: empowered to trade and settle on their own behalf as well as on behalf of clients and other members
- *settling and custodian members*: as above, but acting also as depository or custodian of margin posted in respect of market transactions
- *non-settling members*: authorised to trade on their own behalf or that of third parties, but required to settle operations via a settling member.

Table 1.3   Strippable issues as of July 2000

Issue	Matures	Outstanding
B 5.00%	31/01/2001	13 138
B 4.25%	30/07/2002	10 247
B 5.25%	31/01/2003	14 134
B 3.00%	31/01/2003	9 731
B 4.60%	30/07/2003	6 293
B 4.50%	30/07/2004	10 150
B 3.25%	31/01/2005	9 063
B 4.95%	30/07/2005	5 501
O 6.00%	31/01/2008	18 803
O 5.15%	30/07/2009	12 572
O 4.00%	31/01/2010	11 789
Total		121 421

Millions of euros
Source: Spanish Treasury and authors

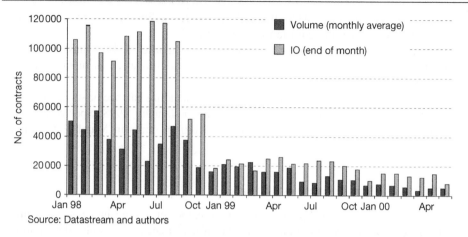

Figure 1.5   Futures contract on the notional 10-year BONO (MEFF RF)

In addition, for each contract traded there exist a set number of market makers whose primary role is to provide the market with liquidity and depth.

The margin participants must post in order to transact in the market is calculated by the MEFF clearing and settlement house, which takes account of the net position of each, i.e. offsetting futures and options operations. By this means, the daily margin requirement is kept considerably lower.

MEFF trading encompasses the following contracts on fixed-income securities:

- *Futures on 5-, 10- and 30-year bonds*, whose underlying asset is a notional bond theoretically issued at par on the expiry date of the futures contract, and maturing in 5, 10 or 30 years according to contract specifications. The basket of underlying bonds deliverable on contract expiry, as listed by MEFF, comprises *Bonos* and *Obligaciones* complying with certain prerequisites as regards residual life, outstanding balance and turnover. The coupons of the notional underlying bonds are 5.50%, 4.00% and 6.50%, respectively, for the futures contracts on 5-, 10- and 30-year bonds.
- *Options on 5-, 10- and 30-year futures*: the underlying assets are the futures contracts on 5-, 10- and 30-year bonds traded on MEFF. Expiry is quarterly (on the third Wednesday in March, June, September and December) and the options work along US lines, i.e. the holder can exercise them at any point up to expiry.

MEFF trading has historically centred on debt futures contracts, more specifically the future on the notional 10-year *Bono*. This contract has attracted a healthy demand since its launch, albeit with some fluctuations. At present, the massive concentration of eurozone demand in the futures contract on the 10-year *Bund* and the resurgence of the contract on the 10-year OAT since mid-year 1999 (swayed by the requirements imposed by French law on collective investment undertakings) has depressed trading in the MEFF benchmark.

1.6   CLEARING AND SETTLEMENT

The Book-Entry System managed by the Bank of Spain handles the clearing and settlement of public debt market transactions. Each market member holds an account in the Book-Entry System, where transactions in its securities are recorded.

1.6.1 Settlement of Operations between Account Holders in the Book-Entry System

The procedure used is one of cash on delivery. During each session, account holders notify the Book-Entry System of transactions conducted through the Bank of Spain Settlement Service, specifying the following points:

- the type of operation
- the securities reference transacted
- the nominal amount
- the price
- the counterparty
- the value date agreed.

The Book-Entry System records this information and, on the value date indicated for settlement, debits or credits the corresponding cash accounts held by account holders at the Bank of Spain. The value date most widely used in *Bono* and *Obligación del Estado* transactions is T + 3, i.e. three working days from transaction. In the case of *Letras del Tesoro*, value and transaction dates tend to coincide.

1.6.2 Settlement of Operations Conducted by Non-Accountholders

Individuals or legal entities who are not members of the public debt market, i.e. who are not account holders in the Book-Entry System, have to channel transactions through a management institution (for direct-account holders, the Bank of Spain itself acts in this capacity). The management institution can be that in which the securities are registered or any other specified. It must notify transactions to the Book-Entry System on the working day prior to the value date established, except where the unit value of the transaction exceeds 500 000 euros, in which case it may notify on the value date itself. Transactions may also be settled against payment on third parties' behalf through the Bank of Spain Settlement Service.

1.6.3 Settlement of Operations Conducted by Non-residents

Non-resident investors can also clear and settle their transactions through EUROCLEAR and CEDEL. These international clearing and settlement systems are linked to Spain's Book-Entry System through the third-party accounts of two management institutions which act as their depositories (one in Spain and the other in the investor's country of residence). The following procedures may apply:

- Transactions between EUROCLEAR or CEDEL clients are cleared and settled internally, without notification to or intervention by the Book-Entry System.
- When the transaction is between one EUROCLEAR and one CEDEL client, clearing and settlement is again internal, though in this case the third-party accounts held at each system's depository will reflect movements in their respective balances on the value date established.
- When the transaction is between a EUROCLEAR or CEDEL and a non-depository individual or entity, two alternatives can arise:

(a) If the intervention of the EUROCLEAR or CEDEL depository is restricted to informing the BSSS of the securities transfer, settlement will be processed by EUROCLEAR or CEDEL.

(b) If the depository is linked to the transaction, it will use the Book-Entry System clearing and settlement service in the form described above.

1.6.4 Book-Entry System Connections with EU Central Depositories and Securities Clearing and Settlement Services

In May 2000, the Book-Entry System was running the following connections in addition to EUROCLEAR and CEDEL:

- Book-Entry System—Clearstream (Germany)
- Book-Entry System—Sicovam (France)
- Book-Entry System—Monte Titoli (Italy)
- Book-Entry System—Negicef (Netherlands).

1.7 TAXATION

1.7.1 Taxation of Non-residents

The interest and capital gains earned on Spanish government debt securities by non-resident individuals and entities are not liable for Spanish tax. For this exemption to apply, however, the following conditions must be met:

(a) The non-resident individual or entity acquiring the income or capital gains does not operate through a permanent establishment in Spain.

(b) The income or capital gains on public debt are not earned through tax havens.

Non-residents holding government debt securities also enjoy exemption from wealth tax on these, provided they do not operate in Spain through a permanent establishment.

1.7.2 Taxation of Residents in Spain

Personal income tax

Letras del Tesoro
- The income gained on the transfer or redemption of *Letras del Tesoro* is treated as capital income.
- No withholding tax is applied.

Bonos and *Obligaciones del Estado*
- The interest earned in coupon payments is treated as capital income and, as such, is taxable in the year of collection.
- Withholding tax of 18% is applied.
- Income from the transfer or redemption of *Bonos del Estado* and *Obligaciones del Estado* is regarded as capital income, subject to personal income tax. Tax will be paid on the difference between the transfer or redemption and acquisition price of the *Bonos* and *Obligaciones* in question.

- Income from the transfer or redemption of *Bonos* and *Obligaciones del Estado* is not subject to withholding tax.

Government debt strips   For tax purposes, stripping involves the splitting of an explicit yield asset (*Bono* or *Obligación*) into several assets at a discount (stripped coupons and principal) and therefore with an implicit yield associated. In the transfer or redemption of segregated coupons and principal, the management institution intervening is obliged to deduct and pay the corresponding withholding tax (18%).

Corporate Income Tax

The income earned by corporate tax payers from government securities (*Letras, Bonos* and *Obligaciones* or strips) will be taxed as standard at a rate of 35%. Income earned on Treasury securities held by corporate tax payers is not liable for withholding tax, provided such securities were issued as of 1 January 1999.

Wealth Tax

The government securities held by wealth-tax payers at each annual close form part of their net worth and are taxed accordingly.

Bond Washing between Residents and Non-residents

In order to discourage bond washing, a withholding tax (18%) is applied to the part of the price equivalent to accrued interest in the case of *Bono* and *Obligación* transfers made within the 30 days prior to coupon maturity. Such liability arises when the buyer is a person or entity not resident in Spain or is a corporate income-tax payer, and when the explicit yield raised from the securities transferred is exempt from withholding tax on the buyer's part.

Withholding tax will not be applied in the following circumstances:

- operations conducted by management institutions with the status of market makers, provided certain conditions are met
- operations conducted by the governing bodies of official futures and options markets as part of the normal functioning of such markets
- operations conducted in the Public Debt Interdealer Brokers trading network, provided certain conditions are met.

1.8 GOVERNMENT DEBT MARKET MAKERS

Market makers comprise a small group of financial institutions with special rights and obligations in the primary and secondary markets. Their ultimate purpose is to boost the liquidity of the secondary market in Book-Entry Public Debt and to co-operate with the General Directorate of the Treasury and Financial Policy in moving government debt securities both within and outside Spain.

The Spanish Public Debt market-maker system has undergone profound reform in recent years, the main elements of which have been an enlargement of market-maker rights and obligations and the extension of eligibility to non-resident institutions.

1.8.1 Market-Maker Rights

1. *Participation in Treasury auctions*: once the general submission deadline at each *Bonos* and *Obligaciones* auction has passed, market makers have an additional 30 minutes in which to present their bids.
2. *Exclusive access to Bonos and Obligaciones auction second rounds*: once the bidding period has closed for each *Bonos* and *Obligaciones* auction, market makers are allowed exclusive access to a second round.
3. *Stripping and reconstitution of government debt securities*: market makers are the only entities authorised to strip and reconstitute strippable government debt securities.
4. *Other debt management operations*: market-maker status is privileged by the General Directorate of the Treasury and Financial Policy when choosing counterparties for its other financial operations, such as swaps or foreign-currency issues.
5. *Access to updated information on the Treasury's financing policy.*
6. *Participation in the setting of issue objectives for medium- and long-term government debt instruments.*
7. *Representation on the Advisory Board of the Public Debt Book-Entry Market.*

1.8.2 Market-Maker Obligations

1. *Participation in auctions*: Each market maker must submit bids for a minimum nominal value of 3% of the amount allotted by the General Directorate of the Treasury and Financial Policy at the last three auctions of each *Bono* or *Obligación del Estado*, at prices no lower than the stop-out rate minus 5 cents in the case of 3-year *Bonos del Estado*; 10 cents for 5-year *Bonos del Estado*; 15 cents for 10-year *Obligaciones del Estado*; and 30 cents for *Obligaciones del Estado* with maturities over 10 years. Auctions at which a single entity has acquired over 50% of the amount issued do not count for these purposes.
2. *Guaranteeing secondary-market liquidity*, by quoting a minimum of 13 *Bono*, *Obligación* and strip references under the price-range, volume and trading-time conditions laid down by the General Directorate of the Treasury and Financial Policy. Market makers must also quote the futures contract on the 10-year *Bono* traded on MEFF Renta Fija.
3. *Furnishing any information requested by the General Directorate of the Treasury and Financial Policy*, on the public debt market in general and their own market-making activity in particular. Specifically, market makers must furnish monthly reports on their direct and third-party transactions, detailing the type of entities their clients are and their geographical base.

1.8.3 Application for Market-Maker Status

Entities wishing to be recognised as market makers must accompany their formal request with a dossier setting out the technical and human resources at their command for market-making functions, and stating their express acceptance of the commitments and conduct required. Market-maker status is officially granted by the General Directorate of the Treasury and Financial Policy subject to a favourable report from the Bank of Spain. A new condition has recently been added, that of having previously operated as a Public Debt Dealer.

1.8.4   Evaluation of Market-Maker Activity

Market-maker activity is evaluated on a monthly basis with regard to performance of the following functions:

- subscription of securities at auctions
- participation in the total monthly turnover of the Book-Entry Public Debt Interdealer Broker trading network (INFOMEDAS) and other electronic platforms where Spanish public debt is traded
- quotation on the Book-Entry Public Debt Interdealer Broker network (INFOMEDAS) and other platforms where Spanish public debt is traded, in view of their growing importance as trading channels at Europe-wide level
- participation in monthly government debt trading between market members in official secondary-debt markets
- participation in the trading conducted by market makers with entities other than account holders in the Book-Entry System
- the stripping/reconstitution of strippable securities
- activity in the 'blind' trading segment and in securities with longer residual lives (especially valued).

1.8.5   Market Makers in Kingdom of Spain Public Debt (March 2000)

Banco Bilbao Vizcaya Argentaria
Banco Popular
Banco Santander Central Hispano
Banesto
Bankinter
Barclays Bank, Spanish branch
Caja de Ahorros y Monte de Piedad de Madrid
Caja de Ahorros y Pensiones de Barcelona
Confederación Española de Cajas de Ahorros
Crédit Agricole Indosuez, Spanish branch
Bank of America International Ltd
Deutsche Bank AG
Dresdner Bank AG
Goldman Sachs International
J.P. Morgan
Merrill Lynch International
Salomon Brothers International Ltd

ANNEXE: THE SPANISH PUBLIC DEBT MARKET

Domestic Public Debt References in Euros, June 2000

Issue	Matures	Outstanding	Strippable	Benchmark	'On-the-run'
B 5.00%	31/01/2001	13 138	***	—	—
B 10.10%	28/02/2001	4 299	—	—	—
B 8.40%	30/04/2001	5 167	—	—	—
O 7.50%	30/07/2001	295	—	—	—
O 11.30%	15/01/2002	2 995	—	—	—
B 7.90%	28/02/2002	6 547	—	—	—
O 10.30%	15/06/2002	3 015	—	—	—
B 4.25%	30/07/2002	10 247	***	—	—
B 5.25%	31/01/2003	14 134	***	—	—
B 3.00%	**31/01/2003**	**9 731**	***	***	—
B 4.60%	30/07/2003	6 293	***	—	***
O 10.90%	30/08/2003	5 289	—	—	—
O 10.50%	30/10/2003	3 973	—	—	—
O 8.00%	30/05/2004	5 066	—	—	—
B 4.50%	30/07/2004	10 150	***	—	—
B 3.25%	**31/01/2005**	**9 063**	***	***	—
O 10.00%	28/02/2005	5 259	—	—	—
B 4.95%	30/07/2005	5 501	***	—	***
O 10.15%	31/01/2006	4 051	—	—	—
O 8.80%	30/04/2006	3 890	—	—	—
O 7.35%	31/03/2007	4 771	—	—	—
O 6.00%	31/01/2008	18 803	***	—	—
O 8.20%	28/02/2009	5 948	—	—	—
O 5.15%	30/07/2009	12 572	***	—	—
Notas 4.78%	10/08/2009	500	—	—	—
O 4.00%	**31/01/2010**	**11 789**	***	***	***
O 8.70%	28/02/2012	1 860	—	—	—
O 6.15%	31/01/2013	11 964	—	—	—
O 4.75%	**30/07/2014**	**6 251**	—	***	***
O 6.00%	**31/01/2029**	**11 112**	—	***	***
Total		213 673			

Millions of euros
Source: Spanish Treasury and authors

International and Foreign-currency Issues, June 2000

Reference	Currency	Coupon	Matures	Frequency	Balance	EUR equiv.	USD equiv.
Euro Bono	JPY	5.750%	23/03/2002	annual	125 000	1 222.4	1 147.7
Euro Bono	JPY	4.625%	22/07/2004	semiannual	150 000	1 466.8	1 377.2
Euro Bono	JPY	4.750%	14/03/2005	annual	150 000	1 466.8	1 377.2
Euro Bono	JPY	3.100%	20/09/2006	annual	150 000	1 466.8	1 377.2
Euro Bono	FRF	6.500%	20/06/2001	annual	6 000	914.7	858.8
Euro Bono	FRF	9.250%	20/12/2004	annual	6 000	914.7	858.8
Euro Bono	FRF	6.625%	31/07/2006	annual	3 000	457.3	429.4
Euro Bono	FRF	6.625%	31/07/2006	annual	6 000	914.7	858.8
Euro Bono	FRF	7.500%	24/05/2008	annual	7 000	1 067.1	1 001.9
Euro Bono	FRF	6.250%	10/04/2012	annual	4 000	609.8	572.5
Euro Bono	DEM	Libor-0.0625	29/06/2002	semiannual	2 000	1 022.6	960.1
Euro Bono	DEM	7.250%	04/03/2003	annual	4 000	2 045.2	1 920.2
Euro Bono	DEM	5.750%	03/01/2007	annual	2 000	1 022.6	960.1
Yankee Bond	USD	9.125%	01/08/2000	semiannual	300	319.5	300.0
Euro Bono	USD	5.750%	18/05/2004	annual	1 000	1 065.1	1 000.0
Global Bond	USD	7.000%	19/07/2005	semiannual	1 500	1 597.6	1 500.0

(Continued)

Reference	Currency	Coupon	Matures	Frequency	Balance	EUR equiv.	USD equiv.
Euro Bono	USD	5.875%	28/07/2008	annual	1 500	1 597.6	1 500.0
Bulldog Bond	GBP	11.750%	24/03/2010	semiannual	60	96.8	90.9
Totals						**19 268.1**	**18 090.8**

Millions of euros
Source: Spanish Treasury and authors

International Issuance Programmes, July 2000

EMTN	Currency	EUR Equiv.	USD Equiv.
Euros	EUR	1695.5 m	1592.0 m
Dollars	USD	83.1 m	78.0 m
Total		1778.6 m	1670.0 m

Source: Spanish Treasury and authors

Outcome of Letras Issues in 2000

Auction date	Instrument	Term	Matures	Days	Settles	Sold	Bids	NC	Bid/cover	Stop rate	Average rate
04-Jan-00	Letras	12 months	05-Jan-01	364	07-Jan-00	316	1548	93	4.9	3.896	3.847
04-Jan-00	Letras	18 months	06-Jul-01	546	07-Jan-00	1119	3160	28	2.8	4.251	4.229
19-Jan-00	Letras	12 months	19-Jan-01	364	21-Jan-00	346	3126	127	9.0	3.842	3.817
19-Jan-00	Letras	18 months	20-Jul-01	546	21-Jan-00	1145	5647	53	4.9	4.200	4.180
26-Jan-00	Letras	6 months	28-Jul-00	182	28-Jan-00	428	1027	—	2.4	3.451	3.437
02-Feb-00	Letras	12 months	02-Feb-01	364	04-Feb-00	312	1858	94	6.0	3.928	3.865
02-Feb-00	Letras	18 months	03-Aug-01	546	04-Feb-00	915	5704	39	6.2	4.251	4.245
09-Feb-00	Letras	6 months	11-Aug-00	182	11-Feb-00	298	1441	—	4.8	3.574	3.564
16-Feb-00	Letras	12 months	16-Feb-01	364	18-Feb-00	632	1541	94	2.4	3.981	3.939
16-Feb-00	Letras	18 months	17-Aug-01	546	18-Feb-00	909	5144	37	5.7	4.299	4.278
01-Mar-00	Letras	12 months	02-Mar-01	364	03-Mar-00	688	2269	73	3.3	3.992	3.987
01-Mar-00	Letras	18 months	31-Aug-01	546	03-Mar-00	1109	4493	28	4.1	4.339	4.323
08-Mar-00	Letras	6 months	08-Sep-00	182	10-Mar-00	726	1062	—	1.5	3.800	3.775
15-Mar-00	Letras	12 months	16-Mar-01	364	17-Mar-00	627	1459	—	2.3	4.196	4.119
15-Mar-00	Letras	18 months	14-Sep-01	546	17-Mar-00	1322	4462	—	3.4	4.431	4.414
29-Mar-00	Letras	12 months	30-Mar-01	364	31-Mar-00	713	1425	75	2.0	4.228	4.204
29-Mar-00	Letras	18 months	28-Sep-01	546	31-Mar-00	885	6271	24	7.1	4.427	4.416
05-Apr-00	Letras	6 months	06-Oct-00	182	07-Apr-00	495	1136	—	2.3	3.902	3.892
12-Apr-00	Letras	12 months	11-Apr-01	362	14-Apr-00	314	1383	86	4.4	4.224	4.209
12-Apr-00	Letras	18 months	12-Oct-01	546	14-Apr-00	1341	5312	28	4.0	4.420	4.414
26-Apr-00	Letras	12 months	27-Apr-01	364	28-Apr-00	453	1783	—	3.9	4.406	4.376
26-Apr-00	Letras	18 months	26-Oct-01	546	28-Apr-00	1031	3733	—	3.6	4.590	4.565
03-May-00	Letras	6 months	03-Nov-00	182	05-May-00	305	940	—	3.1	4.263	4.218
10-May-00	Letras	12 months	11-May-01	364	12-May-00	847	1861	80	2.2	4.627	4.572
10-May-00	Letras	18 months	09-Nov-01	546	12-May-00	571	3806	20	6.7	4.786	4.746
24-May-00	Letras	12 months	25-May-01	364	26-May-00	609	2437	77	4.0	4.834	4.805
24-May-00	Letras	18 months	23-Nov-01	546	26-May-00	653	2980	21	4.6	4.986	4.978
31-May-00	Letras	6 months	01-Dec-00	182	02-Jun-00	385	870	—	2.3	4.563	4.538
07-Jun-00	Letras	12 months	08-Jun-01	364	09-Jun-00	1253	2446	91	2.0	4.730	4.716
07-Jun-00	Letras	18 months	07-Dec-01	546	09-Jun-00	601	2937	19	4.9	4.815	4.809
21-Jun-00	Letras	12 months	22-Jun-01	364	23-Jun-00	440	2837	81	6.4	4.850	4.836
21-Jun-00	Letras	18 months	21-Dec-01	546	23-Jun-00	686	1190	15	1.7	5.042	5.008
28-Jun-00	Letras	6 months	29-Dec-00	182	30-Jun-00	299	789	—	2.6	4.625	4.613
05-Jul-00	Letras	12 months	06-Jul-01	364	07-Jul-00	450	3044	92	6.8	4.921	4.877
05-Jul-00	Letras	18 months	04-Jan-02	546	07-Jul-00	760	3787	26	5.0	5.061	5.023
19-Jul-00	Letras	12 months	20-Jul-01	364	21-Jul-00	376	2978	93	7.9	5.068	5.036
19-Jul-00	Letras	18 months	18-Jan-02	546	21-Jul-00	956	2358	28	2.5	5.248	5.229
26-Jul-00	Letras	6 months	26-Jan-01	182	28-Jul-00	57	1455	—	25.4	4.739	4.714

Millions of euros
Source: Spanish Treasury and authors

Outcome of Bonos *and* Obligaciones *Issues in 2000*

Auction date	Instrument	Coupon	Term	Settles	Matures	Sold	Bids	NC	Bid/ cover	Stop rate	Stop price	Avge rate	Avge price
12-Jan-00	Bonos	3.25%	5 years	17-Jan-00	31-Jan-05	818	1831	12	2.24	5.260	91.180	5.254	91.203
12-Jan-00	Obligaciones	4.75%	15 years	17-Jan-00	30-Jul-14	153	804	2	5.24	6.049	89.850	6.036	89.968
13-Jan-00	Bonos	3.00%	3 years	18-Jan-00	31-Jan-03	780	2783	20	3.57	4.834	94.830	4.836	94.841
13-Jan-00	Obligaciones	4.00%	10 years	18-Jan-00	31-Jan-10	908	2081	7	2.29	5.785	89.450	5.782	89.471
13-Jan-00	Obligaciones	6.00%	30 years	18-Jan-00	31-Jan-29	134	473	2	3.53	6.282	102.050	6.279	102.094
09-Feb-00	Bonos	4.95%	5 years	14-Feb-00	30-Jul-05	811	2169	13	2.67	5.381	95.830	5.371	95.875
09-Feb-00	Obligaciones	4.75%	15 years	14-Feb-00	30-Jul-14	358	622	2	1.74	5.851	92.000	5.841	92.084
10-Feb-00	Bonos	4.60%	3 years	15-Feb-00	30-Jul-03	921	2578	16	2.80	5.044	96.610	5.036	96.633
10-Feb-00	Obligaciones	4.00%	10 years	15-Feb-00	31-Jan-10	597	1338	6	2.24	5.766	87.050	5.763	87.073
01-Mar-00	Bonos	4.95%	5 years	06-Mar-00	30-Jul-05	745	2753	11	3.69	5.321	96.390	5.316	96.414
01-Mar-00	Obligaciones	6.00%	30 years	06-Mar-00	31-Jan-29	432	1013	2	2.35	6.033	100.100	6.032	100.120
02-Mar-00	Bonos	4.60%	3 years	07-Mar-00	30-Jul-03	1040	2419	24	2.33	5.018	96.960	5.015	96.970
02-Mar-00	Obligaciones	4.00%	10 years	07-Mar-00	31-Jan-10	505	1534	5	3.04	5.734	87.550	5.733	87.559
05-Apr-00	Bonos	4.95%	5 years	10-Apr-00	30-Jul-05	912	1586	15	1.74	5.076	97.970	5.066	98.015
05-Apr-00	Obligaciones	4.75%	15 years	10-Apr-00	30-Jul-14	381	718	2	1.88	5.563	95.400	5.559	95.439
06-Apr-00	Bonos	4.60%	3 years	11-Apr-00	30-Jul-03	668	2070	30	3.01	4.807	98.040	4.803	98.051
06-Apr-00	Obligaciones	4.00%	10 years	11-Apr-00	31-Jan-10	1039	1727	4	1.66	5.423	90.150	5.418	90.187
03-May-00	Bonos	4.95%	5 years	08-May-00	30-Jul-05	815	1817	7	2.23	5.350	97.130	5.346	97.147
03-May-00	Obligaciones	6.00%	30 years	08-May-00	31-Jan-29	413	745	—	1.80	5.852	103.600	5.849	103.644
04-May-00	Bonos	4.60%	3 years	09-May-00	30-Jul-03	634	1848	17	2.92	5.196	97.270	5.189	97.291
04-May-00	Obligaciones	4.00%	10 years	09-May-00	31-Jan-10	816	1533	1	1.88	5.711	88.550	5.677	88.781
07-Jun-00	Bonos	4.95%	5 years	12-Jun-00	30-Jul-05	784	2031	9	2.59	5.178	98.360	5.176	98.372
07-Jun-00	Obligaciones	4.75%	15 years	12-Jun-00	30-Jul-14	329	505	0	1.53	5.584	96.100	5.578	96.155
08-Jun-00	Bonos	4.60%	3 years	13-Jun-00	30-Jul-03	781	1575	21	2.02	5.097	98.020	5.092	98.035
08-Jun-00	Obligaciones	4.00%	10 years	13-Jun-00	31-Jan-10	802	1103	2	1.38	5.434	90.900	5.425	90.956
05-Jul-00	Bonos	4.95%	5 years	10-Jul-00	30-Jul-05	819	2311	6	2.82	5.402	97.780	5.400	97.791
05-Jul-00	Obligaciones	6.00%	30 years	10-Jul-00	31-Jan-29	303	556	1	1.84	5.821	105.050	5.816	105.118
06-Jul-00	Bonos	4.60%	3 years	11-Jul-00	30-Jul-03	796	2630	10	3.30	5.197	98.120	5.192	98.133
06-Jul-00	Obligaciones	4.00%	10 years	11-Jul-00	31-Jan-10	700	2546	2	3.64	5.539	90.550	5.534	90.589

Millions of euros

Source: Spanish Treasury and authors

Letras *Issuance Calendar 2000*

Auction date	Instrument	Term	Currency	Matures	Days	Settles
04-Jan-00	Letras	12 months	EUR	05-Jan-01	364	07-Jan-00
04-Jan-00	Letras	18 months	EUR	06-Jul-01	546	07-Jan-00
19-Jan-00	Letras	12 months	EUR	19-Jan-01	364	21-Jan-00
19-Jan-00	Letras	18 months	EUR	20-Jul-01	546	21-Jan-00
26-Jan-00	Letras	6 months	EUR	28-Jul-00	182	28-Jan-00
02-Feb-00	Letras	12 months	EUR	02-Feb-01	364	04-Feb-00
02-Feb-00	Letras	18 months	EUR	03-Aug-01	546	04-Feb-00
09-Feb-00	Letras	6 months	EUR	11-Aug-00	182	11-Feb-00
16-Feb-00	Letras	12 months	EUR	16-Feb-01	364	18-Feb-00
16-Feb-00	Letras	18 months	EUR	17-Aug-01	546	18-Feb-00
01-Mar-00	Letras	12 months	EUR	02-Mar-01	364	03-Mar-00
01-Mar-00	Letras	18 months	EUR	31-Aug-01	546	03-Mar-00
08-Mar-00	Letras	6 months	EUR	08-Sep-00	182	10-Mar-00
15-Mar-00	Letras	12 months	EUR	16-Mar-01	364	17-Mar-00
15-Mar-00	Letras	18 months	EUR	14-Sep-01	546	17-Mar-00
29-Mar-00	Letras	12 months	EUR	30-Mar-01	364	31-Mar-00
29-Mar-00	Letras	18 months	EUR	28-Sep-01	546	31-Mar-00
05-Apr-00	Letras	6 months	EUR	06-Oct-00	182	07-Apr-00
12-Apr-00	Letras	12 months	EUR	11-Apr-01	362	14-Apr-00
12-Apr-00	Letras	18 months	EUR	12-Oct-01	546	14-Apr-00
26-Apr-00	Letras	12 months	EUR	27-Apr-01	364	28-Apr-00
26-Apr-00	Letras	18 months	EUR	26-Oct-01	546	28-Apr-00
03-May-00	Letras	6 months	EUR	03-Nov-00	182	05-May-00
10-May-00	Letras	12 months	EUR	11-May-01	364	12-May-00
10-May-00	Letras	18 months	EUR	09-Nov-01	546	12-May-00
24-May-00	Letras	12 months	EUR	25-May-01	364	26-May-00
24-May-00	Letras	18 months	EUR	23-Nov-01	546	26-May-00
31-May-00	Letras	6 months	EUR	01-Dec-00	182	02-Jun-00
07-Jun-00	Letras	12 months	EUR	08-Jun-01	364	09-Jun-00
07-Jun-00	Letras	18 months	EUR	07-Dec-01	546	09-Jun-00
21-Jun-00	Letras	12 months	EUR	22-Jun-01	364	23-Jun-00
21-Jun-00	Letras	18 months	EUR	21-Dec-01	546	23-Jun-00
28-Jun-00	Letras	6 months	EUR	29-Dec-00	182	30-Jun-00
05-Jul-00	Letras	12 months	EUR	06-Jul-01	364	07-Jul-00
05-Jul-00	Letras	18 months	EUR	04-Jan-02	546	07-Jul-00
19-Jul-00	Letras	12 months	EUR	20-Jul-01	364	21-Jul-00
19-Jul-00	Letras	18 months	EUR	18-Jan-02	546	21-Jul-00
26-Jul-00	Letras	6 months	EUR	26-Jan-01	182	28-Jul-00
02-Aug-00	Letras	12 months	EUR	03-Aug-01	364	04-Aug-00
02-Aug-00	Letras	18 months	EUR	01-Feb-02	546	04-Aug-00
09-Aug-00	Letras	6 months	EUR	09-Feb-01	182	11-Aug-00
16-Aug-00	Letras	12 months	EUR	17-Aug-01	378	04-Aug-00

(*Continued*)

Auction date	Instrument	Term	Currency	Matures	Days	Settles
16-Aug-00	Letras	18 months	EUR	15-Feb-02	560	04-Aug-00
30-Aug-00	Letras	12 months	EUR	31-Aug-01	364	01-Sep-00
30-Aug-00	Letras	18 months	EUR	01-Mar-02	546	01-Sep-00
06-Sep-00	Letras	6 months	EUR	09-Mar-01	182	08-Sep-00
13-Sep-00	Letras	12 months	EUR	14-Sep-01	364	15-Sep-00
13-Sep-00	Letras	18 months	EUR	15-Mar-02	546	15-Sep-00
27-Sep-00	Letras	12 months	EUR	28-Sep-01	364	29-Sep-00
27-Sep-00	Letras	18 months	EUR	28-Mar-02	545	29-Sep-00
04-Oct-00	Letras	6 months	EUR	06-Apr-01	182	06-Oct-00
10-Oct-00	Letras	12 months	EUR	12-Oct-01	364	13-Oct-00
10-Oct-00	Letras	18 months	EUR	12-Apr-02	546	13-Oct-00
25-Oct-00	Letras	12 months	EUR	26-Oct-01	364	27-Oct-00
25-Oct-00	Letras	18 months	EUR	26-Apr-02	546	27-Oct-00
31-Oct-00	Letras	6 months	EUR	04-May-01	182	03-Nov-00
07-Nov-00	Letras	12 months	EUR	09-Nov-01	364	10-Nov-00
07-Nov-00	Letras	18 months	EUR	10-May-02	546	10-Nov-00
22-Nov-00	Letras	12 months	EUR	23-Nov-01	364	24-Nov-00
22-Nov-00	Letras	18 months	EUR	24-May-02	546	24-Nov-00
29-Nov-00	Letras	6 months	EUR	01-Jun-01	182	01-Dec-00
04-Dec-00	Letras	12 months	EUR	07-Dec-01	365	07-Dec-00
04-Dec-00	Letras	18 months	EUR	07-Jun-02	547	07-Dec-00
20-Dec-00	Letras	12 months	EUR	21-Dec-01	364	22-Dec-00
20-Dec-00	Letras	18 months	EUR	21-Jun-02	546	22-Dec-00
27-Dec-00	Letras	6 months	EUR	29-Jun-01	182	29-Dec-00

Source: Spanish Treasury and authors

Bonos *and* Obligaciones *Issuance Calendar 2000*

Auction date	Instrument	Coupon	Term	Target	Currency	Settles	Matures
12-Jan-00	Bonos	3.25%	5 years	750–1000	EUR	17-Jan-00	31-Jan-05
12-Jan-00	Obligaciones	4.75%	15 years	750–1000	EUR	17-Jan-00	30-Jul-14
13-Jan-00	Bonos	3.00%	3 years	1550–1900	EUR	18-Jan-00	31-Jan-03
13-Jan-00	Obligaciones	4.00%	10 years	1550–1900	EUR	18-Jan-00	31-Jan-10
13-Jan-00	Obligaciones	6.00%	30 years	1550–1900	EUR	18-Jan-00	31-Jan-29
09-Feb-00	Bonos	4.95%	5 years	1000–1200	EUR	14-Feb-00	30-Jul-05
09-Feb-00	Obligaciones	4.75%	15 years	1000–1200	EUR	14-Feb-00	30-Jul-14
10-Feb-00	Bonos	4.60%	3 years	1300–1600	EUR	15-Feb-00	30-Jul-03
10-Feb-00	Obligaciones	4.00%	10 years	1300–1600	EUR	15-Feb-00	31-Jan-10
01-Mar-00	Bonos	4.95%	5 years	1000–1200	EUR	06-Mar-00	30-Jul-05
01-Mar-00	Obligaciones	6.00%	30 years	1000–1200	EUR	06-Mar-00	31-Jan-29
02-Mar-00	Bonos	4.60%	3 years	1300–1650	EUR	07-Mar-00	30-Jul-03
02-Mar-00	Obligaciones	4.00%	10 years	1300–1650	EUR	07-Mar-00	31-Jan-10
05-Apr-00	Bonos	4.95%	5 years	1000–1300	EUR	10-Apr-00	30-Jul-05
05-Apr-00	Obligaciones	4.75%	15 years	1000–1300	EUR	10-Apr-00	30-Jul-14
06-Apr-00	Bonos	4.60%	3 years	1500–1800	EUR	11-Apr-00	30-Jul-03
06-Apr-00	Obligaciones	4.00%	10 years	1500–1800	EUR	11-Apr-00	31-Jan-10
03-May-00	Bonos	4.95%	5 years	—	EUR	08-May-00	30-Jul-05
03-May-00	Obligaciones	6.00%	30 years	—	EUR	08-May-00	31-Jan-29
04-May-00	Bonos	4.60%	3 years	—	EUR	09-May-00	30-Jul-03
04-May-00	Obligaciones	4.00%	10 years	—	EUR	09-May-00	31-Jan-10
07-Jun-00	Bonos	4.95%	5 years	—	EUR	12-Jun-00	30-Jul-05
07-Jun-00	Obligaciones	4.75%	15 years	—	EUR	12-Jun-00	30-Jul-14
08-Jun-00	Bonos	4.60%	3 years	—	EUR	13-Jun-00	30-Jul-03
08-Jun-00	Obligaciones	4.00%	10 years	—	EUR	13-Jun-00	31-Jan-10
05-Jul-00	Bonos	4.95%	5 years	—	EUR	10-Jul-00	30-Jul-05
05-Jul-00	Obligaciones	6.00%	30 years	—	EUR	10-Jul-00	31-Jan-29
06-Jul-00	Bonos	4.60%	3 years	—	EUR	11-Jul-00	30-Jul-03
06-Jul-00	Obligaciones	4.00%	10 years	—	EUR	11-Jul-00	31-Jan-10
02-Aug-00	Bonos	—	5 years	—	EUR	07-Aug-00	—
02-Aug-00	Obligaciones	—	15 years	—	EUR	07-Aug-00	—
03-Aug-00	Bonos	—	3 years	—	EUR	08-Aug-00	—
03-Aug-00	Obligaciones	—	10 years	—	EUR	08-Aug-00	—
06-Sep-00	Bonos	—	5 years	—	EUR	11-Sep-00	—
06-Sep-00	Obligaciones	—	30 years	—	EUR	11-Sep-00	—
07-Sep-00	Bonos	—	3 years	—	EUR	12-Sep-00	—
07-Sep-00	Obligaciones	—	10 years	—	EUR	12-Sep-00	—
04-Oct-00	Bonos	—	5 years	—	EUR	09-Oct-00	—
04-Oct-00	Obligaciones	—	15 years	—	EUR	09-Oct-00	—
05-Oct-00	Bonos	—	3 years	—	EUR	10-Oct-00	—
05-Oct-00	Obligaciones	—	10 years	—	EUR	10-Oct-00	—
08-Nov-00	Bonos	—	5 years	—	EUR	13-Nov-00	—
08-Nov-00	Obligaciones	—	30 years	—	EUR	13-Nov-00	—
10-Nov-00	Bonos	—	3 years	—	EUR	15-Nov-00	—
10-Nov-00	Obligaciones	—	10 years	—	EUR	15-Nov-00	—
13-Dec-00	Bonos	—	5 years	—	EUR	18-Dec-00	—
13-Dec-00	Obligaciones	—	15 years	—	EUR	18-Dec-00	—
14-Dec-00	Bonos	—	3 years	—	EUR	19-Dec-00	—
14-Dec-00	Obligaciones	—	10 years	—	EUR	19-Dec-00	—

The face value of the bonds to be issued is subject to change by the GDTFP
Millions of euros
Source: Spanish Treasury and authors

MEFF Bono *Turnover and Open Position*

Date	Turnover		Open Position
	Monthly	Average	
4/1/1992	7 682	591	5 100
5/1/1992	15 511	861	6 571
6/1/1992	65 251	2 966	10 377
7/1/1992	68 061	2 959	12 915
8/1/1992	55 302	2 634	18 104
9/1/1992	87 963	4 108	12 978
10/1/1992	63 778	3 058	11 293
11/1/1992	46 389	2 316	14 138
12/1/1992	47 181	2 291	10 052
1/1/1993	72 529	3 665	16 805
2/1/1993	120 528	6 026	28 958
3/1/1993	138 136	6 695	25 940
4/1/1993	108 593	5 405	34 944
5/1/1993	135 416	6 448	43 551
6/1/1993	208 735	9 488	44 784
7/1/1993	179 660	8 166	60 283
8/1/1993	283 721	13 330	63 216
9/1/1993	429 259	19 512	84 878
10/1/1993	306 588	14 869	102 364
11/1/1993	377 411	18 958	97 431
12/1/1993	333 472	16 949	84 002
1/1/1994	440 004	22 242	100 006
2/1/1994	851 619	42 581	161 359
3/1/1994	1 074 114	47 989	97 079
4/1/1994	670 456	33 523	115 893
5/1/1994	664 431	31 640	137 006
6/1/1994	1 013 115	46 050	97 709
7/1/1994	559 782	27 217	107 357
8/1/1994	653 575	30 106	114 938
9/1/1994	664 728	31 671	55 500
10/1/1994	551 311	27 738	73 602
11/1/1994	426 901	21 085	81 938
12/1/1994	328 575	16 996	46 497
1/1/1995	643 871	30 561	41 388
2/1/1995	595 724	29 786	49 408
3/1/1995	880 968	39 661	49 673
4/1/1995	507 942	27 692	48 881
5/1/1995	703 934	35 195	45 973
6/1/1995	833 711	37 896	29 447
7/1/1995	599 474	28 546	43 507

(*Continued*)

| | Turnover | | |
Date	Monthly	Average	Open Position
8/1/1995	484 931	21 560	51 977
9/1/1995	842 148	40 646	35 265
10/1/1995	542 686	25 552	32 612
11/1/1995	679 395	34 213	48 934
12/1/1995	486 449	30 521	46 808
1/1/1996	1 048 784	47 672	45 819
2/1/1996	976 689	46 509	47 831
3/1/1996	823 234	40 245	40 640
4/1/1996	727 351	39 780	48 144
5/1/1996	750 020	37 518	62 551
6/1/1996	845 312	42 265	61 373
7/1/1996	910 516	39 588	49 569
8/1/1996	693 484	32 837	60 646
9/1/1996	1 121 875	53 423	77 043
10/1/1996	1 381 227	60 053	71 253
11/1/1996	1 044 760	52 238	71 607
12/1/1996	755 565	37 874	81 215
1/1/1997	1 277 149	59 406	68 346
2/1/1997	1 046 184	52 309	78 202
3/1/1997	1 146 069	58 411	71 676
4/1/1997	1 171 350	53 243	73 257
5/1/1997	1 057 951	55 497	101 746
6/1/1997	1 430 291	68 109	90 457
7/1/1997	887 335	40 677	86 360
8/1/1997	874 725	42 984	82 311
9/1/1997	1 212 418	55 110	83 649
10/1/1997	1 238 381	53 842	86 826
11/1/1997	609 193	30 460	109 053
12/1/1997	694 096	32 854	89 048
1/1/1998	1 028 893	50 539	106 141
2/1/1998	895 303	44 765	115 808
3/1/1998	1 212 965	57 216	97 246
4/1/1998	796 305	37 861	91 539
5/1/1998	604 810	31 562	108 771
6/1/1998	981 163	44 598	111 760
7/1/1998	528 622	22 983	118 470
8/1/1998	729 373	34 732	117 084
9/1/1998	1 038 629	47 210	105 079
10/1/1998	715 638	37 690	52 333
11/1/1998	348 709	18 900	55 773
12/1/1998	342 363	15 893	18 610

(Continued)

Date	Turnover		Open Position
	Monthly	Average	
1/1/1999	356 694	21 025	24 312
2/1/1999	395 764	19 788	21 615
3/1/1999	506 534	22 634	16 888
4/1/1999	303 307	15 964	24 953
5/1/1999	333 562	15 884	26 093
6/1/1999	415 356	18 880	21 741
7/1/1999	208 189	9 463	22 053
8/1/1999	181 859	8 702	23 767
9/1/1999	295 071	13 412	23 428
10/1/1999	225 933	10 910	20 339
11/1/1999	212 848	10 615	17 959
12/1/1999	141 277	7 251	10 306
1/1/2000	157 005	7 814	15 141
2/1/2000	146 981	6 999	15 471
3/1/2000	126 953	5 919	13 282
4/1/2000	65 692	3 647	12 610
5/1/2000	106 997	5 236	14 962
6/1/2000	113 404	5 155	8 400

No. of contracts
Source: MEFF

2
The German Government Bond Market

2.1 INTRODUCTION

The German market ranks among the world's largest, and is second in the euro zone after Italy. The historical factors supporting this lead position are the solidity and stability of the country's financial system, the convertibility of its currency and its long tradition of free capital movements.

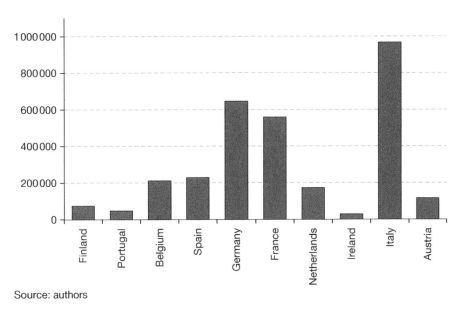

Source: authors

Figure 2.1 Euro-zone public debt markets by size (medium- and long-term debt, in millions of euros)

In order to maintain and consolidate the position of the German debt market ahead of future changes in the worldwide and European contexts, the German authorities have launched a modernisation drive aimed at providing an appropriate framework for ongoing development.

The current organisation of German markets is a result of the combined efforts of participating agents. The Deutsche Terminbörse (DTB) or German futures market (now EUREX Deutschland) introduced electronic trading of options and futures on *Bunds, Bobls* and *Schätze*. The creation of IBIS (the integrated stock-market trading and information system) allowed the intra-day trading of stocks and bonds. IBIS is now being phased out in favour of a new trading system, XETRA, already operational across the stock-exchange

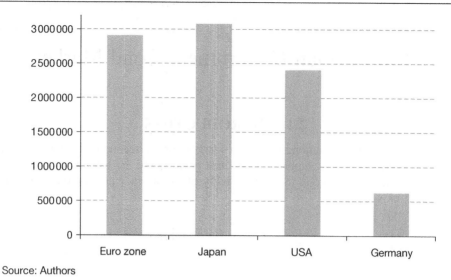

Source: Authors

Figure 2.2   Tradeable medium- and long-term debt as of 31 June 2000 (excluding money-market assets, in millions of US dollars)

network. Finally, in 1993 Deutsche Börse Clearing AG became the centralised channel for order execution, settlement and the promotion of trading on German stock exchanges.

Federal debt management pursues the central goal of raising the funds needed for budget implementation, under market conditions and at the lowest possible cost. The Bundesbank acts as the Federal Government's financial agent, participating in all Federal Government asset issues and playing a key role in the secondary market in federal securities through its price-management operations on German stock exchanges. Given the huge amount of Federal Government securities outstanding and the vital importance of debt management to the competitive standing of any financial centre, it is no surprise that the Federal Finance Ministry and the Bundesbank are constantly striving to enhance the market's efficiency and international competitiveness. This drive has materialised in a succession of measures aimed at (1) widening the range of products available, and (2) improving the liquidity and transparency of the Federal securities market:

- conducting of bond issues through a mix of auction and syndication since 1990
- introduction of a quarterly issuance calendar for all syndicated placements and auctions among members of the Federal Bond Consortium
- creation of new instruments at the long end of the curve, such as the 30-year bond (first issued in 1994, and later discontinued until its reopening in mid-1997)
- regular issuance of special 5-year bonds (*Bobls*) since August 1995
- regular issuance of 6-month bills (*Bubills*) since July 1996
- issue of 2-year notes (*Schätze*) since September 1996
- step-up of issuance volumes for each debt reference
- authorisation of the stripping of certain 10- and 30-year bonds
- the end-1997 disbanding of the Federal Bond Consortium and its replacement with the *Bund* Issues Action Group (BIAG), now in charge of the issuance—at auction only—of 10- and 30-year bonds (*Bunds*), special 5-year bonds (*Bobls*), 2-year notes

(*Schätze*) and 6-month bills (*Bubills*). At the same time, the Bundesbank was authorised to retain a given volume of these securities for sale on the secondary market (stock exchange), pursuant to its market management targets.

2.2   OVERVIEW OF THE GERMAN CAPITAL MARKET

The German bond market is Europe's second largest measured by fixed-income assets in issue, and the fourth largest worldwide after Japan, the USA and Italy. Its current outstanding balance is practically triple the level of 1985, owing in part to the heavy funding requirement imposed by German reunification. The German market is also the euro zone's busiest by volume of operations.

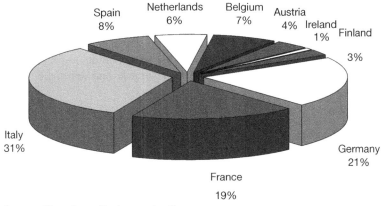

Source: Bloomberg, Reuters and authors

Figure 2.3   Euro-zone medium- and long-term public debt as of June 2000 (Central Government issues, excluding the money market in millions of euros)

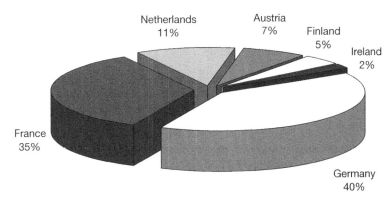

Source: Bloomberg, Reuters and authors

Figure 2.4   AAA-rated medium- and long-term public debt in the euro zone as of June 2000 (Central Government issues, excluding the money market in millions of euros)

Of the volume of fixed-income securities in issue by resident sectors (1998 figures), the lion's share is represented by bank bonds (61%), followed by public-sector (38.8%) and corporate paper (0.2%). The term 'bank bonds' includes mortgage, special and other bonds issued by private- and public-sector mortgage banks, special-purpose credit institutions and commercial banks. 'Public-sector' issuers comprise the Federal Government, State governments and local authorities.

Zero-coupon bonds account for only a small portion (0.3%) of bonds in issue, but floating-rate notes have been coming up fast, reaching a market share of 10%.

Net sales of resident fixed-income issues swelled from 80 billion deutschmarks in 1989 to over 400 billion in 1993—due mainly to the heavy borrowing imposed by reunification—and then settled back to 328 billion deutschmarks in 1998. The share of these sales falling to the Federal Government and the German States (Länder) rose from 34% in 1989 to 60% in 1993, then receded to 18.3% in 1998.

Foreign investors are avid buyers of German debt securities, albeit with a widely fluctuating participation rate: 54% of all buy transactions in 1993, for instance, against 40% in 1997. German credit institutions and individuals remain the biggest investor groups, though their importance has waned slightly in recent years parallel to the rise of collective investment institutions. Conversely, the share of insurance and non-financial companies has been trending consistently downwards.

2.2.1 Legal Framework

Article 115 of the Constitution stipulates that the borrowing of funds to finance the Federal Budget requires the prior approval of Parliament, as enacted in the Annual Budget Law. Any extraordinary requirements arising in a fiscal year will be resourced through an additional or supplementary budget law. The Federal Finance Minister is free to decide which instruments are issued and at which maturities. The same article makes it incumbent upon the Federal Government to ensure that annual borrowings are kept below the capital expenditure budgeted, though the limit may exceptionally be exceeded to tackle persistent economic imbalances. This legislation pursues a twin goal: to ensure that funds are raised for investment spending only and not for consumption, and to allow budgetary policy to pursue a pro- or anti-cycle stance.

2.2.2 Basic Debt-Management Strategies

The fundamental objective of Federal debt management is to ensure that the credit budgeted is available at the right time, under market conditions and with the widest possible distribution, i.e. a broad investor base. The guiding principles of budgetary design and implementation are 'cost efficiency' and 'spending austerity'.

- The Federal Government may resort to the money markets in order to manage its liquidity, and is legally authorised to raise short-term funds amounting to a maximum 8% of the budget. It may also opt to replace these funds with longer-dated alternatives.
- Debt policy pursues the widest possible lender base and, as such, issues an array of instruments at differing maturities, a proportion of them placed directly with individual investors. By encouraging uptake among a broad section of the public, the Federal Government is simultaneously promoting long-term saving.

- The liquidity of Federal securities is assured by high issuance volumes, their subsequent trading on German stock markets and the Bundesbank's commitment to undertake price management operations in line with changing market conditions. By this means, investors can buy and sell the securities in issue, confident that they are transacting at market rates. Another advantage of liquidity is that large volumes can be traded with relative ease.

- The all-important qualities of clarity and transparency are guaranteed by the admission of benchmark securities to trading on German stock exchanges, where they are subject at all times to market sentiment. In addition, issuance procedures are tailored to the needs of the potential investor audience. The Federal Government does not issue solely through auctions—restricted to BIAG members—as this would preclude take-up by the broader retail base, but also conducts tap placements in OTC markets and sells securities directly on the stock-exchange network, as part of its market management repertoire.

- Other characteristics of Federal Government borrowing strategy are the redenomination into euros of all securities issued as of 1 January 1999 and its non-recourse to indexed issues, because of the attendant inflationary risk.

2.2.3 The Role of the Bundesbank

Section 20 (2) of the Bundesbank Law states: 'Special Federal Funds and Land Governments must conduct Bond and Treasury Bill issuance through the Bundesbank or, failing this, consult in advance with the Bank'.

Parliament thereby empowers the Bundesbank to act as the principal banker for the public sector. Not only does it manage securities issuance, it also carries out advisory, brokerage and co-ordination functions. The bank is also empowered to block or modify certain issues which may have a harmful impact on the market or adverse implications for monetary aggregates. Put another way, it will raise no objections to any security issue consistent with monetary policy objectives.

Standard practice is for Federal securities to be issued via the Bundesbank. By this means, the Special Federal Funds can raise most of the resources they need to redeem their debt via bonds issued by the Federal Government. State governments use credit institutions as their primary issuance channel, after due consultation with the Bundesbank. Local authorities are outside the remit of this legislation, but their issuance in any case is relatively small scale.

2.2.4 Debt Registration and Administration

Federal Government loans and special funds are managed by the Federal Debt Administration (FDA), an autonomous federal agency under the Ministry of Finance. Its statutory obligations are:

- the monitoring of Federal Government borrowing to ensure it does not overstep the legally established bounds
- the recording of debt securities
- management of the Federal Debt Register
- debt servicing, i.e. payment of interest accrued and the return of principal upon maturity.

Recently, a growing number of investors have appeared as individual lenders on the Federal Debt Register, alongside the German stock-exchange clearing house and institutional investors. Investors acquiring Federal Securities—including those issued by the Special Federal Funds—can opt to hold a direct account with the Register, free of charge. The FDA will then reinvest their assets through the Bundesbankon maturity or interest payment dates.

2.3   ASSETS ISSUED BY THE FEDERAL GOVERNMENT

2.3.1   Issuers

In the early 1990s, a total of nine issuers placed their securities through the Bundesbank, with the backing of a Federal Government guarantee. Since 1998, however, Special Funds have raised most of the cash for their debt redemptions through the securities issued by the Federal Government (sole issuer as of 1995). Special Fund, Treuhand Agency and Currency Conversion Equalisation Fund issues all retain outstanding balances. These borrowers have the same credit-worthiness as the Federal Government itself.

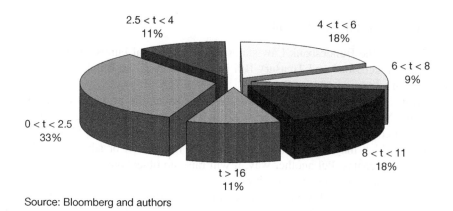

Source: Bloomberg and authors

Figure 2.5   Federal Government debt by term (*Bubills, Bunds, Bobls* and *Schätze*)

A brief description of the issues outstanding is as follows:

- *Republic of Germany Federal Government Bund*: Federal Government issues to finance federal budgets.
- *Federal Government Bund-Erblastentilgungsfonds or ELF*: a fund set up to meet the financial liabilities incurred by the former GDR.
- *Federal Government Bund-Bundeseisenbahnvermögen or BEV*: arising from the Railways Reorganisation Act of 1993, decreeing the merger of the former *Deutsche Reichsbahn* and *Deutsche Bundesbahn* funds. The Federal Government is liable for the debt issued by the former GDR and FRG railways.
- *Federal Government Bund-Sondervermögen or ERP*: a fund established for the reconstruction and improvement of the German economy, especially in the nine new Länder created after reunification, by issuing credit for new business start-ups and the modernisation of private enterprises.

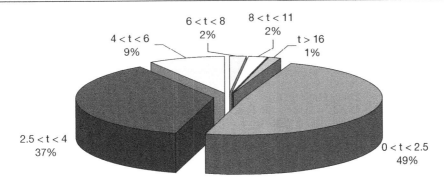

Figure 2.6 Special Fund debt by term (Treuhand, Unity, ERP, etc.)

- *Federal Government Bund-Entschädigungsfonds*: a fund created to compensate individuals and companies for the non-restoration of property held in the former GDR. Compensation takes the form of tradeable 'indemnity' bonds.
- *Federal Government Bund-Fonds Deutsche Einheit or FDE*: the 'Unity Fund' arising from the 1990 Treaty of Reunification between the GDR and FRG to further the two countries' economic, monetary and social union. Monies raised are assigned to the new Länder for the purpose of budgetary stabilisation. Payments under the fund ceased in 1994.
- *Ausgleichfonds Währungsumstellung (AFW) or Currency Conversion Equalisation Fund*: created to manage the rights granted to ex-GDR banks and export firms in relation to the conversion of their currency. The fund's management was transferred to the ELF in January 1995.
- *Treuhand Agency (Treuhandanstalt) or THA*: up to December 1994.
- *Deutsche Bundespost or DBP*: up to December 1994. Following the privatisation of Germany's postal service, fund liabilities were transferred to Deutsche Telecom AG. This change does not impair the credit-worthiness of the bonds issued by the German Federal Postal Service, as the Federal Government is ultimately responsible for all liabilities carried at the time of privatisation.

2.3.2 Main Federal Government Instruments

The Federal Government uses six types of instruments to raise funds for budget financing (see Table 2.1).

Federal securities share the following characteristics:

- *Fixed annual coupon* (except certain floating-rate notes (FRNs), Funding Bonds, Federal Savings Bonds Type B and Treasury Discount Paper).
- *Closed maturity, i.e. without early redemption option* (except Funding Bonds, bonds issued by the Currency Conversion Equalisation Fund and those issued by the Indemnity Fund).
- *Usable for direct investment* by mutual funds and life insurance hedging funds, as collateral for Lombard-rate loans and, with the exception of Federal Savings Bonds and Financing Paper, transactable in open market operations with the Bundesbank.

Table 2.1   Classification of German Federal securities

A. Federal securities tradeable on secondary markets

   I.   Bonds (*Bunds–Anleihen*)
      1. Bonds issued by the Federal Republic of Germany
      2. Bonds issued by the Federal Republic of Germany
          Unity Fund (FDE)
      3. Bonds issued by the Federal Republic of Germany
          Special Fund (ERP)
      4. Bonds issued by the Federal Railways (*Bundesbahn*)
      5. Bonds issued by the Federal Postal Service (*Bundespost*)
      6. Bonds issued by the Treuhand Agency (THA)
  II. Special five-year Federal bonds (*Bundesobligationen* or *Bobls*)
 III. Federal Treasury bonds (*Schatzanweisungen*)
      1. Federal Treasury bonds (*Schätze* or BSA)
      2. Treasury bonds issued by the Federal Postal Service (DBP)
  IV. Special five-year Treuhand bonds (*Treuhand-obligationen* or *Tobls*)
   V. Bonds issued by the Federal Postal Service (*Postobligationen*)
  VI. Other issues
      1. Funding Bonds issued by the Federal Republic of Germany
      2. Bonds issued by the Currency Conversion Equalisation Fund
      3. Bonds issued by the Indemnity Fund

B. Other Federal securities not tradeable on secondary markets

   I.   Federal Treasury Discount Paper (*Bubills*)

Source: authors

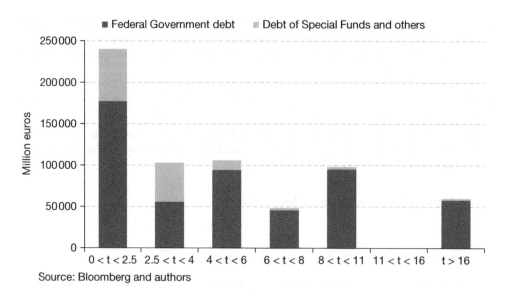

Source: Bloomberg and authors

Figure 2.7   Distribution of total German public debt, June 2000

- *Primary marker acquisition of tap-sold assets at no charge to the final investor*, since the issuer itself pays credit institutions a placement or sale commission.
- *Federal securities are issued as 'claims on registered debt' represented by book entries in the Federal Debt Register.*

The five instruments with benchmark status on German and, in some cases, European markets are described in detail below.

Federal Bonds (Bundesanleihen or Bunds)

Issued for the first time in 1952, the benchmark status of Federal Bonds gives them a key role within the German capital market and in transactions with non-resident investors. The name 'Federal Bonds' is applied to two types of securities: the bonds—or *Bunds*—issued by the Federal Government and the bonds issued by the Federal Funds.

Federal Bonds are auctioned by the Bundesbank among members of the BIAG. The lines currently issued have maturities of 10 or 30 years.

Bund yield is calculated as follows:

$$P = \frac{C}{q} + \frac{C}{q^2} + \cdots + \frac{C}{q^n} + \frac{R}{q^n} \text{ in which } \frac{1}{q^n} = \frac{1}{\left(1 + \dfrac{r}{100}\right)^n} = \text{discount factor, and}$$

where

P = acquisition price
C = coupon in %
n = number of years to maturity
R = redemption price
r = yield in %

Special 5-Year Bonds (Bundesobligationen or Bobls)

These have been issued since 1979, and their importance, like that of *Bunds* themselves, lies in their benchmark status for the medium-term segment of the curve. Issuance is by tap placement or continuous sale on the OTC market, followed up with 'American' auctions held by the Bundesbank.

Issue procedure is as follows: a fixed-coupon line is first opened for market sale; its price is continually readjusted in line with market conditions over the issuance period. The length of this period depends on the precise conditions prevailing, i.e. on the need for coupon changes, but may be no greater than three months per line. The purchaser range during tap selling is limited to individuals and non profit organisations. Since 1995, a certain volume of each line (between 5 and 6 billion euros) has been held back until after the suspension of tap selling (around 1 billion euros usually placed). This amount is then issued at auction to the BIAG. Auctions are held in February, May, August and November, and securities are then automatically listed for trading on German stock exchanges.

Bobl yield is calculated in the same way as that of *Bunds*:

$$P = \frac{C}{q} + \frac{C}{q^2} + \cdots + \frac{C}{q^n} + \frac{R}{q^n} \text{ in which } \frac{1}{q^n} = \frac{1}{\left(1 + \dfrac{r}{100}\right)^n} = \text{discount factor, and}$$

where

P = acquisition price
C = coupon in %
n = number of years to maturity

R = redemption price
r = yield in %

Federal Treasury Notes (Bundesschatzanweisungen *or* Schätze)

Schätze are assets dated two years, issued at quarterly auctions in March, June, September and December. The procedure in this case is a one-off auction (i.e. no tap selling as in the case of *Bobls*), and bidding is reserved exclusively for members of the BIAG, though any investor can later purchase notes through a BIAG member or direct on the secondary market (following their admission to stock exchange trading).

The yield of *Schätze* is arrived at by the following formula (the same as for *Bunds* and *Bobls*):

$$P = \frac{C}{q} + \frac{C}{q^2} + \cdots + \frac{C}{q^n} + \frac{R}{q^n} \quad \text{in which} \quad \frac{1}{q^n} = \frac{1}{\left(1 + \dfrac{r}{100}\right)^n} = \text{discount factor, and}$$

where

P = acquisition price
C = coupon in %
n = number of years to maturity
R = redemption price
r = yield in %

Federal Savings Bonds (Bundesschatzbriefe)

These are Federal Government assets issued by tap placement or direct market sale. Their 1969 launch was a response to the government's policy of seeking the widest possible take-up of Federal asset holdings among the German population, and the purchaser range is accordingly restricted to individuals and non-profit organisations.

Two types of Savings Bonds are currently issued: Type A, with six-year maturities and paying annual interest according to a pre-set programme; and Type B, maturing in seven years, with interest payment solely upon redemption (i.e. functioning like a seven-year zero coupon bond).

Yield on Type A bonds is calculated as follows:

$$P = \frac{C_1}{q} + \frac{C_2}{q^2} + \frac{C_3}{q^3} + \frac{C_4}{q^4} + \frac{C_5}{q^5} + \frac{C_6}{q^6} + \frac{R}{q^7}$$

$$\text{in which} \quad \frac{1}{q^n} = \frac{1}{\left(1 + \dfrac{r}{100}\right)^n} = \text{discount factor, and}$$

where

P = acquisition price
$C_{1\ldots6}$ = bond coupon, in %, in each year
n = number of years to maturity
R = redemption price
r = yield in %

Their defining feature is that interest accumulates over time according to a pre-set schedule, creating an added incentive to hold to maturity. In the event of any major change in market prices, issue of the original line's tranches is broken off and a new line created in tune with market conditions.

Type B bonds, as zero-coupon instruments, conform to the following yield formula:

$$P = \frac{R}{\left(1 + \dfrac{r}{100}\right)^n} \text{ where } R = 100 + \text{compound interest}$$

Savings Bonds are not traded on German stock exchanges and, as such, have no secondary market. As an alternative, bonds can be resold to the Federal Government as of one year from issue, in maximum lots of DM 10000/month and at a price equal to par plus accumulated interest.

Federal Treasury Discount Paper (Unverzinsliche Schatzanweisungen *or* Bubills)

These are assets issued at discount with a maturity of six months. Their yield is the difference between nominal value and acquisition price. *Bubills* are aimed primarily at institutional investors and other central banks, though their purchase is open to any investor. They are auctioned by the Bundesbank among BIAG members in the months of January, April, July and October, and may then be traded on secondary markets.

Bubills come under the price and yield formulae for assets issued at and maturing in less than one year, which are as follows:

$$\text{Acquisition price: } 100 = P \times \left(1 + r \times \frac{d}{360 \times 100}\right)$$

$$\text{Yield: } r = \left(\frac{100}{P} - 1\right) \times \frac{360 \times 100}{d}$$

where d = number of days to maturity

Remaining assets issued at discount include Federal Treasury Financing Paper and Treasury Bills:

- *Federal Treasury Financing Paper*: sold via tap issuance on the open market, with maturities of 12 and 24 months. Financing Paper cannot be acquired by credit institutions and is not available for secondary-market trading.
- *Treasury Bills*: normally dated three days, these assets are for the exclusive use of the Bundesbank in its monetary policy operations and, as such, are considered Bundesbank paper despite their Federal origin. Their interest rate represents the floor rate for all other German interest rates, and the Bundesbank uses them to drain liquidity from the system.

2.3.3 Structure of the Outstanding Balance of Federal Government Debt

The Federal Government debt position has undergone a radical shift since the 1980s (60% loans against notes in 1980 versus 95% securities in 1998). The factors driving this change were:

Table 2.2 Total outstanding balance of German public debt (1980–April 2000)

Amount	1980	1985	1990	1995	1996	1997	1998	1999	2000
Bunds	94 293	207 857	441 233	712 622	771 382	852 527	951 753	541 764	562 709
Bobls	8 879	73 640	126 916	174 413	179 277	181 930	205 105	124 071	125 737
Federal Savings Bonds	24 083	25 921	31 024	78 453	96 386	99 300	92 706	41 618	41 043
FDE	—	—	9 000	54 000	45 000	45 000	45 000	23 008	23 008
AFW	—	—	—	65 044	69 161	75 406	77 383	39 347	39 450
Indemnity Fund	—	—	—	—	10	59	147	136	160
ERP	—	—	—	11 000	11 000	11 000	11 000	5 624	5 624
THA or Treuhand	15 222	18 469	27 734	160 220	156 052	155 402	130 302	52 817	52 817
BEV (railways)	8 734	18 351	36 981	39 366	35 500	30 200	25 000	12 782	10 737
DBP (postal service)	12 160	27 475	40 264	96 116	86 763	77 274	68 076	29 463	29 086
State governments	—	—	—	121 096	126 903	122 190	120 582	62 621	64 531
Local authorities	327	184	150	1 625	2 105	2 255	2 315	1 220	1 220
Total	130 736	272 336	555 362	1 261 089	1 303 876	1 371 313	1 431 558	768 782	789 342

Percentage	1980	1985	1990	1995	1996	1997	1998	1999	2000
Bunds	72.1%	76.3%	79.4%	56.5%	59.2%	62.2%	66.5%	70.5%	71.3%
Bobls	6.8%	27.0%	22.9%	13.8%	13.7%	13.3%	14.3%	16.1%	15.9%
Federal Savings Bonds	18.4%	9.5%	5.6%	6.2%	7.4%	7.2%	6.5%	5.4%	5.2%
FDE	—	—	1.6%	4.3%	3.5%	3.3%	3.1%	3.0%	2.9%
AFW	—	—	—	5.2%	5.3%	5.5%	5.4%	5.1%	5.0%
Indemnity Fund	—	—	—	—	0.0%	0.0%	0.0%	0.0%	0.0%
ERP	—	—	—	0.9%	0.8%	0.8%	0.8%	0.7%	0.7%
THA or Treuhand	11.6%	6.8%	5.0%	12.7%	12.0%	11.3%	9.1%	6.9%	6.7%
BEV (railways)	6.7%	6.7%	6.7%	3.1%	2.7%	2.2%	1.7%	1.7%	1.4%
DBP (postal service)	9.3%	10.1%	7.3%	7.6%	6.7%	5.6%	4.8%	3.8%	3.7%
State governments	—	—	—	9.6%	9.7%	8.9%	8.4%	8.1%	8.2%
Local authorities	0.3%	0.1%	0.0%	0.1%	0.2%	0.2%	0.2%	0.2%	0.2%
Total	100%	100%	100%	100%	100%	100%	100%	100%	100%

To 1998, figures in millions of deutschmarks
From 1999, figures in millions of euros
Source: Bundesbank and authors

- the rise of asset securitisation, in Germany and worldwide
- investors' growing preference for fungible securities permitting large-volume trading on liquid markets
- the 1984 abolition of coupon tax, which acted as a strong demand stimulus among foreign investor groups
- the creation of the futures market DTB to localise trading in futures contracts on Federal securities, as well as other assets.

These changes alone explain why tradeable Federal securities (*Bunds*, *Bobls* and *Schätze*) now account for 80% of the total volume issued by the Federal Government.

The outstanding balance of Federal debt has also undergone a major structural change, such that securitised assets now constitute 97%, compared to just 46% in 1980. The result is that the share falling to loans against notes has slumped from the highs of 1980 to a meagre 2.4% at the time of writing. Federal Bonds, meanwhile, represented over half the outstanding total at the 1997 close.

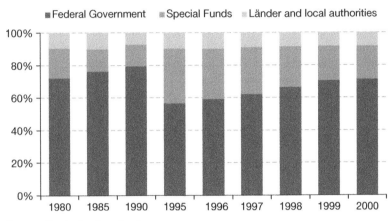

Source: Bundesbank and authors

Figure 2.8   Composition of German public debt (1980–2000)

2.4   THE PRIMARY MARKET

2.4.1   Federal Securities Issuance Planning

In theory, any issuer is free to decide both the instrument and the issue volume as well as issue characteristics and date, although various conventions have been imposed to harmonise public sector issuance. Steps prior to issuance are as follows:

- The issue is included in the Public Debt Issuance Committee programme.
- The Capital Market Central Committee is notified.
- The issue is included in a quarterly issuance calendar.
- A prior announcement of each issue is made.

Public Debt Issuance Committee: the committee is composed of representatives of the Federal Ministry of Finance, Federal Ministry of the Economy, State governments and organisations representing cities, towns, municipalities and rural districts. A Bundesbank representative is invited to attend these meetings. The committee's task is to co-ordinate during a specific time period (usually one quarter) all bond issue requests made by central government, regional and local authorities, and to draw up an issuance calendar that is not made public. The committee's aim is to avoid a glut of issues that might overwhelm the capital markets.

Capital Market Central Committee: this committee is not convened at pre-set intervals. It is composed of representatives from those banks whose importance as market makers and underwriters give them an influential role in the capital market. As the banking agency which borrowers must notify of their intent to issue securities, the Capital Market Central Committee is in a privileged position to make recommendations regarding in public- and private-sector issuance planning. The primary aim of such recommendations is to preclude market tensions arising from new issues.

Issuance Calendar: since fourth quarter 1993, the Bundesbank and the Ministry of Finance have jointly published the Federal Government's quarterly issuance schedule. This calendar appears during the ten days preceding the start of each quarter, and includes additional information on the volume of securities coming up for maturity and the interest payments due. It is intended to facilitate decision-making by domestic and foreign investors. It may be subject to review in the event of unforeseen circumstances which counsel the cancellation of a programmed issue or the scheduling of new issues. Each issue is announced one week in advance and details are given of the opening dates for bid submission, allotment dates, value dates, the volume envisaged and, where relevant, the start date of listing on the stock exchange.

2.4.2 Federal Securities Issuance Procedures

The success of securities issues hinges on an efficient placement procedure. Several such procedures exist in Germany, depending on the type of security involved and the government's debt management objective.

- *Bunds*, *Schätze*, *Bubills* and certain *Bobl* issue volumes are placed through auctions conducted among BIAG members.
- *Bobls*, Federal Savings Bonds and Treasury Financing Paper are sold on tap with no pre-set issue period and up to a previously established volume.
- In *Bunds*, *Schätze* and *Bobl* issues—by auction in the first two cases, or by tap issue in the third—the Bundesbank withholds a portion of the volume, prior to listing, for market management operations and phased sale on German stock exchanges. The Bundesbank can top up such amounts at any time.

The main characteristics of each procedure are described below.

Auctions among BIAG Members

Federal bonds (*Bunds*) used to be issued through the Federal Bond Consortium by a combined auction/syndication system, whereas *Bobls*, *Schätze* and *Bubills* were issued exclusively by auction. Under this system, any German credit institution with a giro account at any State Central Bank could participate in auctions.

Since January 1998, however, the issuance of *Bunds*, *Schätze*, *Bubills* and certain volumes of *Bobls* has been conducted by auction among BIAG members. German credit institutions, German branches of foreign credit institutions, broker–dealers and investment banks can take part in these auctions provided they fulfil the following requirements:

- authorisation to participate in issues under the terms of the German Banking Act
- possession of a giro account at a State Central Bank and a custody account with Deutsche Börse Clearing AG, the German clearance and settlement house
- a proven capacity to place *Bunds, Bobls, Schätze* and *Bubills*. This means, in essence, that each entity must subscribe at least 0.05% of total auction volumes during one calendar year, with a weighting factor assigned to each type of security (1 for *Bubills*, 4 for *Schätze*, 8 for *Bobls* and 25 for 10- and 30-year *Bunds*). This membership prerequisite is closely monitored by the Bundesbank, which publishes an annual ranking of BIAG members according to their securities placement quota. Those failing to reach the minimum quota are dropped from the list, although they may be readmitted in future (the 2000 ranking is shown in Table 2.9).

The auction procedure commences (T − 5) with the Bundesbank's announcement of the issue, which gives details of the security to be issued (maturity, issue volume, date and duration of the auction).

The key date in the process is that of the invitation to bid (T − 0), when the main issue characteristics are established:

- coupon
- the date the coupon begins to accrue interest and the first coupon payment date
- issue volume
- minimum bid volume: 1 000 000 euros
- deadline for presentation of bids: before 11.00 local time on the day the auction is resolved
- bid denomination, as a percentage of nominal value
- issue value date and date of listing on the German exchanges: in both cases T + 3.

BIAG members send their bids by e-mail to the Bundesbank or any State Central Bank. These can be either competitive (with the option of submitting several bids at different prices) or non-competitive.

The Bundesbank resolves the auction (T + 1) according to the bids received. Allocation is via the 'American' method: the issuer sets a minimum price and allots all higher competitive bids at their stated price. Non-competitive bids are allotted at the weighted average price of accepted competitive bids. In cases where demand outstrips supply, the issuer makes a pro rata allocation. Conversely, in cases of underbidding or bid prices out of step with market conditions, the issuer may choose not to make any allocation at all. The volume the Bundesbank will set aside for market-management operations is established upon resolution of the auction. Bidders are informed of the results immediately after resolution.

The issue is inscribed in the Federal Debt Register on the day after auction resolution (T + 2), while value date and listing follow one day later (T + 3). On this date, the price of the securities acquired must be debited to the bidder's account and credited to the issuer's account. The sale of unplaced securities and securities withheld for market-management operations also begins on this date.

Figure 2.9 shows the procedure for securities issuance by auction.

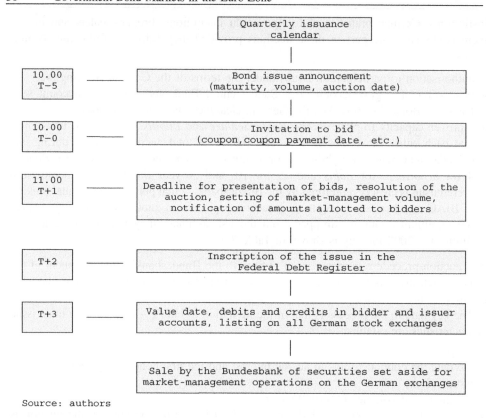

Source: authors

Figure 2.9   Securities issuance by auction

Tap Issues

This system, used to issue *Bobls*, Savings Bonds and Treasury Financing Paper, consists of continuous direct sale on the market to credit institutions and State Central Banks during an unspecified time period. The Bundesbank sets the terms of offer and adjusts them periodically, even daily if necessary, to suit market conditions.

The advantage of this issuance system is that it enables the government to raise conjunctural financing, and simultaneously to spread the burden or market recourse more or less continuously over a given period, thus avoiding excessive market tensions on specific dates. The drawback is that the selling period must be extended substantially when the issue volume is large.

Market-Management Operations (Sale on the Exchanges)

The Bundesbank invariably retains a portion of *Bund*, *Bobl* and *Schätze* issue volumes for their phased sale—market-management operations—on the German stock exchanges. The volumes involved have scaled up enormously in recent years, making this an increasingly valuable tool for providing the Federal debt market with greater depth and liquidity. Furthermore, it gives the Federal Government greater flexibility in covering its financing requirements.

This type of operation is included here rather than in the section on the Bundesbank's secondary-market activities because its underlying implications are of an issuance nature.

Topping-up Issues

This variant allows the issuer to open up a new tranche of a given line after its issuance is closed. There are two ways of doing so: (a) by assigning a certain number of securities to the Bundesbank for market-management operations, and (b) by means of a new auction using the standard procedure described above. This type of operation comes into its own when a specific issue requires a liquidity boost (provided the original coupon is in line with the market conditions at top-up time). The Bundesbank used this procedure on many occasions during 1999 and 2000, primarily to ensure that the 10-year *Bund* (the authentic euro-zone benchmark) had the balance it needed to meet keen Europe-wide demand.

2.4.3   Characteristics of *Bund, Bobl, Schätze* and *Bubill* Issues

Bunds

- *Issue procedure*: 'American' auction among BIAG members. The normal pattern is of one 10-year *Bund* issue per quarter, joined on occasion by a 30-year *Bund*.
- *Presentation of competitive bids*: from the start of the invitation to bid (T − 0) up to 11.00 local time on the auction date (T + 1). Bids should be sent by e-mail to the Bundesbank or State Central Banks, and expressed as a percentage of nominal value to two decimal places, with a variation of 0.01 percentage points.
- *Minimum amounts of bids*: 1 000 000 euros and multiples.
- *Announcement of target volume*: five days before the invitation date (T − 5). Volumes envisaged usually stand at around 5 billion euros (the Bundesbank targets a volume in issue for each line of 15 billion euros).
- *Auction results*: posted one day after the invitation (T + 1).
- *Payment/value date*: two days after the auction is resolved (T + 3).
- *Admission to trading*: on payment date (T + 3).
- *Interest basis*: Current/Current.
- *Bund auction calendar*: the Bundesbank announces the 10-day period for its auctions in a quarterly issuance calendar, then gives a week's notice of the exact date.

Bobls

- *Issue procedure*: the Bundesbank uses a combination of tap sales and an 'American' auction among BIAG members. In the first case, the selling or placement period for a given line—for instance, the 130—runs from the day (T − 1) before the auction of the previous line—the 129—to one day (T − 1) prior to the auction of the 130 itself. Once tap selling is closed, the Bundesbank proceeds to auction securities among BIAG members (T + 1).
- *Presentation of bids*: from the start of the invitation to bid (T − 0) to 11.00 local time on the auction resolution date (T + 1). Bids should be sent by e-mail to the Bundesbank or State Central Banks, and expressed as a percentage of nominal value to two decimal places, with a variation of 0.01 percentage points.
- *Minimum amount of bids*: (1) on tap, 100 euros; (2) at auction, 1 000 000 euros.

Table 2.3   *Bund* issue (28/4/99): *Bund* 4% 4/2009 (in millions of euros)

Bids	14 897
Competitive bids	8 371
Non-competitive bids	6 526
Weighted average price of total bids	101.06%
Allocation	4 545.75
Stop-out price	101.10%
Weighted average price	101.11%
Average rate (Current/Current)	3.86%
Retained for market-management operations	743.5
Increase in amount outstanding	5 000
Amount of previous issue	5 000
Total volume issued	10 000

Source: authors

- *Announcement of target volume*: on the closing date of tap selling (T − 0).
- *Auction results*: published by the Bundesbank on auction date (T + 1).
- *Payment*: two days (T + 3) after the auction is resolved.
- *Admission to trading*: on payment date (T + 3).
- *Interest basis*: Actual/Actual; as of the start of tap issuance.
- *Bobl issuance calendar*: February (17/2/99), May (19/5/99), August and November. The Bundesbank announces the 10-day period for its auctions in a quarterly issuance calendar, then gives a week's notice of the exact date. Up to 1999, new lines were issued four times a year (in February, May, August and November), but this was reduced to two only as of second quarter 2000 (one per semester) with top-up in alternate quarters.

Schätze

- *Issue procedure*: 'American' auction among BIAG members, normally on a quarterly basis (March, June, September and December).

Table 2.4   *Bobl* issue (19/5/99): *Bobl* 3.25% 2/2004 line 130; Tap selling as of 17/2/99; Start of interest accrual: 17/2/99 (in millions of euros)

Bids	17 207
Competitive bids	10 768
Non-competitive bids	6 529
Weighted average price of total bids	99.72%
Allocation	5 680
Stop-out price	99.68%
Weighted average price	99.71%
Average rate (Current/Current)	3.31%
Tap sales	750
Retained for market-management operations	1 568
Total volume issued of line 130	8 000

Source: authors

- *Presentation of competitive bids*: from the invitation to bid (T − 0) up to 11.00 local time the day the auction is resolved (T + 1). Bids should be sent by e-mail to the Bundesbank or State Central Banks, and expressed as a percentage of nominal value to two decimal places, with a variation of 0.01 percentage points.
- *Minimum amount of bids*: 1 000 000 and multiples.
- *Announcement of target volume*: five days (T − 5) before the invitation date. Volumes envisaged usually stand at around 5 billion euros.
- *Auction results*: published one day (T + 1) after the invitation.
- *Payment/value date*: two days (T + 3) after the auction is resolved.
- *Admission to trading*: on payment date (T + 3).
- *Interest basis*: Current/Current.
- *Schätze auction calendar*: the Bundesbank announces the 10-day period for its auctions in a quarterly issuance calendar, then gives a week's notice of the exact date.

Bubills

- *Issue procedure*: 'American' auction between members of the BIAG, normally on a quarterly basis (January, April, July and October).
- *Presentation of competitive bids*: from announcement of the invitation to bid (T − 0) up to 11.00 local time on auction resolution date (T + 1). Bids should be sent by e-mail to the Bundesbank or State Central Banks, and expressed in percentage terms to three decimal places, with a variation of 0.005 percentage points.
- *Minimum amount of bids*: 1 000 000 euros and multiples.

Table 2.5 *Schätze* issue (16/3/99) (in millions of euros)

Bids	19 326
Competitive bids	10 859
Non-competitive bids	8 467
Weighted average price to total bids	100.11%
Allocation	4 238.4
Stop-out price	100.13%
Weighted average price	100.18%
Average rate (Current/Current)	2.91%
Retained for market-management operations	761.6
Total volume issued	5 000

Source: authors

Table 2.6 *Bubills* issue (14/4/99) (in millions of euros)

Bids	16 229
Competitive bids	14 390
Non-competitive bids	1 839
Weighted average price of total bids	98.751%
Allocation	5 033
Stop-out price	98.760%
Weighted average price	98.767%
Average rate (Current/360)	2.47%

Source: authors

- *Announcement of issue target*: five days (T − 5) before the invitation date. Volumes envisaged usually stand at around 5 billion euros.
- *Auction results*: published one day (T + 1) after the invitation.
- *Payment*: two days (T + 3) after the auction is resolved.
- *Admission to trading*: on payment date (T + 3).
- *Interest basis*: Current/360.
- *Bubills auction calendar*: the Bundesbank announces the exact date of auctions in its quarterly issuance calendar. The normal practice is to issue four lines a year on a quarterly basis.

2.4.4   Publication of Quarterly Issuance Calendars

The Bundesbank publishes its issuance calendar for the next quarter (for example: July, August and September) during the last 10 days of the preceding month (in this case, the closing days of June) on www.bundesbank.de/index_e.htm, alongside the volume of securities maturing and the interest payments to be met.

2.5   THE SECONDARY MARKET IN FEDERAL SECURITIES

2.5.1   Introduction

The secondary market in Federal securities leads the world in liquidity and depth. Trading, overwhelmingly concentrated in *Bunds*, *Bobls* and *Schätze*, is localised in German stock exchanges and OTC markets.

In these trading forums, Federal securities are quoted as a percentage of nominal value to two decimal places, with a tick of 0.01 bp (1 basis point) and a spread running normally from 3 to 5 bp. Almost all trades, as detailed below, are closed at the price set by specialist institutions in the first segment of the secondary market.

In the interest of maximum transparency, the Bundesbank and German exchanges publish a series of indicators or indices on Federal securities, chief among them: (i) the yield of bonds in issue, stated as a weighted average of the yield of all securities outstanding; (ii) the yields of Federal securities across a range of maturities, usually the corresponding benchmark instrument; (iii) the German bond price index (REX), based on a portfolio of synthetic bonds with prices derived from the yield structure of the Federal securities traded and, finally, (iv) a yield index (REXP), factoring in accrued interest. (All these indices, updated minute by minute, can be consulted on the web pages of the German stock exchanges.)

2.5.2   Secondary-Market Organisation: Trading Segments

Germany has eight stock exchanges, with FWB (the Frankfurt Stock Exchange) leading the field by trading volumes and listed securities. The organisational hub of the system comprises Deutsche Börse AG and Eurex Frankfurt AG (a subsidiary of Eurex Zurich AG, owned 50/50 by Schweizer Börse and Deutsche Börse AG), which operates in the Eurex Deutschland futures market (formerly DTB) providing a joint trading platform for the German and Swiss futures markets.

There is, then, seamless co-ordination between the Frankfurt spot market (FWB) and the Eurex futures market, taking in their respective clearing houses (Deutsche Börse Clearing

AG and Eurex Clearing AG), conducive to the ongoing development of the German Federal securities market.

Germany's stock exchanges comprise four trading segments:

1. the official or primary trading market
2. the privately organised regulated market
3. the open market
4. the new market, for young, innovative companies.

Only the first of these four is relevant to Federal securities trading, i.e. the official or primary trading market (*Amtlicher Handel*). Federal securities are admitted to continuous trading on this market segment at the close of their issuance period (T + 3) and suspended from trading 15 working days before redemption, of which advance notice is given in the official bulletin. Trading is conducted through the electronic XETRA system, fully operational since end-1998 and with the following main characteristics: (i) the concentration of liquidity in a single centralised market, (ii) transparent execution of orders and transactions, (iii) decentralised access via computer terminals with remote access capability, and (iv) back-up liquidity provided by a number of designated institutions.

Stock-exchange member companies divide into three categories, each with its own defined functions:

- *credit institutions, investment banks and broker–dealers*, empowered to conduct both proprietary and third-party trades
- *specialists (Kursmakler)*, which channel trading in listed Federal securities and fix official market prices. Specialists also undertake to quote prices continuously between 10.30 and 13.30 local time.
- *brokers (Freimakler)*, acting as intermediaries in listed security transactions and with price-fixing functions in the second (regulated) and third (open-market) segments. These institutions can also engage in proprietary trading.

2.5.3 Daily Fixing of Official Secondary-Market Prices

The daily fixing of official Federal security prices is a key feature of the German stock-exchange system. These prices set the standard for settling operations with clients, the valuation of positions and their accounting entries. The system works on the principle of 'maximum execution'; that is, the official price fixed must channel the greatest possible trading volume (greatest number of transactions matched). Price-fixing time represents the peak period for trading, though transactions may also be crossed before or after.

The process works as follows: at 11.00 each day local time, specialists fix the prices of each Federal security admitted to first-segment trading on the basis of all orders received up to that time. This procedure of bunching together all sell and buy orders at the same point in the day favours small or open-price orders which might otherwise go through at inflated rates.

2.5.4 Market-Management Operations

The Bundesbank is mandated to conduct Federal security price-management operations on German exchanges on behalf of Federal issuers. This intervention does not involve open-market operations with monetary policy aims, nor does it seek to influence market trends or secure a given yield for Federal securities. Its sole purpose is to provide the greatest possible liquidity to the secondary-market trading of Federal securities and to maintain a trading environment that is favourable to new issues.

2.5.5   The Supervision of German Markets

Supervisory functions are performed at two different but interrelated levels. Under the Stock Exchange Act, local bourses come under the supervision of the competent State authorities, in conjunction with stock-exchange supervisory committees. At Federal level, stock-exchange and OTC trading are monitored by the Federal Securities Supervision Board (BAWe), with responsibility for:

- identifying and sanctioning insider trading
- guaranteeing the publication of any relevant event which affects listed companies and may exert a significant influence on the formation of prices
- monitoring compliance with the general and specific rules binding on financial services firms, in particular those relating to customer transactions and the rendering of financial services
- monitoring compliance with rules on the notification and publicising of changes in the voting rights structure of listed companies
- maintaining wide-ranging co-operation with supervisory authorities in other countries
- ensuring the deposit of sales prospectuses for unlisted securities.

2.5.6   The German Strips Market

Germany's strips market was a relatively late starter compared to its French (1990), Belgian (1992) and Dutch (1993) counterparts. The stripping of three 10- and 30-year Federal bonds in issue was finally authorised in mid-1997. The stripping of 10- and 30-year bonds and the launch of new 30-year lines were a response by the Federal Government to investors' keen interest in strip facilities in long segments of the curve. As a prop to strips trading, Federal Bonds now have fixed dates for the payment of interest and principal (4 January and 4 July respectively) and, as such, may have 'long' or 'short' coupons depending on their date of issue. By this means, the Federal Government is providing investment opportunities across the whole length of the curve up to 30 years, even though it only issues at specific maturities (6 months and 2, 5, 10 and 30 years). There are currently 10 strippable lines, as detailed Table 2.7.

2.5.7   The German Futures Market

Germany's financial futures market, DTB (now EUREX Deutschland), dates back to 1990. It offers a wide range of products for the hedging and arbitrage of positions in deposits, bonds, shares, etc., and a correspondingly broad range of futures and options contracts on capital-market assets, shares and indices. As Table 2.8 shows, the main contracts traded on the EUREX are futures and options on bonds (61.64% of market turnover in April 1999). The growth in trading volumes, relative and absolute, recorded between April 1998 and April 1999 testifies to the strength and liquidity of the EUREX, which have shot it to the lead position in European futures, ahead of the London market LIFFE. This trading expansion has particularly favoured the futures contract on the *Bund* (+53.75%)

Table 2.7   Strippable *Bund* lines as of June 2000

Security	Outstanding
6.25% Bund 4/1/2024	10 225 837
6.00% Bund 4/1/2007	15 338 756
6.00% Bund 4/7/2007	15 338 756
6.50% Bund 4/7/2027	11 248 241
5.25% Bud 4/1/2008	15 338 756
4.75% Bund 4/7/2008	8 691 961
4.125% Bund 4/7/2008	13 804 880
3.75% Bund 4/1/2009	14 000 000
4.00% Bund 4/7/2009	11 000 000
4.50% Bund 4/7/2009	20 000 000
5.375% Bund 4/1/2010	20 000 000
5.25% Bund 4/7/2010	8 000 000
5.625% Bund 4/1/2028	14 316 172
4.75% Bund 4/7/2028	11 000 000
6.25% Bund 4/1/2030	7 000 000
Total	195 303 359

Millions of euros
Source: Bloomberg and authors

and *Bobl* (+20.76%), while *Schätze* volumes have actually contracted slightly (−2.73%). As regards remaining futures segments, note the trading slump in futures and options on shares listed on Germany's DAX (−16.17%) and the Swiss SMI (−19.40%).

Trading is conducted over a fully computerised platform which supports decentralised access (via PC terminal) to the global network.

The settlement of positions, whether by daily marking to market or on contract expiry, is underwritten by EUREX Clearing AG. This clearing house acts as counterparty to all market transactions and it calculates and monitors the margins (in the form of cash or securities) and guarantees that each counterparty must post relative to its current position.

EUREX bond futures contracts share the same characteristics as those traded on virtually all other European markets, i.e. a basket of deliverable bonds, cheapest-to-deliver (CTD), conversion factor, etc.

2.6   CLEARING AND SETTLEMENT

Before Federal securities clearing and settlement procedures are studied in detail, the German system of safe custody should be mentioned briefly. Public-sector bonds are generally issued as book entries representing a claim on the debt carried on the Federal Debt Register (FDA), and with identical legal status to paper certificates. Claims on registered debt can be of two types:

- *Individual claims*, where lenders figure free of any charge on the Federal Debt Register, in the form of a named account with the same characteristics as a bank custody account.
- *Collective claims*, appearing in the Federal Debt Register as a trust/deposit in favour of Deutsche Clearing AG, which, in turn, transfers these claims to the banks—via the securities clearing and settlement system—as individual participations in the "collective claim", administered by the banks on their own behalf or on behalf of third parties.

Table 2.8 EUREX Deutschland: Comparative Data April 1999–April 1998

	31/4/99	31/03/99	% Apr./Mar.	31/4/98	Var. % 98/99
Futures on EURIBOR (1 month)	10 121	11 507	12.04%	—	—
Futures on EURIBOR (3 months)	205 060	340 513	39.78%	—	—
Futures on EURO-LIBOR (3 months)	—	—	—	—	—
Futures on EUROMARCO (3 months)	—	—	—	47 372	−99.96%
Options on EURIBOR futures (3 months)	250	890	71.91%	—	−100.00%
Options on EUROMARCO futures (3 months)	—	—	−100.00%	300	−100.00%
Total money market	**215 549**	**352 910**	**−38.92%**	**49 611**	**334.48%**
Futures on Euro-*Schätze*	866 325	1 311 290	−33.94%	890 501	−2.73%
Futures on Euro-*Bobl*	3 053 359	4 043 683	−24.49%	2 528 519	20.76%
Futures on Euro-*Bund*	10 468 984	13 983 102	−25.13%	6 809 072	53.75%
Futures on Euro-*Buxl*	—	10	−100.00%	—	—
Options on Euro-*Schätze* futures	35 344	40 157	−11.99%	18 614	89.88%
Options on Euro-*Bobl* futures	55 756	54 892	1.57%	188 381	−70.40%
Options on Euro-*Bund* futures	1 800 956	2 116 311	−14.90%	210 511	755.52%
Rollover *Schätze* (Mar./Jun.)	—	12 399	—	—	—
Rollover *Bobl* (Mar./Jun.)	—	47 788	—	—	—
Rollover *Bund* (Mar./Jun.)	—	100 964	—	—	—
Total bond market	**16 330 799**	**21 799 108**	**−25.09%**	**10 721 664**	**52.32%**
Options on DAX shares	3 106 764	3 093 232	0.44%	3 705 937	−16.17%
Options on SMI (Swiss Monetary Index) shares	2 480 103	2 523 015	−1.70%	3 077 135	−19.40%
Total options on shares	**5 586 867**	**5 616 247**	**−0.52%**	**6 818 638**	**−18.06%**
Futures and options on stock-exchange indexes	4 359 642	6 044 924	−27.88%	3 435 740	26.89%
Total of index-linked products	**4 359 642**	**6 044 924**	**−27.88%**	**3 435 740**	**26.89%**
Total EUREX	**26 492 857**	**33 813 189**	**−21.65%**	**21 026 311**	**52.32%**
Money market	0.81%	1.04%	−38.92%	0.24%	334.48%
Bond market	61.64%	64.47%	−25.09%	50.99%	52.32%
Stocks and shares market	21.09%	16.61%	−0.52%	32.43%	−18.06%
Index-linked products	16.46%	17.88%	−27.88%	16.34%	26.89%

Millions of euros
Source: Deutsche Börse

The procedure is as shown in Figure 2.10.

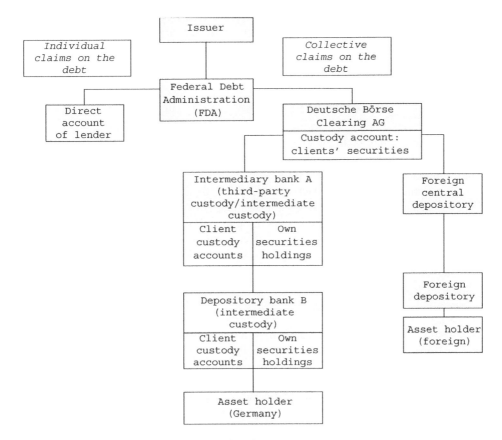

Figure 2.10   Federal securities clearing and settlement system

2.6.1   Deutsche Börse Clearing AG *(Deutscher Kassenverein)*

Deutsche Börse Clearing AG, together with its branches in the Berlin, Dusseldorf, Frankfurt, Hamburg, Hanover, Munich and Stuttgart stock exchanges, acts as a central depository for securities, kept under collective custody, and as a clearing and settlement system. Its status is that of a specialist bank performing restricted functions and subject to the supervision of the Federal Bank Supervision Board. Its remit is: (i) to perform all securities transfers arising from sale-purchase operations, and (ii) to service the debt under its administrative charge, such that all payments of interest or principal are settled in a timely manner and duly transferred to the securities' depositors.

Domestic Settlement of Operations

The standard rule for the clearing and settlement of all transactions on the German stock exchanges, unless otherwise specified by contract parties, is to settle operations on T + 2 by delivery against payment. As a guarantee of this principle, the Deutsche Börse Clearing

AG will only deliver securities when the corresponding (cash) payment has been credited through the depository bank's giro accounts with the corresponding State Central Bank. In this way, the seller of the securities is safeguarded against any loss of ownership prior to payment, while the buyer is assured receipt of its securities. Transactions closed on markets other than the stock exchanges can also be settled, in some cases on a same-day or real-time basis, through Deutsche Börse Clearing AG.

International Settlement of Operations

In the case of cross-border operations, Deutsche Börse Clearing AG must either entrust securities to the custody of foreign central depositories or act on their behalf as a 'third-party custodian'. Under long-standing agreements, foreign clearing houses are allowed to hold Federal securities on their own or clients' behalf in Deutsche Börse Clearing AG, empowering them to settle German securities. By the same token, German banks and broker–dealers can use these foreign institutions for the settlement of proprietary and customer trades with non-resident investors through their respective custody accounts with Deutsche Börse Clearing AG. The value date convention for cross-border transactions is $T + 3$ (though this may vary according to the convention used by the foreign central depository) and delivery against payment is applied as standard.

Central Securities Lending System

In conclusion, the *central securities lending system* open to all account holders in the Deutsche Börse Clearing AG should be mentioned. By using this system, sellers can transfer securities ahead of their ownership, paying an assignment commission to the lender. Lender risk—arising from borrowers defaulting on the return of the securities—is covered by a collateral arrangement. This system, which is peculiar to Deutsche Börse Clearing AG, should not be confused with the interbank repo market in Federal securities.

2.7   TAXATION

2.7.1   Personal Income Tax

In Germany, the main factor deciding the tax liability or otherwise of income earned on Federal security holdings (interest) is the investor's resident or non-resident status. Investors are considered resident if Germany is their normal place of residence for at least 183 days in a calendar year or if their economic interests are based in the country. All others, i.e. non-residents, pay taxes under the legislation of their country of residence, supplemented in some cases by international double-taxation agreements. German residents enjoy a special allowance known as the 'savers' deduction' (DM 6000) and another for 'investment expenses' (DM 100), both of which are doubled in the case of joint tax returns.

Any increase or decrease in the value of holdings is taxed not as income but as a capital gain or loss, except when regarded as of speculative origin. Speculative operations are defined for this purpose as those in which less than six months elapses from the time of purchase to the time of sale. The capital gains earned on operations of this type—the difference between acquisition and sale price less the 'investment expenses' deduction—are exempt from tax if the total gain attributable to a given tax year is less

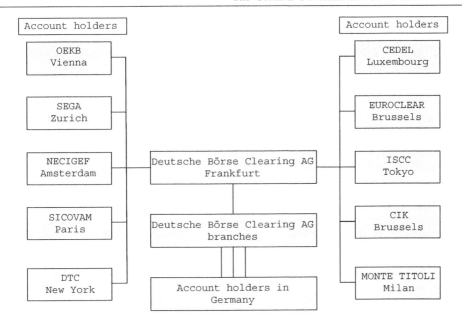

Figure 2.11 International links between custody agencies

than DM 1000. Regular capital gains raised from speculative operations can also be offset by regular losses incurred in the same tax year.

2.7.2 Withholdings

Since 1993, withholding taxes have been applied to income from investment in German securities and the interest earned on investment in foreign securities. Withholdings are made at source by the paying channel (securities depositories and custodians, the FDA) and must be added to the assessment base to calculate the tax rate applying. They are later returned to investors entitled to a tax rebate.

The interest on German or foreign securities paid in Germany to resident taxpayers is subject to a 30% withholding tax, increased in 1995 by a 75% 'solidarity tax' imposed because of the country's reunification. Non-residents and certain classes of German institution are exempt from this general withholding tax.

In the case of OTC transactions, a 35% withholding tax is applied to both residents and non-residents. The return of this tax, in the latter case, will depend on the bilateral agreements or international treaties to which their country of residence is a signatory.

2.8 SPECIALISTS, BROKERS AND BIAG MEMBERS

Germany differs from most euro-zone countries in its lack of a market-maker system. The place of the market-maker role is taken by the BIAG, formed by institutions specialising in the placement of Federal securities issued at Bundesbank auctions. The group's membership is currently down to 59, after the mergers and acquisitions of 1999, one resignation and the exclusion of 10 institutions on account of their below-par subscription activity. The Bundesbank published its last ranking of the BIAG's 59 members (Table 2.9) on 21 December 1999, though without specifying the quota ascribed to each.

The BIAG members are joined by a group of secondary-market specialists (*Krusmakler*) and brokers (*Freimakler*) with intermediation and official price-fixing functions—specialists in the first trading segment and brokers in the second and third—and with certain price-quoting obligations over pre-set trading hours.

Table 2.9   Ranking of BIAG members (December 1999)

1	Deutsche Bank	31	DGZ DekaBank
2	Dresdner Bank	32	SGZ Bank
3	Bayerische Hypo- und Vereinsbank	33	Crédit Suisse First Boston
4	Bayerische Landesbank Girozentrale	34	Hesse Newman & Co.
5	Westdeutsche Landesbank Girozentrale	35	Barclays Bank PLC
6	Morgan Stanley Bank AG	36	WGZ Bank
7	Norddeutsche Landesbank Girozentrale	37	Istituto Bancario San Paolo di Torino SpA
8	Goldman, Sachs & Co.		
9	Deutsche Genossenschaftsbank	38	BHF Bank
10	Bankgesellschaft Berlin	39	Vereins- und Westbank
11	Landesbank Baden-Württemberg	40	Landesbank Hessen-Thüringen Girozentrale
12	Paribas		
13	Salomon Brothers	41	Landesbank Sachsen Girozentrale
14	Landesbank Berlin Girozentrale	42	Hamburger Sparkasse
15	ABN AMRO Bank AG	43	Nomura Bank GmbH
16	Société Générale SA	44	GZB Bank
17	Commerzbank	45	Cooperative Centrale Raiffeisen Boerenleenbank
18	Banque Nationale de Paris		
19	J.P. Morgan	46	BfG Bank AG
20	Banca Monte dei Paschi di Siena SpA	47	Warburg Dillon Read AG
21	Merrill Lynch Capital Markets Bank Limited	48	HSBC Trinkaus und Burkhardt
		49	Landesbank Saar Girozentrale
22	Lehman Brothers Bankhaus	50	Bank of America
23	Landesbank Rheinland-Pfalz Girozentrale	51	Bank of Tokyo Mitsubishi
		52	Kreissparkasse Köln
24	ING Bank NV Deutschland Branch	53	Stadtsparkasse Köln
25	Hamburgische Landesbank Girozentrale	54	Merck, Finck & Co.
		55	National Bank
26	Landesbank Schleswig-Holstein Girozentrale	56	M.M. Warburg & Co.
		57	Banca Commerciale Italiana
27	Bremer Landesbank Kreditanstalt Oldenburg	58	Reuschel & Co.
		59	Schmidt Bank Kommanditgesellschaft auf Aktien
28	Baden-Württembergische Bank		
29	Deutsche Apotheker- und Ärztebank		
30	Deutsche Siedlungs- und Landesrentenbank		

Source: Bundesbank

ANNEXE: THE GERMAN PUBLIC DEBT MARKET

Outcome of Bund, Bobl *and* Schätze *Issues in 2000*

Auction	Instrument	Coupon	Term	Target	Settles	Matures	Format	Sold	Total bids	Non Comp	Bid/sold	Stop rate	Stop price	Avge rate	Avge price
05-Jan-00	Bund	5.375%	10 years	9 000	07-Jan-00	04-Jan-10	Auction	5 881	8 786	2 326	1.49	—	98.930	5.500	99.020
19-Jan-00	Bund	6.25%	30 years	5 000	21-Jan-00	04-Jan-30	Auction	2 567	3 802	939	1.48	—	99.950	6.240	100.060
16-Feb-00	Bobl	4.25%	5 years	6 000	18-Feb-00	18-Feb-05	Auction	4 745	9 621	2 226	2.03	—	95.840	5.200	95.860
15-Mar-00	Schätze	4.50%	2 years	5 000	17-Mar-00	15-Mar-02	Auction	4 476	14 785	3 763	3.30	—	99.960	4.520	99.960
23-Mar-00	Bund	6.25%	30 years	2 000	23-Mar-00	04-Jan-30	Reopening	2 000	2 000	—	1.00	—	Market	Market	—
12-Apr-00	Schätze	4.50%	2 years	1 000	12-Apr-00	15-Mar-02	Reopening	1 000	1 000	—	1.00	—	Market	Market	—
12-Apr-00	Bobl	4.25%	5 years	1 000	12-Apr-00	18-Feb-05	Reopening	1 000	1 000	—	1.00	—	Market	Market	—
03-May-00	Bund	5.25%	10 years	10 000	05-May-00	04-Jul-10	Auction	6 309	10 412	2 443	1.65	—	99.260	5.340	99.290
17-May-00	Bobl	5.00%	5 years	5 000	19-May-00	20-May-05	Auction	4 773	12 181	3 372	2.55	—	98.830	5.260	98.850
14-Jun-00	Schätze	5.00%	2 years	5 000	16-Jun-00	14-Jun-02	Auction	4 400	7 018	2 365	1.60	—	100.240	4.870	100.250
05-Jul-00	Bund	5.25%	10 years	10 000	07-Jul-00	04-Jul-10	Auction	8 123	9 243	2 215	1.14	—	99.500	5.280	99.730
16-Aug-00	Bobl	5.00%	5 years	5 000	18-Aug-00	19-Aug-05	Auction	5 414	14 224	2 754	2.63	—	99.120	5.180	99.140
13-Sep-00	Schätze	5.00%	2 years	5 000	15-Sep-00	13-Sep-02	Auction	4 723	11 465	2 040	2.43	—	99.740	5.130	99.750
14-Sep-00	Bund	5.25%	10 years	2 000	04-Jul-00	04-Jul-10	Reopening	2 000	2 000	—	1.00	—	Market	Market	—
14-Sep-00	Bund	5.00%	5 years	1 000	19-Aug-00	19-Aug-05	Reopening	1 000	1 000	—	1.00	—	Market	Market	—
18-Oct-00	Bund	5.25%	10 years	10 000	20-Oct-00	04-Jan-11	Auction	7 891	23 805	5 081	3.02	—	100.150	5.210	100.27
24-Oct-00	Bund	5.50%	30 years	5 000	25-Oct-00	04-Jan-31	Auction	3 951	7 548	1 761	1.91	—	99.510	5.520	99.600

Source: Bundesbank and authors

Outcome of Bubill *Issues in 2000*

Auction	Instrument	Term	Target	Matures	Days	Settles	Format	Sold	Bids	NC bids	Bid/cover	Bid/target	Stop rate	Avge rate
12-Jan-00	Bubilis	6 months	5 000	14-Jul-00	182	14-Jan-00	Auction	4 811	8 001	353	1.7	1.6	—	3.410
12-Apr-00	Bubilis	6 months	5 000	13-Oct-00	182	14-Apr-00	Auction	5 125	6 365	545	1.2	1.3	—	3.950
12-Jul-00	Bubilis	6 months	5 000	12-Jan-01	182	14-Jul-00	Auction	4 873	10 421	761	2.1	2.1	—	4.600
11-Oct-00	Bubilis	6 months	5 000	20-Apr-01	189	13-Oct-00	Auction	4 861	8 610	1 566	1.8	1.7	—	4.880

Source: Bundesbank and authors

Characteristics of Federal Government Securities issued by the Bundesbank

	Bunds	Bobls	Schätze	Savings Bonds	Bubills
Issue frequency	two or three lines a year (topping-up option)	two lines a year (topping-up option)	four lines a year (topping-up option)	—	quarterly auctions (four lines)
Procedure	'American' auction among BIAG members	sales on tap and 'American' auction among BIAG members	'American' auction among BIAG members	tap issue	'American' auction among BIAG members
Issue dates	Irregular	semiannual (February and August)	quarterly (March, June, Sep, Dec)	continuous	quarterly (Jan, Apr, Jul, Oct)
Minimum denomination	0.01 euros	0.01 euros	0.01 euros	DEM 0.01	1 000 000 euros
Minimum bid at issue	Auction: 1 000 000 euros	Tap: 100 euros Auction: 1 000 000 euros	Auction: 1 000 000 euros	DEM 1 000	Auction: 1 000 000 euros
Target outstanding amount	15 to 20 billion euros	5 to 8 billion euros	5 to 7 billion euros	open	5 billion euros
Maximum bid	unrestricted	unrestricted	unrestricted	DEM 500,000 per person and working day	unrestricted
Interest payment	annual	annual	annual	Type A: annual Type B: on redemption	issued at a discount

Interest basis	Current/Current	Current/Current	Current/Current	Current/Current	Current/360
Maturity	10 years 30 years	5 years 3 months	2 years	Type A: 6 years Type B: 7 years	six months
Redemption	at par	at par	at par	Type A: at par Type B: at redemption value (par + interest)	at par
Purchaser range	unrestricted	At issue: individuals and non-profit organisations After auction: unrestricted	unrestricted	individuals and non-profit organisations	unrestricted
Early redemption	after admission to stock exchanges, at market prices	after admission to stock exchanges, at market prices	after admission to stock exchanges, at market prices	after first year, resale to Federal Government (Bundesbank), to max. DM 10000 per month, at par plus interest	possibility of sales in secondary market
Transferability to third parties	at any time	during selling on tap: authorised buyers only. After close of selling: unrestricted	at any time	at any time; only to authorised counterparties	at any time
Materialisation	book entries in the Federal Debt Register				
Selling agents	commercial banks and State Central Banks				
Safe custody	banks, savings banks, credit co-operatives, State Central Banks and Federal Debt Administration				

Source: Bundesbank and authors

3
The Austrian Government Bond Market

3.1 INTRODUCTION

The Austrian public debt market is one of the smallest in the European Union, yet its public debt/GDP ratio (70%) ranks with those of the medium-sized markets. It has more than doubled in size since 1990, and has a current outstanding total of approximately 82.5 billion euros.

Despite its small size compared to other issuers, Austria's fixed-income market (public and private) stands far ahead of its stock-market capitalisation. Specifically, the total volume of fixed-income issues is 144.3 billion euros, whereas Vienna Stock Exchange capitalisation was only 32.1 billion as of May 2000. Furthermore, government issues have grown much faster than the Austrian fixed-income market as a whole, such that the outstanding volume of public debt is more than 60% of the total market, against 37.5% in 1990. This chapter focuses on the central government debt market, although the Austrian Länder and municipalities also raise finance through debt issuance, albeit sporadically and in residual volumes only.

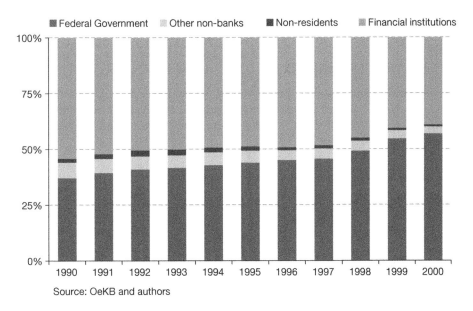

Figure 3.1 Composition of the Austrian public debt market as of July 2000

After Austria's public deficit exceeded 5% of GDP in 1994 and 1995, a fiscal consolidation programme was initiated to comply with Maastricht conditions. As a result, the deficit was reined back to 2.1% in 1998, while the volume of public debt in issue (which since 1993 had exceeded the 60% threshold imposed by convergence criteria) dropped

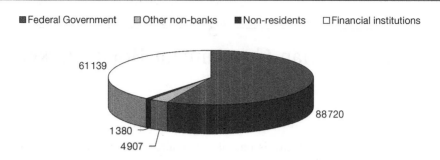

Source: OeKB and authors

Figure 3.2 Composition of the Austrian public debt market as of July 2000 (in millions of euros)

from 69.5% of GDP in 1996 to 63.1% at the beginning of 1999. The Stability Programme presented by Austria envisages that both the public deficit and public debt issuance will continue to decrease as far as 1.4% and 60% of GDP respectively in the year 2002.

Such is Austria's economic interdependence with Germany, and the close tie between the Austrian schilling and deutschmark exchange rates, that it is almost possible to talk of a monetary union between the two countries since 1970. This circumstance, together with the 1999 start-up of the third phase of EMU, has resulted in only a minimal yield spread between German and Austrian bonds. However, cracks began to show in this traditional relationship during the opening months of 2000, when a coalition between the government and an extreme right-wing party sent spreads widening to upwards of 25 bp.

3.2 ASSETS ISSUED BY THE AUSTRIAN TREASURY

Until 1986, the Austrian Treasury's medium- and long-term issues took the form of serial bonds, i.e. bonds with various maturity dates scheduled at regular intervals until the issue is retired. Since then, all medium- and long-term issues have comprised bullet bonds, redeemable only upon maturity.

3.2.1 Federal Bonds (*Bundesanleihen* or BAs)

These assets pay a fixed annual coupon registered by book entry in the Austrian Book-Entry System, operated by the Oesterreichische Kontrollbank AG. (The Oesterreichische Kontrollbank AG, OeKB, is a private entity owned by the major Austrian banks and one foreign bank. The government created the OeKB as the body responsible for the entry, settlement and clearance of securities. Book entry of securities issued by the Austrian Treasury is handled by the Book-Entry System, WSB.) Federal Bonds have 1- to 50-year maturities (usually 5, 10 and 30 years), and since 1 January 1999 have been drawn up in euros. The minimum denomination is 1000 euros and interest is calculated on a Current/Current basis, i.e. according to the exact number of days between coupons, for issues conducted in 1999 and coupons start to accrue in that year. The Austrian government's *Bundesanleihen* are strippable into coupons and principal and may only be redeemed upon maturity.

Since 28 January 1999, Austrian government bonds have been issued under the Debt Issuance Programme (DIP), a dual procedure comprising either auction or syndication among a certain number of Austrian and international banks. The first tranche of each line is usually syndicated and the remaining tranches are issued at auction (though issue through a banking syndicate is also possible). Participating entities in both cases are a group of 27 banks (8 Austrian and 19 foreign) chosen as market makers by the Austrian Treasury according to a series of criteria set out in section 3.8 below.

Bundesanleihen are quoted at a clean price to two decimal places, and the yield formula is as follows:

$$P + Cc = \sum_{i=1}^{n} F_i \times R^{\frac{-d_i}{b}}$$

where d is the exact number of days between value date and each respective coupon payment date on a Current/Current basis, and b is the number of days between coupon payments, also on a Current/Current basis. The term R is equivalent to $1/(1+y)$, in which y is the IRR or yield.

y itself is derived from the following formula:

$$y = 100 \times (R - 1)$$

3.2.2 Austrian *Bundesobligationen* (aOBLs)

These securities, issued prior to the introduction of the auction system (1988), are designed for individual investors and have the same characteristics as the *Bundesanleihen* (fixed coupons, etc.). They are drawn up in Austrian schillings and were not redenominated into euros due to their low outstanding balance and short remaining term. As of May 2000, there were 14 aOBL series outstanding for a total amount of 9.27 billion schillings (674 million euros). The average life of these issues is 4.64 years and the average balance is approximately 662 million schillings (48 million euros).

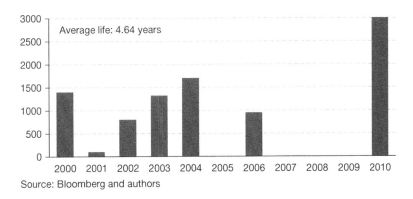

Source: Bloomberg and authors

Figure 3.3   aOBL maturities as of May 2000 (in millions of Austrian schillings)

3.2.3 Austrian Treasury Bills (ATBs)

ATBs are money-market assets issued through the multi-currency Austrian Treasury Bill Programme created in March 1999 under British legislation. Citibank is the main agent. Clearance and settlement of ATBs is performed through EUROCLEAR and CEDEL,

Table 3.1   The Austrian Treasury Bill Programme

Maturities	7 to 365 days (364 for pounds sterling)
Currency	Any currency
Dealers	Any dealer
Interest rate	At discount, fixed, floating, indexed, etc. (normally at discount)
Minimum denomination	100 000 euros (however, denominations in other currencies are also accepted)
Type of bill	Global bearer bill
Status of the bill	Pari passu[1]
Negative pledge	Yes
Cross default	No[2]
Listing	Bills are not listed on any stock exchange, unless otherwise agreed
Working days	Euro: TARGET and London Other currencies: the most relevant financial centre for the currency and London
Main agent	CITIBANK, NA, London
Settlement system	EUROCLEAR and CEDEL
Applicable legislation	British

[1]Clause whereby the borrower undertakes not to grant a new creditor more advantageous guarantees or conditions than those granted to the lender in whose contract said clause is included.
[2]Clause denouncing a breach of obligations to third parties.
Source: authors

which also act as depositories for the securities. Maturities can vary from 7 to 365 days, and interest can be at discount, fixed, floating, indexed, etc.

This programme was created to give investors a short-term investment product with payment in only two days (value date $T + 2$). Issues are conducted by auction or direct placement (tap issue) among entities designated by the Austrian Treasury (*Oesterreichische Bundesfinanzierunsagentur*, hereafter OeBFA). The maximum outstanding balance permitted in the 1999 ATB programme was two billion euros. The characteristics of the Austrian Treasury Bill Programme are summarised in Table 3.1.

As of May 2000, the Austrian Treasury had issued 75 ATBs, 54 of which were denominated in dollars, 1 in pounds sterling, 2 in Swiss francs and 18 in US dollars. It is possible to issue lines with extensible maturity (i.e. automatically renewable), although a clause

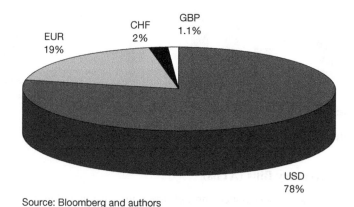

Source: Bloomberg and authors

Figure 3.4   ATB issues by currency as of July 2000

Table 3.2   The Austrian MTN programme

Maturities	7 days to 50 years
Currency	Any currency
Dealers	Any dealer
Interest rate	Fixed, variable, zero-coupon, linked to an index or to a formula
Denomination	Subject to any relevant legislation as agreed between the Austrian government and the dealer
Type of note	Bearer or registered
Note status	Pari passu[1]
Negative pledge	Yes
Cross default	No[2]
Listing	In Luxembourg or where specified in each issue
Working days	Euro: TARGET Other currencies: the relevant financial centre for the currency
Main agent	CITIBANK, NA, London
Settlement system	EUROCLEAR, CEDEL (registered bills only) or as specified in the issue
Applicable legislation	British

[1]Clause whereby the borrower undertakes not to grant a new creditor more advantageous guarantees or conditions than those granted to the lender in whose contract said clause is included
[2]Clause denouncing a breach of obligations to third parties
Source: authors

is included that enables the issuer to opt unilaterally against renewal 180 days before the next-up maturity date (when, in theory, the bill would automatically be renewed).

The formula for calculating ATB yields in the secondary market is as follows (standard for assets issued at discount in the euro area):

$$P_0 = \frac{100}{\left(1 + \dfrac{R}{100} \times \dfrac{d}{360}\right)}$$

where d is the number of days (on a Current/360 basis) between the bill's value and maturity dates.

3.2.4   MTN Programme (Medium-term International Note Issuance Programme)

This programme, also introduced in March 1999, permits an interval of just three days between launch and payment date. Notes issued under its aegis have a ceiling balance of five billion euros. Programme features are summarised in Table 3.2.

Only four issues for an amount of eight billion Austrian schillings (581.4 million euros) were outstanding as of May 2000, with coupons ranging from 3.75% to 4.40% and an average residual life of one year.

3.3   OVERVIEW OF THE AUSTRIAN PUBLIC DEBT MARKET

Following the redenomination of most *Bundesanleihen* issues from Austrian schillings into euros, the amount of debt in foreign currencies has been reduced to 23%, and more than half the international issues within this percentage are denominated in euro-legacy

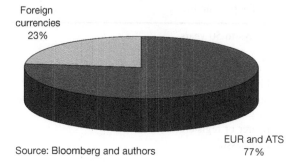

Figure 3.5   Total outstanding balance of Austrian debt by currency (July 2000)

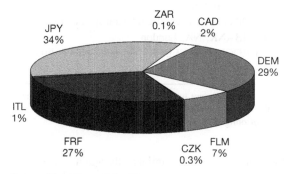

Figure 3.6   Austrian Federal Government international issues (July 2000)

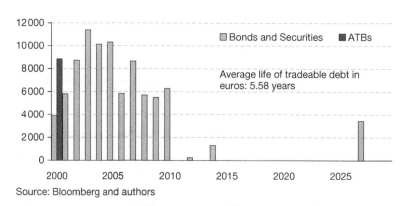

Figure 3.7   Maturities curve of Austrian debt as of March 2000 (domestic issues, in millions of euros)

currencies. The result, as in most euro-zone member states, has been a sharp reduction in exchange risk.

The majority of Austria's domestic issues are composed of *Bundesanleihen* or BAs (with an outstanding balance of 85.5 billion euros as of May 2000), topped up by the ATB programme (5917 billion euros) and residual aOBL issues (1156 billion euros).

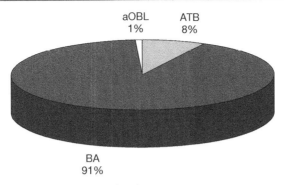

aOBL
1%

ATB
8%

BA
91%

Source: Bloomberg and authors

Figure 3.8   Distribution of Austrian domestic debt as of July 2000

Austria's maturities curve does not differ much from that of the other core countries
(Spain, Germany, France, Belgium and Holland), and the average life of domestic debt
(ATBs, aOBLs and BAs) is approximately 5.58 years.

3.4   THE PRIMARY MARKET

3.4.1   BA Issuance Procedure

From January 1989 to April 1990, Austrian Federal Government public debt was issued
by one procedure only: an 'American' price-based auction. In April 1990, this system
was replaced by a yield-based 'American' auction, with one underwritten or syndicated
tranche (approximately half the volume issued yearly was underwritten by a syndicate of
market makers). The definitive auction system, which continues to date, was instituted in
February 1991.

Issuance of Austrian *Bundesanleihen* has been conducted since January 1999 by a dual
procedure comprising both 'American' auctions and a Debt Issuance Programme (DIP)
implemented through a banking syndicate. The first tranche of a new line is usually issued
through the Debt Issuance Programme (DIP) and placed with a banking syndicate formed
of market makers selected by the Treasury. The remaining tranches of the same issue or
line (fungible within each series) are issued by auction (*Auktion*).

3.4.2   DIP or BA Issuance Programme

The reason for using a syndicated placement system (the DIP)—also used, with variants,
by other euro-zone treasuries—is to ensure that each line attains the critical mass or
outstanding balance to encourage investor take-up at subsequent auctions.

Under the Debt Issuance Programme (DIP), only those entities participating in auctions
may act as managers or co-managers. The syndicate itself can vary with each issue. This
programme enables the Austrian Federal Government to react swiftly and flexibly to
specific market circumstances and changing investor demand. The characteristics of the
Debt Issuance Programme via banking syndicate are as shown in Table 3.3.

Table 3.3   The Austrian Debt Issuance Programme

Maturities	Not to exceed 50 years (usually 5, 10 and 30 years)
Currency	Euro
Dealers	Auction participants
Interest rate	Fixed on a Current/Current basis, payable annually
Denomination	1000 euros
Type of bill	Global bearer bill
Negative pledge	Yes
Cross default	No
Listing	On the Vienna Stock Exchange at least
Working days	TARGET
Main agent	Oesterreichische Kontrollbank AG
Settlement system	Oesterreichische Kontrollbank AG
Applicable legislation	Austrian
Strips	Possible

Source: authors

3.4.3   BA Auctions

Since February 1991 (date of the most recent modification), auction issuance has been conducted as follows:

- *Issuance calendar*: at each year-end, the Austrian Federal Financing Agency (*Oester-reichische Bundesfinanzierungsagentur*) announces the nominal issue volume forecast for the following year and the corresponding issuance calendar (in 1999, for instance, the issuance volume targeted was 15 to 18 billion euros). Auctions are usually held every six weeks, on Tuesdays. Settlement takes place three working days after the auction (usually the following Friday or $T + 3$). Trading on the secondary market begins one working day after settlement date (the Monday following the auction or $T + 4$).
- *Announcement of issue characteristics*: five working days prior to the day of the auction $(T - 5)$, the Treasury announces the bond maturity (including the date interest begins to accrue and coupon payment dates) and the target issue volume (minimum one billion euros, unless the annual target volume for the reference in question has been used up). Prior to the announcement, market makers can submit recommendations to the government regarding issue conditions.
- *Auction participants*: only appointed market makers can attend the auctions. This group currently consists of 27 entities (8 domestic and 19 foreign institutions) Other institutions wishing to acquire the assets in issue must do so through a market maker (market-maker rights and obligations are described in full in section 3.8 below).
- *Presentation of competitive bids*: each of the 27 banks chosen must subscribe bids for at least 1/27th part of the issue volume announced, to ensure that coverage is complete. No participant, however, may request more than 30% of the total issue amount. Bids must specify both volume and yield. The yield (in net terms) sought by the subscriber must be stated to two decimal places (three decimal places, if desired, for issues with maturities exceeding 10 years). Bids from auction participants must be communicated to the Oesterreichische Kontrollbank AG before 11.00 (local time) on the auction date. Multiple bids specifying different yields may be submitted. Once bids are in, the Austrian Treasury reserves the right to cancel the issue up to 12.00 hours (local time). If this occurs, the auction is automatically convened for the following week (five working

days after the original date). Since May 1998, bids have been placed electronically through the Austrian Direct Auction System (ADAS). The Oesterreichische Kontroll-bank AG calculates the auction result and sends it through ADAS to the Treasury (*Bundesfinanzierungsagentur*) and participating entities.

- *Coupon and official issue price*: bids are sorted in ascending order of yield. Once the target amount is reached, the Oesterreichische Kontrollbank AG calculates the average yield for all bids under the issue limit. The coupon is then determined by rounding off this average yield to the nearest 0.05%, to give an average price (expressed in units of 5 bp) with the least possible deviation from par. The official issue price of a bond—the amount to be paid by the subscribing entity—is equal to the average price plus a variable sales commission in line with asset maturity. The commission for 5-year bonds is 1.05%, for 10-year bonds 1.5% and for maturities over 14 years 2%.

- *Allocation of competitive bids*: accepted competitive bids are allotted at the bid yield, as translated into the corresponding coupon price. Bids at the lowest price accepted (stop-out) may be subject to pro rata allocation. Those entities allotted less than 15 million euros can make non-competitive bids up to 15 million euros (including the amount allotted in the competitive auction). If the total number of bids in the non-competitive tranche exceeds 10% of the competitive round, a downward pro rata allocation will be effected until the 10% threshold is reached. If bids exceed 100 million euros in the non-competitive tranche, and the volume of the competitive auction is under 1 billion euros, a downward pro rata allocation of the non-competitive tranche will be effected as far as 100 million euros. Allocation in the non-competitive tranche is at the average price accepted in competitive bidding.

- *The Treasury's auction share*: since January 1998, the issue volume of each BA tranche has been increased by 10%. This incremental volume is retained by the Treasury—in the government's name—and later sold in the secondary market on a discretionary basis (open-market operations). This system resembles that used by the Bundesbank when it retains a given amount of issue volume for market-management operations. The differ-ence is that, in Austria's case, the amount is on top of, not part of, the volume announced.

An example of an Austrian government *Bundesanleihen* auction is given in Table 3.4.

Table 3.4 Auction of the second tranche of the 4.3% line, maturing 15/7/2003

Auction resolution date	7 September 1999
Payment/value date	10 September 1999
Payment of first coupon	15 July 2000
Maturity	15 July 2003
Total amount of issue	1650 million euros
Amount of competitive auction	1500 million euros
Allotted to the Treasury	150 million euros
Official issue price	100.85%
Accrued interest (57 days)	0.66967...%
Final yield for investor	4.05357%
Maximum rate accepted (marginal)	4.32%
Pro rata at marginal rate	25.72%
Allotted to Austrian banks	394.6 million euros (26.3%)
Allotted to foreign banks	1105.4 million euros (73.7%)

Source: authors

3.5   THE SECONDARY MARKET

The bulk of Austrian Treasury Bond trading (approximately 95%) is conducted on the over-the-counter (OTC) market. OTC trading is primarily through the interbank market structure or directly between institutional investors. In 1991, an electronic Direct Settlement System was created to channel OTC market transactions. Remaining trading is conducted on the Vienna Stock Exchange, which until 1999 (and the introduction of the German Stock Exchange XETRA system) had a partial electronic trading system (PATS) and a complete electronic trading system (EQOS). On 5 November 1999, the XETRA trading platform was introduced in place of the two previous systems. EuroMTS, a third trading environment, is limited to the most liquid lines of Austrian *Bundesanleihen*.

Turnover figures provided by the Vienna Stock Exchange and the semi-official or OTC market show that securities trading in Austria is heavily biased towards fixed-income assets (Austrian Federal Government and private issues) in preference to equities, and that fixed-income security trading is overwhelmingly centred on the OTC segment. Although no data are available for this last market from 1997 onwards, it is clear that trading of fixed-income securities on the Vienna Stock Exchange contracted sharply as of that year, such that 1999 turnover was roughly 30% lower than that for 1997. It seems highly unlikely that OTC trading has fallen by anything like the same extent.

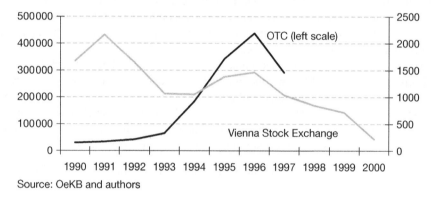

Source: OeKB and authors

Figure 3.9   Fixed-income securities traded on the Austrian market (in millions of euros)

BAs are quoted on the secondary market as a percentage of nominal value to two decimal places, both on the Vienna Stock Exchange and on the Reuters and Bloomberg pages of market makers participating in the OTC segment. Austrian bond transactions are settled three working days after the operation (T + 3). Trading commissions in the secondary market (including brokerage fees, bank commissions and turnover tax) amount to 0.75% of total turnover.

3.5.1   The Repo Market

The Austrian Treasury offers market makers the option of carrying out repo operations on Austrian government debt to compensate these entities for fulfilling their market-making obligations. In 1991, this facility was extended to bonds issued by other Austrian issuers and to certain corporate borrowers.

Table 3.5 Turnover in Austrian fixed-income securities

Year	Vienna SE	%	OTC market	%	Total
1990	1675	5.3%	29 975	94.7%	31 650
1991	2161	6.0%	34 120	94.0%	36 281
1992	1645	3.8%	42 044	96.2%	43 689
1993	1062	1.6%	65 484	98.4%	66 546
1994	1049	0.6%	184 209	99.4%	185 258
1995	1379	0.4%	343 215	99.6%	344 595
1996	1463	0.3%	437 737	99.7%	439 200
1997	1036	0.4%	292 016	99.6%	293 052
1998	842	—	—	—	—
1999	713	—	—	—	—
2000	216	—	—	—	—

Millions of euros
Source: OeKB

3.5.2 The Strips Market

The separate trading of the coupons and principal of new BA lines was authorised as of October 1996, on the initiative of the Central Securities Depository (OeKB). Information on stripping and reconstitution of Austrian Treasury Bonds is available on the Reuters OeKB03 page. Despite Treasury and OeKB efforts, stripped volumes have not substantially increased since the start-up of this investor facility.

References strippable into coupons and principal are shown in Table 3.6, together with their outstanding balance and stripped volume as of November 1999.

3.5.3 The Derivatives Market

In 1998 the Vienna Stock Exchange decided to abolish the government bonds futures market (AGB). The feeling was that the introduction of the euro and the concentration of liquidity in the German *Bund* contract traded on the EUREX (formerly Deutsche

Table 3.6 Strippable references as of November 1999

Reference	Outstanding balance	Stripped volume
BA 96-06/7	1134	55
BA 97-07/5	1466	0
BA 97-27/6	3443	186
BA 98-08/1	5707	0
BA 98-03/2	7455	0
BA 98-05/3	6186	0
BA 99-14/1	1320	0
BA 99-09/2	5500	0
BA 99-04/3	4415	0
BA 99-10/4	2200	0

Millions of euros
Source: authors

Terminbörse or DTB) would rob this market of its investor appeal, as events would later confirm.

3.5.4 Debt Exchanges

The Austrian Federal Government repurchases or exchanges insufficiently liquid bonds (generally on the point of maturing and with coupons at odds with market rates) for 'on-the-run' assets. These exchanges are offered to market makers on an irregular basis, i.e. with no pre-set programme.

3.6 CLEARING AND SETTLEMENT

3.6.1 Domestic Settlement

Domestic clearance and settlement of securities is performed by the Arrangement Bureau, under the Oesterreichische Kontrollbank AG. The Bureau settles operations conducted on the Vienna Stock Exchange on a T + 3 value basis, i.e. three working days after the transaction.

The large percentage of securities turnover falling to OTC market transactions (approximately 95% of fixed-income and 40% of equities trading) prompted the Oesterreichische Kontrollbank AG to develop the Direct Settlement System (DS) for this type of operation, accounted for in the Austrian Central Securities Depository (WSB or Wertpapiersammelbank). The WSB is operated by the Oesterreichische Kontrollbank AG and is responsible for the custody and transfer of securities (through a book-entry system) and for accounting for securities and deposit settlement, using information furnished by the Austrian clearance system and the Direct Settlement System (DS).

3.6.2 Settlement of International Operations

Settlement of international operations (between non-residents or between residents and non-residents) takes place via the connections the Oesterreichische Kontrollbank AG maintains with other foreign clearance and settlement houses, such as CEDEL, EURO-CLEAR, SICOVAM and Deutsche Börse Clearing AG. As for domestic transactions, settlement takes place three working days after the operation (T + 3).

3.7 TAXATION

3.7.1 Investors Resident in Austria

Since 1993, a withholding tax has been applied to interest earned on any investment in Austrian Federal Government securities. The amount withheld, initially 22%, was increased to 25% in 1996.

Interest is also subject to personal income tax (in the case of natural persons). If the interest proceeds from domestic securities and the investor is a legal entity residing in Austria, it is liable for corporate income tax, with the exception of bonds issued from 1 January 1999 onwards.

Nonetheless, there are some exemptions to the application of this withholding tax to accrued interest (though not to personal or corporate income taxes). The following are exempt:

- interest on bonds redenominated into euros issued before 1994
- interest on bonds in foreign currencies issued before 1989 and not redenominated into euros
- interest on bonds redenominated into euros issued by foreign financial institutions before October 1992.

3.7.2 Non-resident Investors in Austria and Investors with Tax Residence Abroad

The interest earned by non-residents on holdings of Austrian Federal Government bonds is not liable for any tax or withholding whatsoever, and coupons are paid gross.

3.8   MARKET MAKERS

The category of market maker was first introduced in 1989, and 27 financial institutions (8 Austrian and 19 foreign) currently fulfil this role. The selection of market makers depends ultimately on the Treasury, backed by a recommendation from the Oesterreichische Kontrollbank AG.

3.8.1 Eligibility for Market-Maker Status

Institutions applying for market-maker status in Austrian Treasury Bonds must meet a series of requirements concerning their:

- capitalisation
- geographical base
- scope of business and human resources
- trading in Austrian and other fixed-income securities.

3.8.2 Market-Maker Obligations

Market makers must:

- subscribe bids at auction for a minimum 1/27th of the volume announced by the Treasury
- perform market-making functions, i.e. offer bid and ask prices for a range of Austrian debt references during specified trading hours (previously a contractual obligation was acquired along with market-maker status, but this has been abolished)
- make periodic reports to the Treasury on their debt-market activity, including trading details.

3.8.3 Special Privileges or Rights derived from Market-Maker Status

Market makers receive a commission of 10 bp on the price of their allocations in Treasury security auctions. They have the exclusive right to participate in Austrian Treasury securities auctions.

3.8.4 Market Makers in Austrian Public Debt

Austrian Banks

Bank für Arbeit und Wirtschaft AG
Bank of Austria AG

Österreichische Postsparkasse AG
Österreichische Volksbanken-AG
Raiffeisen Zentralbank Österreich AG
Raiffeisenlandesbank Oberösterreich Reg. GmbH
Erste Bank der Österreichischen Sparkassen AG
Oberbank AG

Foreign Banks

ABN AMRO Bank NV
CDC Marchés
Banque Paribas
Bayerische Hypo-und Vereinsbank AG
DG Bank (Deutsche Genossenschaftsbank) AG
Commerzbank AG
Crédit Agricole Indosuez
Crédit Suisse First Boston (Europe) Ltd
Deutsche Bank AG
Dresdner Bank AG
Goldman Sachs International
HSBC Markets Ltd
ING Bank NV
Morgan Stanley & Co. International Ltd
Nomura International PLC
Salomon Brothers International Ltd
Société Générale SA
UBS AG

ANNEXE: THE AUSTRIAN PUBLIC DEBT MARKET

Austrian Federal Government Bundesanleihen Issues, 1999 and 2000

Auction	Reference	Tranche	Matures	Format	Sold	Outstanding
12/01/1999	3.9% BA 1998-2005/3	3rd	20/10/2005	Auction	2200	6185
13/01/1999	4.125% BA 1999-2014/1	1st	15/01/2014	DIP*	1100	1100
16/02/1999	6.25% BA 1997-2027/6	6th	15/07/2027	Auction	1100	2989
18/02/1999	4.0% BA 1999-2009/2	2nd	15/07/2009	DIP*	1100	1100
16/03/1999	4.0% BA 1999-2009/2	2nd	15/07/2009	Auction	2750	3850
06/04/1999	3.4% BA 1999-2004/3	3rd	20/10/2004	DIP*	1100	1100
04/05/1999	3.4% BA 1999-2004/3	3rd	20/10/2004	Auction	1665	2765
11/05/1999	4.125% BA 1999-2014/1	1st	15/01/2014	DIP*	220	1320
22/06/1999	4.0% BA 1999-2009/2	2nd	15/07/2009	Auction	1650	5500
27/07/1999	3.4% BA 1999-2004/3	3rd	20/10/2004	Auction	1650	4415
07/09/1999	4.3% BA 1998-2003/2	2nd	15/07/2003	Auction	1650	7454
25/10/1999	5.5% BA 1999-2010/1	1st	15/01/2010	DIP*	2200	2200
23/11/1999	5.5% BA 1999-2010/2	2nd	15/01/2010	Auction	550	2750
11/01/2000	5.5% BA 1999-2010/3	3rd	15/01/2010	Auction	1650	4410
12/01/2000	5.5% BA 2000-2007	1st	20/10/2007	DIP*	3000	3000
08/02/2000	3.4% BA 1999-2004/3	4th	20/10/2004	Auction	660	5075
10/02/2000	5.5% BA 1999-2010/4	4th	15/01/2010	Auction	1650	6060
14/03/2000	5.5% BA 2000-2007	2nd	20/10/2007	Auction	1655	5243
04/04/2000	5.875% BA 1996-2006/7	—	17/07/2006	Auction	2750	4299
02/05/2000	6.25% BA 1997-2027/6	7th	17/07/2027	Auction	550	4112
13/06/2000	5.5% BA 1999-2010/4	5th	17/01/2010	Auction	1650	7710
04/07/2000	3.9% BA 1998-2005/3	4th	20/10/2005	Auction	1650	7836
05/09/2000	6.25% BA 1997-2027/6	7th	15/07/2027	Auction	1100	5242
10/10/2000	5.5% BA 1999-2010/4	4th	15/01/2010	Auction	1100	8810

Millions of euros
*Debt Issuance Programme
Source: OeBFA and authors

Benchmark and 'on-the-run' Issues in the Austrian Public Debt Market, October 2000

Reference	Coupon	Matures	Outstanding	'On-the-run'
Bund 1997/2002	4.625	23/05/2002	1453.5	—
Bund 1998/2003	4.300	15/07/2003	7454.8	*
Bund 1999/2004	3.400	20/10/2004	5075.0	—
Bund 1998/2005	3.900	20/10/2005	7835.9	*
Bund 1996/2006	5.875	15/07/2006	4299.1	*
Bund 2000/2007	5.500	20/10/2007	5243.0	*
Bund 1998/2008	5.000	15/01/2008	5707.4	—
Bund 1999/2009	4.000	15/07/2009	5500.0	—
Bund 1999/2010	5.500	15/01/2010	8810.0	*
Bund 1999/2014	4.125	15/01/2014	1320.0	—
Bund 1997/2027	6.250	15/07/2027	5242.2	*

Millions of euros
Source: OeBFA and authors

4
The Belgian Government Bond
Market

4.1 INTRODUCTION

The organisational structure of the Belgian Treasury centres on two institutions performing differentiated functions: the Debt Agency and the Public Debt Department.

- The *Debt Agency*, founded in October 1998, is responsible for the operational and strategic management of Federal Debt. Its functions include: (i) the undertaking of all financial operations in money and capital markets, including auctions and other issuance formats, and all types of funding operations; (ii) the establishment of public debt management strategy, control and management of credit risk, co-ordination of debt management with the objectives of the National Budget, provision of legislative input and development and promotion of public debt products; and (iii) the management of back-office procedures and IT systems.
- The *Public Debt Department* handles relations with other public issuers and additional administrative functions of vital importance, such as the Public Debt Book-Entry System.

As at most European Treasuries, the new competitive environment engendered by the euro prompted a drive to modernise trading and enhance the appeal of public debt instruments. The Belgian Ministry of Finance and the Debt Agency have introduced the following changes:

- Regular announcement of bond (OLO) and bill (BTC) issue targets at auction, with the undertaking to maintain a regular presence in the market under maximum conditions of transparency.
- Reduction of the number of OLOs in issue, as a spur to market liquidity, and the establishment of standardised maturity and coupon payment dates—28 March and 28 September. To this end, the Belgian Treasury has since 1999 been implementing a large-scale exchange programme, involving both OLOs and several series of Philippe bonds with maturities under 12 months.
- Enlargement of the range of instruments available to investors via the creation of BTBs (short-term securities dated under three months).
- Conversion of eurocurrency OLOs (especially those in deutschmarks and French francs) into euros, such that almost all these instruments are now euro-denominated.
- Extending the holding and distribution of Belgian public debt securities to the widest possible investor base, targeting both residents and non-residents. This mission is entrusted to a group of market makers and recognised dealers specialising in the placement and distribution of government debt securities to different market segments.

Belgium's Stability Programme 1999–2002 envisages the elimination of the country's public deficit and, with it, a reduction in the public debt/GDP ratio to approximately

100% within five years. This ratio, 114.4% at the 1999 close, is currently the highest in the euro zone after Italy's 119%. But the Treasury is confident that lesser issuance requirements (only 27 billion euros) and accelerating economic growth (a projected 3.4%) will deliver an end-2000 ratio of 110.8%, assuming a general government deficit in the range 0.5%–0.8%.

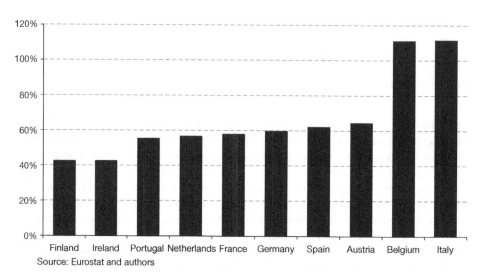

Source: Eurostat and authors

Figure 4.1   Euro zone public debt/GDP forecasts for December 2000

4.2   ASSETS ISSUED BY THE BELGIAN TREASURY

4.2.1   Linear Obligations (OLOs or Bonds)

Also known as Linear Bonds, these are medium- and long-term securities (up to 30 years) drawn up in euros and redeemable on maturity, with fixed or floating coupons, represented by entries in the National Bank of Belgium (NBB) Book-Entry System and issued in tranches which themselves make up fully fungible lines. These assets may be stripped and reconstituted as of a pre-set outstanding amount, and are eligible for inclusion in exchange and/or early redemption programmes. At present, almost all OLOs have a fixed coupon and principal redeemable on maturity. The one exception is the OLOs FRN line, at a floating rate linked to the three-month Euribor.

OLOs have been auctioned twice monthly since February 2000 (monthly up to 1999), excepting the first tranches of new lines, which are now issued through a banking syndicate.

Primary and secondary market transactions are routed through the Bank of Belgium Clearance and Settlement System. Settlement of operations in both primary and secondary markets takes place three working days after transaction date (T + 3). A core group of market makers and specialised or recognised dealers undertakes to guarantee the placement of securities and their secondary-market liquidity. Any individual or legal entity can acquire OLOs, though only market makers and specialised institutions can bid directly at auctions.

OLOs are quoted at a clean price based on the following equation:

$$P + Cc = \sum_{t=1}^{t=N} \frac{F(t)}{(1+R)^t}$$

where

$F(t)$ = bond flows in the year t
R = yield
P = ex-coupon price in %
Cc = accrued coupon calculated as Current/Current
N = years to maturity

4.2.2 Treasury Certificates (BTCs or Bills)

These are short-term bills maturing in 3, 6 and 12 months, drawn up in euros and issued weekly at a discount via yield-based auctions. They are represented by entries in the National Bank of Belgium Book-Entry System.

As with OLOs, primary and secondary market transactions are channelled through the Bank of Belgium Clearance and Settlement System, while their placement and secondary-market liquidity is likewise underwritten by a core group of market makers and specialised institutions. Treasury Certificates can be purchased by any individual or legal entity, though only market makers can submit bids at auction.

Their price is based on the following calculation:

$$P = \frac{N}{1 + R \times \dfrac{d}{360 \times 100}}$$

where

N = nominal or redemption value
d = exact no. of days between value and redemption dates, calculated as Current/360
R = yield at issue
P = amount payable

4.2.3 Belgian State Notes (BSNs)

These are medium- and long-term securities whose maturities vary throughout their lifetime. Their principal is redeemable at each maturity date and they pay fixed annual coupons. BSNs are drawn up in Belgian francs and, since 1999, in euros also, and represented by book entries or security certificates. They are neither strippable nor exchangeable for new lines. Lines issued prior to 1 January 1999 will not be redenominated in euros, though all BSNs issued since March 1999 are drawn up solely in euros.

These securities were designed with retail investors in mind. Primary market access is therefore restricted to individual investors, public institutions, non-profit organisations and companies whose main business is neither financial nor insurance activity. Their secondary-market trading, however, is open to any type of investor. BSNs are quoted on the Brussels Stock Exchange, and the Securities Regulation Fund handles their regulation and supervision. This segment of the public debt market is fairly short on liquidity.

The placement of BSNs is via a panel of financial institutions selected by the Ministry of Finance (for a full list, see the section on market makers, 4.8). Issues are on the fourth of March, June, September and December each year, and can comprise any three of the following series:

- 5-year BSNs extensible to 7 years, paying a fixed coupon throughout their lifetime
- 3-, 5- and 7-year BSNs, with upwardly revisable coupons (guaranteed minimum coupon)
- 5-year BSNs, with annually revisable coupons
- 8-year BSNs, paying a fixed coupon throughout their lifetime.

The Treasury must compulsorily issue a series of 5-year BSNs extensible to 7, and may then choose any two of the other three. Thirty lines were in issue at 31 March 2000, six of them denominated in euros and the remainder in Belgian francs. The outstanding balance of all BSN lines amounts to 5.20 billion euros, with an average life of 4.78 years.

4.2.4 Belgian Treasury Bills (BTBs)

BTBs are securities issued at a discount with maturities of under 12 months, though in practice all instruments issued are dated three months or less. BTBs were originally drawn up in the currencies of OECD member countries, but the rules were redrawn in September 1998 to allow issuance in Belgian francs, a facility subsequently extended to euros. They are represented by entries in an accounting system to which CEDEL and EUROCLEAR have access.

These instruments have a comparable status to BTCs or bills, except in their issuance procedures (on tap), their distribution (via seven institutions designated by the Belgian Treasury) and their duration (BTCs have standard maturities at 3, 6, and 12 months, while BTB maturities are tailored to market demand and the funding needs of the Treasury).

BTBs are issued by the Kingdom of Belgium, while their placement, payment and entry in the Public Debt Register is handled by the National Bank of Belgium. Their purpose is solely to satisfy the Treasury's need for extremely short-term finance and their issuance is therefore occasional only. Finally, note that BTBs can be acquired by any individual or legal entity and have the same tax treatment as BTCs (see the section on taxation, 4.5).

4.2.5 Traditional Loans (Philippes)

These notes, originally issued in terms of 3 to 7 years, are drawn up in Belgian francs and pay a fixed annual coupon. They are represented by book entries or in materialised form and are traded on the Belgian Stock Exchange, but in low volumes only. Philippes have not been redenominated in euros, owing mainly to their dual materialised–dematerialised format and the short residual life of the securities outstanding—the longest dated matures in November 2004. In addition, their low outstanding balance robs them of much of their liquidity. Precisely for these reasons, the Belgian Treasury has since 1999 been exchanging them for the more liquid OLOs.

Philippes were issued up to 1995, and there are no plans to resume the programme. They came into being, essentially, to meet the needs of individual investors, though any financial institution is free to acquire them. Their issuance was discontinued following the reorganisation and relaunch of the Treasury's product range, with OLOs targeted on the professional investor and BSNs for the retail segment. The last fourteen lines issued were nicknamed 'Philippe' in honour of Finance Minister Philippe Maystadt, and their market identification is via the name 'Philippe' and a corresponding number.

Nine series were circulating in March 2000, with an average life of 2.33 years and a total outstanding balance of 1.26 trillion Belgian francs (31.28 billion euros). The maturities of still extant instruments range from June 2000 to November 2004.

4.3 OVERVIEW OF THE BELGIAN PUBLIC DEBT MARKET

Belgium occupies fifth place in the euro zone by outstanding amount of debt issued, behind Italy, Germany, France and Spain. The total in issue stood at around 245 billion euros in March 2000, breaking down as 162 billion in OLOs and almost 35 billion in BTCs. The remainder of the outstanding balance (23.2%) comprises BSNs, BTBs, Philippes and foreign-currency issues. Average duration, at 3.88 years, is among the lowest in the euro zone, while average life is calculated at 4.89 years. Practically all (96.85%) of Belgium's government debt securities are drawn up in euros, against just 3.2% in foreign currencies.

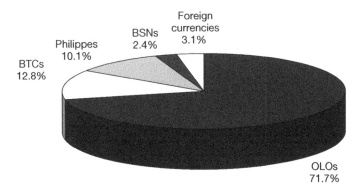

Source: Bloomberg and authors

Figure 4.2 Composition of Belgian public debt as of August 2000 (euro equivalent)

The composition of foreign-currency debt is the legacy of a former policy favouring eurocurrency issues. Specifically, 26.2% of the country's more than 7.77 billion euros (equivalent) in foreign-currency issues is denominated in deutschmarks and French francs, against 45% in US dollars, 16% in Japanese yen and 12% in Swiss francs. The average life of these issues (euro equivalent) is approximately 3.14 years.

The OLOs making up the largest slice of Belgium's public debt comprise 21 series, with maturities falling between August 2000 and March 2028 and an average life of 6.46 years. The average balance outstanding comes to 7.74 billion euros, while over 67% of the total amount is bunched in 11 issues averaging over 8 billion euros.

The strong contraction in public debt/GDP (from 135.9% in 1993 to 114.4% at the 1999 close) has been accompanied—as in almost all other European domestic debt markets—by a marked shift in debt composition. The proportion of debt with a remaining term longer than one year climbed from 70% in 1990 to over 88% in 1999, and indeed the reduction in public debt/GDP was due in its entirety to a sharp decline in short-term recourse. Insistence on this strategy line over the year 2000 should ensure further progress

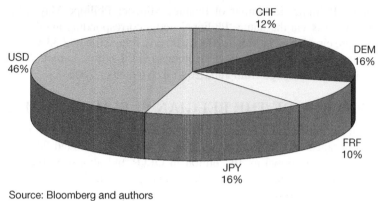

Source: Bloomberg and authors

Figure 4.3   Composition of Belgian foreign-currency debt as of August 2000

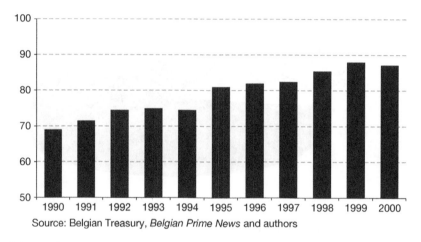

Source: Belgian Treasury, *Belgian Prime News* and authors

Figure 4.4   Belgian public debt maturing in over one year as of August 2000

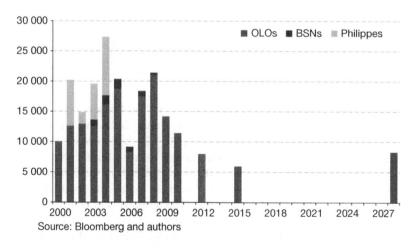

Source: Bloomberg and authors

Figure 4.5   Belgian debt maturities curve as of August 2000

in lengthening residual life, thereby reducing the exposure of public finances to exogenous fluctuations in short-term interest rates.

Another consequence of the strategy deployed has been a reduction in the cost of annual refinancing (the proportion of total debt that must be refinanced in the following year). This cost dropped from 39.3% of the total in 1993 to just 22.5% at the 1999 close. The upshot is that in March 2000 the maturities curve of Belgian euro-denominated public debt (OLOs and BTCs) exhibited a funding profile free of major accumulations.

4.4   THE PRIMARY MARKET

4.4.1   Issuance Procedures for Belgian Treasury Securities

The Belgian Treasury uses two main methods of securities issuance: (1) the auction system (comprising a first competitive tranche via the 'American' or multi-price system and a second non-competitive tranche reserved exclusively for market makers), and (2) direct placement or tap issues. Though the auction system is used as standard, the features of both methods are briefly described here.

The Auction System

In the first, competitive tranche, the Treasury sorts all bids submitted—specifying price and volume—in descending order and sets the minimum price it will accept (i.e. the highest rate it will pay) for the securities on offer. This stop-out price determines which bids will enter the auction. Accepted bids, those at a price higher than the stop-out or marginal rate, are allotted at the price specified in the bid. The procedure is thus a competitive one along 'American' lines. Bids made at the stop-out price may be distributed pro rata if the Treasury so decides.

Once this competitive phase has concluded, the Treasury holds a second, non-competitive round reserved exclusively for market makers (and, in certain circumstances, specialist institutions), in which the subscriptions submitted specify volumes only (i.e. are non-competitive). Allocation is at the average weighted price resulting from the bids accepted in the competitive round. This second, subscription tranche is called one working day after the competitive auction (T + 1) for BTCs and two working days after (T + 2) in the case of OLOs.

Direct Placement or Tap Issue

The Treasury places its securities with a group of specialist institutions—market makers and others—who then distribute them in secondary markets, seeking out the widest possible investor base. The Debt Agency announces its asking price for each issue, and institutions specify the amounts they are willing to acquire at the stated rate. The operation is closed when the Treasury reaches its target volume, or when market conditions preclude sufficient placement, and the weighted average price of accepted bids is announced immediately afterwards. The Treasury can also vary its asking price while the direct-sale period is open.

Issue Syndication

This technique has been used on three occasions since 1999 (OLO 3.75% 2009 in January 1999, OLO 4.75% 2005 in September 1999 and OLO 5.75% 2010 in January 2000).

The Treasury secures sufficient liquidity from the first tranche onwards by getting more securities onto the market. From 2000 on, all first tranches of new OLO lines will be issued through a syndicate.

4.4.2 Characteristics of Belgian Treasury Security Issues

This section focuses on OLOs and BTCs in view of their primary importance in the Belgian market. Both are issued via competitive auctions followed by a second, non-competitive round in which only market makers may participate.

OLOs

- *Auction announcement*: the Treasury publishes an annual auctions calendar at the start of each year.
- *The auction*: until the 1999 close, auctions were held on the last Monday of each month. From 2000 on, however, issues have been spaced out to every two months, again on the last Monday.
- *Presentation of competitive bids*: five days before the auction $(T - 5)$, as of 17.00 local time, the Treasury declares the bidding period open. The day before the auction is held, it announces the volume range to be issued. The deadline for submission of competitive bids is 12.00 on the auction date $(T - 0)$. The announcement is posted on Reuters BELG/MENU, Bloomberg BELG and Telerate 36 350.
- *Minimum amount of bids*: competitive bids must be for a minimum of 1 000 000 euros and all subsequent bids in multiples of 100 000 euros.
- *Bidders*: only market makers (primary dealers) and recognised dealers are eligible to participate in the competitive auction.
- *Announcement of volume limits*: one working day before the auction $(T - 1)$, the Treasury announces the maximum and minimum amounts to be issued. The amounts stated usually refer to the two or three series issued on the same day.
- *Auction results*: the Treasury releases the preliminary results of each competitive auction at 12.45 local time on the same day. Complete results are posted on its own screens by 14.00.
- *Auction resolution*: the Treasury sets a stop-out price separating accepted from rejected bids, then allots the accepted bids at the price subscribed. Bids presented at the stop-out price may be distributed pro rata, in which case the amounts allotted are rounded off to the nearest 100 000 euros, with a minimum of 1 000 000 euros per bid.
- *Second rounds*: reserved exclusively for market makers, and either ordinary or extraordinary. The former are held between 15.00 and 15.30 local time on the working day immediately following the auction $(T + 1)$. The Treasury allocates non-competitive bids at the weighted average price resulting from accepted bids in the competitive round (those above the stop-out price). Extraordinary second rounds are held between 15.00 and 15.30 on the second working day after the competitive auction $(T + 2)$ and follow the same allocation procedure.
- *Payment of amounts allotted*: the third working day after the auction $(T + 3)$.
- *Basis for principal and interest rates*: Current/Current.

The following is an example of an OLOs auction:

Announcement

Announcement date	26 March 1999
Type of auction	Auction with second round
Auction date	29 March 1999
Payment	1 April 1999
Securities to be issued	OLO 9% 28/3/03 and OLO 3.75% 28/3/09
Minimum bid	1 million euros
Amount to be issued	1100–1300 million euros for each reference

Resolution of competitive tranche (29/3/99)

OLO 9% 28/3/03		OLO 3.75% 28/3/09	
Amount bid	1260 m euros	Amount bid	1379 m euros
Amount allotted	469 m euros	Amount allotted	657.5 m euros
Highest/lowest bid	120.48/120.66	Highest/lowest bid	95.26/95.54
Min. price accepted	120.66	Min. price accepted	95.46
Allotted at min. price	100%	Allotted at min. price	100%
Weighted avge price	120.66/3.377%	Weighted avge price	95.473/4.317%

Resolution of second round (30/3/99)

OLO 9% 28/3/03		OLO 3.75% 28/3/09	
Amount bid	94.2 m euros	Amount bid	207.8 m euros
Amount allotted	35 m euros	Amount allotted	83.9 m euros
Weighted avge price	3.377%	Weighted avge price	4.317%

BTCs

- *Auction announcement*: the Treasury publishes its annual auctions calendar for 3-, 6- and 12-month BTCs at the start of each year.
- *Announcement of amount to be issued*: two working days before the BTC auction date $(T - 2)$, the Treasury announces its overall upper and lower limits for the three lines to be issued.
- *Auction*: new 6- and 12-month lines are issued weekly on Tuesdays (or the next working day in the case of public holidays). Since mid-1999, new lines of 3-month BTCs have been issued on a fortnightly basis, reopened weekly.
- *Presentation of competitive bids*: at 11.00 local time on the day before the auction $(T - 1)$, the Treasury announces the opening of competitive bidding on Reuters BELG, Bloomberg BELG and Telerate 36 354. The deadline for submission is 12.00 local time on the auction day $(T - 0)$.
- *Minimum amount of bids*: 1 000 000 euros and multiples of 100 000 euros thereafter.
- *Auction results*: posted by the Treasury at 12.45 on Reuters BELG/TC, Bloomberg BELG and Telerate 36 355.

- *Auction resolution*: the Treasury sets a yield limit at which it is prepared to sell. Allocation is via the 'American' or multi-price system, in which each bid is allotted at the yield stated by the investor, working up from the lowest to the maximum rate. Allocation of bids made at the marginal rate may be distributed on a pro rata basis, rounded off to multiples of 100 000 euros, with a minimum 1 000 000 euros per bid.
- *Second rounds*: restricted exclusively to market makers and held between 15.00 and 15.30 local time on the Wednesday after the auction (T + 1). Subscriptions are allotted at the weighted average rate resulting from the competitive round.
- *Payment*: two working days after the auction (T + 2).
- *Basis for interests and principal*: the amount payable is the discounted value of the allotted bid, on the basis of Current/360.

The following is an example of a BTC auction:

Announcement

	3-month BTC	6-month BTC	12-month BTC
Announcement date	19/04/1999	19/04/1999	19/04/1999
Auction date	20/04/1999	20/04/1999	20/04/1999
Value date	22/04/1999	22/04/1999	22/04/1999
Maturity date	22/07/1999	30/09/1999	20/04/2000
Amount of securities maturing	1365.2 m euros		

Resolution of first round (20/4/99)

	3-month BTC	6-month BTC	12-month BTC
Amount bid	3903 m euros	2651.5 m euros	2920 m euros
Amount allotted	489.2 m euros	304.2 m euros	308.1 m euros
Min./max. yield bid	2.47%/2.55%	2.52%/2.57%	2.59%/2.63%
Marginal yield	2.49%	2.53%	2.59%
Weighted avge yield	2.48%	2.53%	2.59%
Allotted at marginal yield	37.46%	49.55%	30.05%

Resolution of second round (21/4/99)

	3-month BTC	6-month BTC	12-month BTC
Amount allotted	34.4 m euros	1.0 m euros	31.4 m euros
Weighted avge yield	2.48%	2.53%	2.59%

BTBs

- *Issue*: direct placement (tap issue) among a number of specialist institutions, as listed in the section on market makers (4.8).
- *Announcement*: Reuters BELG/MENU and Dow Jones 21 390.

BSNs

- *Issue*: placement is via a panel or syndicate of recognised dealers selected annually by the Ministry of Finance. A list of these specialist institutions can be found in the section on market makers (4.8).

Philippes

- *Issue*: issuance of these instruments was discontinued in 1995.

4.4.3   OLO and Traditional Loan Exchanges

The Belgian Treasury has been programming exchange auctions since May 1999, in a bid to boost market liquidity and simultaneously to smooth out the maturities curve of total public debt. The main objectives pursued are:

1. To smooth out the maturities curve of OLOs and Philippe bonds.
2. To offer investors a wider range of options.
3. To enlarge its primary market presence.
4. To replace insufficiently liquid lines nearing maturity with others having a residual life of more than 18 months.

Participation in the Belgian Treasury's exchange operations is purely voluntary, though restricted to market makers and recognised dealers.

The exchange programme started with OLOs, but since January 2000 has also taken in Philippe bond lines maturing within 18 months. Each line can, in theory, be exchanged up to twelve times from the moment its residual life drops below 18 months to the month prior to its final redemption.

OLO and Philippe bond exchanges take place on one or several Mondays a month, depending on the number of lines up for exchange and the accumulation of maturities over the next twelve months.

Procedures for OLO and Philippe Exchange Operations

- *Announcement*: after 16.00 local time on the Tuesday before the exchange (T − 4), the Treasury posts the codes of the lines to be exchanged on Reuters BELG/EXHG, Bloomberg BELG and Telerate 21 392 or 21 393.
- *Communication of exchange price*: on the day of the exchange (T − 0), the price is announced in terms of the bonds to be issued in replacement of the withdrawn reference(s). The Treasury sets a price for each line offered in exchange for the line(s) with residual life (lives) under 18 months. This price represents the nominal amount payable, in terms of the bond offered, at a nominal unit value of 100 euros for the OLO line being repurchased.
- *Presentation of bids*: the deadline for submission is 13.00 local time on the day of the exchange (T − 0).
- *Resolution*: results are announced in two stages: first the percentage allotted is announced at around 13.15, then the amounts issued at around 15.00 local time.
- *Payment*: the Thursday after the exchange (T + 3).

Table 4.1   Exchange operations in 1999

Month	Exchange	Code	Lines withdrawn
May	17	239	8.25% June, 1999 (OLO 1)
	17	287	4% January, 2000 (OLO 27)
June	14	287	4% January, 2000 (OLO 27)
July	12	287	4% January, 2000 (OLO 27)
August	09	287	4% January, 2000 (OLO 27)
	23	247	10% August, 2000(OLO 3)
September	13	287	4% January, 2000 (OLO 27)
	20	247	10%,August, 2000 (OLO 3)
October	04	287	4% January, 2000 (OLO 27)
	11	247	10% August, 2000 (OLO 3)
	18	267	7% 2000 (Philippe X)
November	15	287	4% January, 2000 (OLO 27)
	22	247	10% August, 2000 (OLO 3)
December	06	287	4% January, 2000 (OLO 27)
	13	247	10% August, 2000 (OLO 3)

Source: authors

Table 4.2   Exchange operations scheduled for 2000

Month	Exchange	Code	Lines withdrawn
January	10	247	10.00% August, 2000 (OLO 247)
February	7	278	7.75% December, 2000 (OLO 21)
	28	267	7.00% June, 2000 (Philippe X)
March	6	247	10.00% August, 2000 (OLO 247)
	6	278	7.75% December, 2000 (OLO 21)
April	3	285	5.00% March, 2001 (OLO 25)
	17	267	7.00% June, 2000 (Philippe X)
May	8	247	10.00% August, 2000 (OLO 247)
	8	278	7.75% December, 2000 (OLO 21)
June	5	267	7.00% June, 2000 (Philippe X)
	26	285	5.00% March, 2001 (OLO 25)
July	3	247	10.00% August, 2000 (OLO 247)
	3	278	7.75% December, 2000 (OLO 21)
August	7	285	5.00% March, 2001 (OLO 25)
	28	252	9.00% June, 2001 (OLO 7)
September	4	278	7.75% December, 2000 (OLO 21)
October	2	285	5.00% March, 2001 (OLO 25)
	30	252	9.00% June, 2001 (OLO 7)
November	6	278	7.75% December, 2000 (OLO 21)
December	4	285	5.00% March, 2001 (OLO 25)
	18	252	9.00% June, 2001 (OLO 7)

Source: authors

Instrumentation of Exchange Operations

The exchange offer is made at a predetermined price calculated according to the following formula: the difference between the price of the OLO offered and the price of the OLO withdrawn on the day of transaction—including accrued interest.

The exchange price thus represents the nominal amount in old OLOs (the asset to be withdrawn) offered for every 100 euros nominal of the OLOs which the applicants wish to acquire.

The Setting of Exchange Prices

Example of an exchange held on 17/5/99 (see Table 4.3):

- Line maturing within 12 months (to be withdrawn): OLO series 287 4% January, 2000
- One of the series offered in exchange: OLO series 259 July, 2002

Prices at 17/5/99:

- Series 287: 100.97 + accrued interest (1.2602) = 102.230
- Series 259: 116.57

Fixed price at which series 287 will be exchanged for 259: the difference between the ex-coupon price of the new OLO and the price plus accrued interest of the OLO withdrawn:

$$P = \frac{116.57}{102.23} \times 100 = 114.00$$

Table 4.3 Resolution of exchange offer of 17/5/99

OLO/OLO	Exchange price	% accepted	Amount accepted: new OLO	Amount withdrawn: old OLO
287/259	114.00	—	—	—
287/251	117.90	—	—	—
287/265	114.45	—	—	—
287/273	112.20	100	70 000	78 540
287/283	116.05	100	91 600	106 301.8
287/257	127.40	—	—	—
287/288	108.25	100	75 000	81 187.5
287/291	100.65	100	61 000	61 396.5
239/259	107.70	100	23 700	25 524.9
239/273	106.05	100	85 000	90 142.5
239/257	120.40	100	39 300	47 317.2
239/291	95.10	100	39 500	37 564.5

Source: authors

4.5 THE SECONDARY MARKET

4.5.1 Overview

Belgium's secondary market in public debt has seen major changes in recent years, following from the introduction of market makers (primary dealers) and recognised dealers in Treasury securities. Trading, once centred on the Brussels Stock Exchange, is now mainly conducted on the newly created MTS Belgium (started up in first quarter 2000). The idea of launching an electronic market comparable to EuroMTS and Italy's pioneering MTS SpA came from the Treasury and the market makers, desirous of boosting the liquidity of secondary-market trading. Three main reasons underlie the choice of the MTS system:

- MTS is the only electronic network between market makers operating throughout the euro zone ('blind' or 'Interdealer–Broker' market).
- MTS provides a route for national market makers' obligations to quote prices over a pre-set range of securities on a continuous basis.
- MTS is a pan-European trading platform, facilitating the connection of domestic platforms both to EuroMTS, and to each other. The number of counterparties can thus be enlarged on both sides of the transaction.

As with all other platforms affiliated to EuroMTS, trading on MTS Belgium is constrained to the most liquid public debt references (usually 'on-the-run' OLOs) with an outstanding balance exceeding 5 billion euros.

OLOs account for the bulk of trading in Belgian Treasury securities, and will do so increasingly in the years ahead (at the expense of BTCs) as the Treasury presses on with its strategy of lengthening average debt life. Specifically, around 83% of total turnover is represented by OLOs, with repo transactions strongly to the fore (70% of OLO turnover). Conversely, repos take a considerably smaller share of market turnover in BTCs (ranging from 20% to 40%).

Total gross turnover in OLOs and BTCs (both spot and repo transactions) contracted sharply in the first half of 1999, but built up again in the first two quarters of 2000 to reach the average level recorded since 1997 (approximately 195 billion euros). It should be stressed, however, that this recovery has been overwhelmingly led by OLOs, while trading in BTCs continues to languish. This bias in favour of OLOs will, if anything, increase in the years ahead, on the likely scale-down of BTC issuance (facilitated by an improvement in Belgium's fiscal accounts).

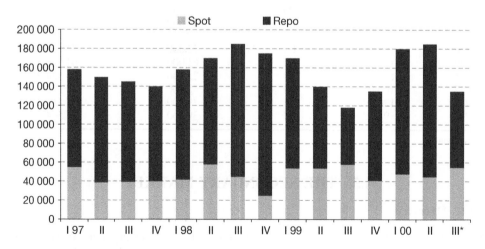

* Data to end August 2000

Source: Belgian Treasury, *Belgian Prime News* and authors

Figure 4.6   Turnover in OLOs (quarterly average in millions of euros)

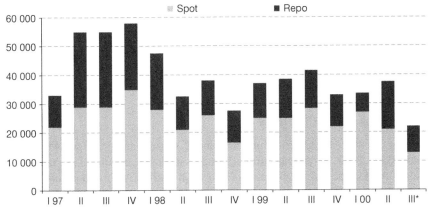

* Data to end August 2000

Source: Belgian Treasury, *Belgian Prime News* and authors

Figure 4.7   Turnover in BTCs (quarterly average in millions of euros)

4.5.2   Internationalisation of the OLOs Market

The advent of the euro has spurred greater internationalisation of the public debt market, measured in the increased participation of international borrowers in the trading and holding of Treasury securities. This trend has been especially marked in Belgian Treasury securities (particularly OLOs), due to other factors which have enhanced their attractiveness in comparison with other euro-zone markets:

- the syndicated issue of various OLO references (widely distributed among foreign investors)
- the widening of the spread at which Belgian assets have traditionally traded relative to the German *Bunds* (from 10 bp in 1997 to around 30 bp at the time of writing), as Belgian investors increasingly diversify their portfolios into euro-zone private and sovereign assets
- the circumstantial fact of several OLO series (most markedly the 30-year) trading at a positive spread to the IRS curve, an effect produced by the internal upsets of 1999 (the dioxins scandal).

Global turnover figures, covering both spot and repo transactions, show that foreign investors' share of OLOs has swelled from 25% in 1998 to over 45% at the 1999 close. These figures, however, are not truly representative of the securities holdings of this investor group, since most trading in Belgian Treasury securities consists of ordinary and blocked repo transactions, in which the change of ownership is temporary only. For an accurate take on foreign investors' OLO holdings, it is necessary to look at the balance sheets of Belgian credit institutions, and what these shows is that OLO holdings dropped by over 10% between 1998 and mid-1999 (from 97.9% to 81.1%).

4.5.3   Repo Transactions in OLOs and BTCs

As previously stated, repo transactions constitute the main trading variant in the securities issued by the Belgian Treasury (OLOs in particular). Gross turnover in OLO and

BTC repos advanced strongly between 1997 and 1999 (from 1.66 to around 1.85 billion euros).

Transaction numbers, in contrast, receded significantly between 1997 and 1999 (from over 43 500 in 1997 to around 30 000 in 1999), though average volumes were, logically enough, higher: over 55 million euros at end-1999 against 37 million in 1997. The most widely used transaction term is seven days (accounting for over 80% of repo trading).

4.5.4 The Strips Market in OLOs

The stripping of certain OLO series into coupons (IO strips) and principal (PO strips) was first authorised in 1992, to replicate similar systems in France and the USA, modernise the market and broaden the range of options open to investors. As in other euro-zone strips markets on debt securities, the power to attend stripping and/or reconstitution requests is restricted to market makers and recognised dealers. Applications must be lodged with the National Bank of Belgium (NBB), as the only institution authorised to strip and reconstitute debt securities.

The outstanding amount of OLOs totalled 162 billion euros in April 2000. Of the 20 fixed-rate lines issued, seven are strippable, with an outstanding balance of 81.09 billion euros. The proportion of strips to total strippable OLOs comes out at 4.313%, dropping back to 2.15% against total OLOs. This percentage denotes a stripping volume appreciably lower than in France or Spain.

Table 4.4   The strips market in OLOs

Securities code	Characteristics	Outstanding at 31/3/00	Stripped volume	% of stripped to outstanding amount
285	OLO 5% 28/3/2001	7 607	180.8	1.81%
251	OLO 9% 28/3/2003	12 440	746.8	6.20%
294	OLO 4.75% 28/9/2005	4 024	0	0
286	OLO 6.25% 28/3/2007	8 307	290.3	4.28%
257	OLO 8.5% 1/10/2007	8 166	1636.4	19.78%
288	OLO 5.75% 28/3/2008	12 092	101.2	0.69%
295	OLO 5.75% 28/9/2010	5 000	0	0
282	OLO 8% 28/3/2015	5 359	99.4	1.78%
291	OLO 5.5% 28/3/2028	6 234	216.8	3.67%
Total strippable lines		**81 099**	**3497**	**4.313%**
Stripped amount vs. total outstanding amount of OLOs				2.151%

Millions of euros
Source: authors

4.6   CLEARING AND SETTLEMENT

4.6.1   National Bank of Belgium Settlement System

The settlement system is designed for the clearance and settlement of transactions in OLOs, BTCs and BTBs, and based on the principles of (i) delivery versus payment, (ii) twofold notification and (iii) automatic securities loans for system participants.

• *Principle of delivery versus payment*: this gives system members the guarantee of simultaneous settlement of securities and payment.

- *Principle of twofold notification*: this requires counterparties to furnish mutual information on all aspects of the operation, using a standard reporting format.
- *Automatic lending of securities*: this enables the holders of securities, if they so wish, to assign them to other system members and vice versa. The system functions as a 'funds pool', in which both borrowers and lenders are assured full confidentiality.

The settlement system takes in only those securities represented by book entries, either directly in the National Bank of Belgium Book-Entry System or in the accounts of institutions authorised by the Ministry of Finance as book-entry system account holders. Account holders must belong to one of the following categories:

- credit institutions incorporated under Belgian law
- Belgian subsidiaries of credit institutions incorporated under the law of any EU member state
- Belgian subsidiaries of credit institutions incorporated under the law of any non-EU member state
- credit institutions incorporated or running a permanent establishment in the Grand Duchy of Luxembourg
- securities broker–dealers recognised by the Banking and Finance Commission, in accordance with secondary-market legislation
- Belgian subsidiaries of investment services firms incorporated under the law of any other EU member state
- Belgian subsidiaries of investment services firms incorporated under the law of any non-EU member state
- the National Bank of Belgium
- EUROCLEAR (Clearstream)
- CEDEL.

4.6.2 Members and Others Participating in the National Bank of Belgium Settlement System

The entities participating in the system are divided into direct members, sub-members and account holders, depending on their status and their capacity to conduct operations (i) on their own behalf and that of third parties, (ii) on their own behalf only, or (iii) as simple intermediaries in Belgian Treasury securities transactions, as well as on whether they are empowered to settle their operations directly with the National Bank of Belgium Book-Entry System.

1. *Direct or settling members* are those institutions settling directly with the NBB Book-Entry System. They comprise:

   - credit institutions belonging to the BLEU (Belgium–Luxembourg Economic Union)
   - stock exchanges within the BLEU
   - the Treasury
   - the National Bank of Belgium
   - the Rediscount and Guarantee Institute
   - CEDEL and EUROCLEAR (solely in the case of members affiliated to these two systems and belonging to the BLEU area).

2. *Sub-members* are obliged to settle their own or third-party operations through a direct member (of their own choice).
3. *Account holders*: eligibility for account-holder status is restricted to existing direct or sub-members, certain of whom may be authorised solely to conduct operations on their own behalf (the Treasury, for instance).

4.7 TAXATION

Whether or not withholding tax is applied to interest earned on the holding of Belgian Treasury securities (and other securities) depends on the X-N assessment system. This system codes all book-entry operations in the securities (OLOs, BTCs, etc.) admitted into the NBB settlement system, such that neither sellers nor buyers need concern themselves with the tax status of their counterparty. Book entries (representing securities transactions) are separated into those exempt from withholding tax—X accounts—and those subject to withholding—N accounts. In other words, withholding tax is applied or otherwise according to the counterparty's status.

Table 4.5 The X-N assessment system

Exempt from withholding tax (X)	Non-exempt (N)
Resident companies	Charities
Mutual funds	Foundations
Insurance firms	Other non-profit organisations
Taxpayers liable for non-residents' tax	Foreign institutions of a like nature
Non-residents	Residents
The Federal State and Federal authorities	All others not classified X
The semi-public social security system and comparable bodies	—

Source: authors

4.8 MARKET MAKERS, RECOGNISED DEALERS AND BSN PLACEMENT SPECIALISTS

Because of the importance of these entities in the primary-market subscription, placement and distribution of OLOs and BTCs, they merit a separate section in this chapter on the Belgian public debt market. The institutions specialising in BSN placements are also covered briefly here, in view of their prominent role in this market segment.

4.8.1 Primary Dealers or Market Makers

The category of market maker was created essentially with the following aims: (1) the primary-market promotion of BTCs, OLOs and OLO strips, (2) the assurance of these securities' secondary-market liquidity, and (3) the promotion of Belgian public debt assets within and beyond national borders.

Market-Maker Obligations

In the primary market:

• regular participation in BTC and OLO auctions.

In the secondary market:

- an active role in the market, to ensure its liquidity
- the quoting of firm bid and ask prices at third-party request
- continuous posting of prices on their screens, under market conditions
- assistance in the promotion of BTCs and OLOs, thereby maximising their placement within Belgium and abroad.

Other obligations:

- regular reporting to the Treasury on their public debt market activities.

Market-Maker Rights and Privileges

- the exclusive right to the name of 'Market Maker in Belgian Government Debt Securities'
- the exclusive right (alongside recognised dealers) to participate in public debt competitive auctions and exchanges
- the exclusive right to participate in the second round of BTC auctions (at the weighted average rate resulting from the first round) and OLO auctions (at the weighted average rate resulting from the first round)
- the exclusive right (shared on occasion with recognised dealers) to apply to the Treasury for the stripping or reconstitution of OLOs
- privileged status as counterparties in Treasury public debt management operations.

Market Makers in Belgian Public Debt

ABN AMOR Bank NV, Amsterdam
ARTESIA BANKING CORPORATION, Brussels
Banque Bruxelles Lambert SA, Brussels
Banque Générale du Luxembourg, Luxembourg
Banque et Caisse d'Epargne de l'Etat, Luxembourg
Banque Générale du Luxembourg SA, Luxembourg
Barclays Capital, Paris
CDC Marchés, Paris
Deutsche Bank AG, Frankfurt
Dexia Capital Markets, Brussels
Fortis Bank, Brussels
Goldman Sachs International, London
J.P. Morgan Securities Ltd, London
KBC Bank NV, Brussels
Morgan Stanley & Co. International Ltd, London
Paribas Capital Markets, London
Société Générale, Paris
Warburg Dillon Read, London

4.8.2 Recognised Dealers

This specialist group was created as part of the Treasury's drive to encourage the take-up of certain securities in particular market segments. Their function is thus to ensure the placement of Treasury securities in the specific segments targeted.

Recognised-Dealer Obligations

- promotion of Treasury securities
- assistance in boosting the liquidity of the secondary market in public debt securities by quoting firm prices at investors' request
- regular reporting to the Treasury on their market activities.

Recognised-Dealer Rights and Privileges

- the exclusive right to the name of 'Recognised Dealer in Belgian Government Debt Securities'
- the exclusive right (alongside market makers) to participate in public debt competitive auctions and exchanges
- the right to apply for the stripping and/or reconstitution of OLOs, as expressed in a formal request to the Treasury
- privileged status as counterparties in Treasury public debt management operations.

Recognised Dealers in Belgian Public Debt

Banca d'Intermediazione Mobiliare IMI SpA, Milan
Commerzbank AG, Frankfurt
Caixa Geral de Depósitos, Lisbon
HSBC Markets Ltd, London
Nomura International PLC, London
Tokyo-Mitsubishi International PLC, London

4.8.3   BSN Placement Specialists

The primary function of these institutions, selected annually via public tender, is to place BSNs among retail investors. The 1999 list of institutions specialising in BSN placement was as follows:

Artesia Banking Corporation, Brussels
AXA Bank Belgium
Banque Bruxelles Lambert SA
Banque de la Poste
Banque Nagelmackers
Bonnewijn, Renwart, Van Goethem et Cie SA
Oostvlaams Beroepskrediet
Crédit Agricole SA
Crédit Communal de Belgique
Crédit Professionnel du Hainaut

Deutsche Bank (Crédit Lyonnais)
Société de Bourse de Buck & Cie
Société de Bourse Dierickx, Leys & Cie
Fortis Bank, Brussels
KBC
Société de Bourse J. Leleux & CIE SA
Banque Van de Put & CCVA
Société de Bourse Riga & Cie SA
Banque d'Epargne Westkrediet SA
West-Vlaamse Bank

ANNEXE: THE BELGIAN PUBLIC DEBT MARKET

Belgian Public Debt References and Benchmarks, August 2000

Issue	Line	Matures	Outstanding	Strippable	Benchmark	'On-the-run'
OLO 10.00%	247	02/08/2000	4 463.47	—	—	—
OLO 7.75%	278	22/12/2000	5 557.32	—	—	—
OLO 5.00%	285	28/03/2001	4 617.80	***	***	—
OLO 9.00%	252	27/06/2001	8 041.84	—	—	—
OLO FRN	293	22/04/2002	2 000.00	—	—	***
OLO 8.75%	259	25/06/2002	10 978.84	—	—	—
OLO 9.00%	251	28/03/2003	12 625.81	***	***	—
OLO 7.25%	265	29/04/2004	10 747.18	—	—	—
OLO 7.75%	275	15/10/2004	5 447.45	—	—	—
OLO 6.50%	273	31/03/2005	9 614.33	—	—	—
OLO 4.75%	294	28/09/2005	9 132.90	*** (*)	***	***
OLO 7.00%	283	15/05/2006	8 253.75	—	—	—
OLO 6.25%	286	28/03/2007	9 337.03	***	—	—
OLO 8.50%	257	01/10/2007	8 177.26	***	—	—
OLO 5.75%	288	28/03/2008	12 705.80	***	—	—
OLO 7.50%	268	29/07/2008	8 375.96	—	—	—
OLO 3.75%	292	28/03/2009	14 187.30	***	—	—
OLO 5.75%	295	28/09/2010	11 429.00	***	***	***
OLO 8.00%	262	24/12/2012	7 971.60	—	—	—
OLO 8.00%	282	28/03/2015	5 950.99	***	***	—
OLO 5.50%	291	28/03/2028	8 320.14	***	***	***
Total			177 935.74			

Millions of euros
(*) not yet strippable
Source: Belgian Treasury and authors

Philippe Bond or Traditional Loan References Outstanding, August 2000

Series	Code	Outstanding August 2000	
		BEF	Euros
PHI 7.50% 2001	263	61 810	1 532
PHI 7.00% 2001	269	30 445	755
PHI REV 2003	271	238 867	5 921
PHI 8.00% 2001	276	187 025	4 636
PHI 8.00% 2001	277	25 045	621
PHI 8.00% 2002	280	77 190	1 913
PHI REV 2004	284	386 879	9 590
Total		1 007 261	24 969

Millions of euros
Source: Belgian Treasury and authors

Belgian State Note (BSN) References, August 2000

Series	Matures	BEF	Euros
900	18/06/2003	12 250.0	303.7
901	18/06/2003	4 387.7	108.8
902	18/09/2003	13 250.0	328.5
903	18/09/2003	6 670.8	165.4
904	18/12/2003	5 650.0	140.1
905	18/12/2004	2 324.0	57.6
906	18/03/2004	5 925.0	146.9
907	18/03/2004	2 588.0	64.2
908	04/06/2004	15 400.0	381.8
909	04/06/2004	4 032.3	100.0
912	04/12/2004	12 675.0	314.2
913	04/12/2004	6 550.0	162.4
914	04/03/2005	9 950.0	246.7
915	04/03/2005	6 550.0	162.4
916	04/06/2005	10 500.0	260.3
917	04/06/2005	6 250.0	154.9
918	04/09/2005	8 325.0	206.4
919	04/09/2005	12 250.0	303.7
920	04/12/2005	4 550.0	112.8
921	04/12/2005	5 925.0	146.9
922	04/03/2006	5 203.8	129.0
923	04/03/2006	4 725.0	117.1
924	04/06/2006	4 639.1	115.0
925	04/06/2006	2 625.0	65.1
926	04/09/2006	8 935.3	221.5
927	04/09/2006	5 163.5	128.0
928	04/12/2006	5 163.5	128.0
929	04/12/2007	5 274.4	130.8
930	04/03/2007	10 968.4	271.9
931	04/03/2008	5 671.8	140.6
932	04/06/2007	10 185.8	252.5
933	04/06/2008	3 792.0	94.0
934	04/09/2007	8 068.0	200.0
935	04/09/2008	2 138.0	53.0
Total		238 557.0	5,914

Millions of euros

Source: Belgian Treasury and authors

Outcome of OLO Issues in 2000

Date	Instrument	Coupon	Term	Target	Settles	Matures	Format	Sold	Total bids	Bid/sold	Stop rate	Average rate
18-Jan-00	OLO	5.75%	10 years	5000	21-Jan-00	28-Sep-10	Syndicate	5000	—	—	Bund + 31 bp	—
27-Mar-00	OLO	4.75%	5 years	2500–3000	30-Mar-00	28-Sep-05	Auction	762	1919	2.52	—	5.238
27-Mar-00	OLO	5.75%	10 years	2500–3000	30-Mar-00	28-Sep-10	Auction	1580	3491	2.21	—	5.578
27-Mar-00	OLO	5.50%	30 years	2500–3000	30-Mar-00	28-Mar-28	Auction	388	916	2.36	—	5.841
29-May-00	OLO	4.75%	5 years	2000–2500	01-Jun-00	28-Sep-05	Auction	1170	1565	1.34	—	5.343
29-May-00	OLO	5.75%	10 years	2000–2500	01-Jun-00	28-Sep-10	Auction	1170	2164	1.85	—	5.577
31-Jul-00	OLO	4.75%	5 years	2000–2500	03-Aug-00	28-Sep-05	Auction	1245	1655	1.33	—	5.415
31-Jul-00	OLO	5.75%	10 years	2000–2500	03-Aug-00	28-Sep-10	Auction	956	1551	1.62	—	5.550
31-Jul-00	OLO	5.50%	30 years	2000–2500	03-Aug-00	28-Mar-28	Auction	244	484	1.98	—	5.767

Millions of euros
Source: Belgian Treasury and authors

Outcome of BTC Issues as of March 2000

Date	Term	Matures	Days	Format	Sold	Bid	Bid/cover	Stop rate	Average rate
04-Jan-00	3 months	06-Apr-00	91	Auction	945	3683	3.9	3.230	3.220
04-Jan-00	6 months	06-Jul-00	182	Auction	285	495	1.7	3.450	3.450
04-Jan-00	12 months	07-Dec-00	336	Auction	900	1095	1.2	3.800	3.790
11-Jan-00	3 months	06-Apr-00	84	Auction	639	4036	6.7	3.210	3.210
11-Jan-00	6 months	06-Jul-00	175	Auction	445	1500	3.7	3.430	3.430
11-Jan-00	12 months	11-Jan-01	364	Auction	591	1485	3.0	3.820	3.810
18-Jan-00	3 months	20-Apr-00	91	Auction	741	2575	3.8	3.190	3.190
18-Jan-00	6 months	06-Jul-00	168	Auction	457	1775	4.4	3.430	3.430
18-Jan-00	12 months	11-Jan-01	357	Auction	355	740	2.5	3.810	3.800
25-Jan-00	3 months	20-Apr-00	84	Auction	604	3211	5.3	3.210	3.200
25-Jan-00	6 months	06-Jul-00	161	Auction	297	2950	9.9	3.430	3.420
25-Jan-00	12 months	11-Jan-01	350	Auction	500	1710	3.4	3.820	3.820
01-Feb-00	3 months	11-May-00	98	Auction	519	2002	3.9	3.380	3.370
01-Feb-00	6 months	06-Jul-00	154	Auction	396	1530	3.9	3.550	3.540
01-Feb-00	12 months	11-Jan-01	343	Auction	495	1825	3.7	3.940	3.930
08-Feb-00	3 months	11-May-00	91	Auction	668	2691	4.3	3.370	3.370
08-Feb-00	6 months	24-Aug-00	196	Auction	451	2825	7.1	3.620	3.610
08-Feb-00	12 months	08-Feb-01	364	Auction	493	2270	5.0	3.970	3.970
15-Feb-00	3 months	18-May-00	91	Auction	443	3774	8.5	3.370	3.360
15-Feb-00	6 months	24-Aug-00	189	Auction	525	2025	4.1	3.610	3.610
15-Feb-00	12 months	08-Feb-01	357	Auction	416	2245	5.4	3.970	3.970
22-Feb-00	3 months	18-May-00	84	Auction	1008	4158	4.1	3.510	3.510
22-Feb-00	6 months	24-Aug-00	182	Auction	297	1400	4.7	3.730	3.720
22-Feb-00	12 months	08-Feb-01	350	Auction	198	1895	9.6	4.090	4.080
29-Feb-00	3 months	08-Jun-00	98	Auction	674	2544	3.8	3.510	3.500
29-Feb-00	6 months	24-Aug-00	175	Auction	409	2325	6.5	3.720	3.720
29-Feb-00	12 months	08-Feb-01	343	Auction	400	2221	5.6	4.020	4.010
07-Mar-00	3 months	08-Jun-00	91	Auction	605	2715	4.5	3.540	3.540
07-Mar-00	6 months	28-Sep-00	203	Auction	198	2670	13.5	3.740	3.730
07-Mar-00	12 months	08-Mar-01	364	Auction	624	1260	2.0	4.100	4.090
14-Mar-00	3 months	15-Jun-00	91	Auction	605	2035	3.4	3.670	3.670
14-Mar-00	6 months	24-Aug-00	161	Auction	396	1865	4.7	3.840	3.830
14-Mar-00	12 months	08-Mar-01	357	Auction	450	860	1.9	4.200	4.190
21-Mar-00	3 months	15-Jun-00	84	Auction	504	2857	5.7	3.650	3.650
21-Mar-00	6 months	21-Sep-00	182	Auction	539	1770	3.5	3.830	3.820
21-Mar-00	12 months	08-Mar-01	350	Auction	500	2160	4.3	4.120	4.120
28-Mar-00	3 months	06-Jul-00	98	Auction	625	3150	5.0	3.710	3.710
28-Mar-00	6 months	21-Sep-00	175	Auction	306	2550	8.3	3.870	3.870
28-Mar-00	12 months	08-Mar-01	343	Auction	416	2300	5.5	4.180	4.180
04-Apr-00	3 months	06-Jul-00	91	Auction	514	2154	4.3	3.720	3.720
04-Apr-00	6 months	21-Sep-00	168	Auction	364	828	2.3	3.870	3.870
04-Apr-00	12 months	08-Mar-01	336	Auction	361	1912	6.4	4.160	4.160
11-Apr-00	3 months	13-Jul-00	91	Auction	445	1775	4.0	3.770	3.760
11-Apr-00	6 months	21-Sep-00	161	Auction	200	2020	10.1	3.900	3.900
11-Apr-00	12 months	12-Apr-01	364	Auction	396	1970	5.0	4.210	4.200
18-Apr-00	3 months	13-Jul-00	84	Auction	454	2613	5.8	3.810	3.810
18-Apr-00	6 months	21-Sep-00	154	Auction	250	1270	5.1	3.930	3.920
18-Apr-00	12 months	12-Apr-01	357	Auction	365	1280	3.5	4.210	4.210
25-Apr-00	3 months	13-Jul-00	77	Auction	475	1850	3.9	3.880	3.870
25-Apr-00	6 months	26-Oct-00	182	Auction	306	1770	5.8	4.070	4.070
25-Apr-00	12 months	12-Apr-01	350	Auction	313	1730	5.5	4.320	4.320
02-May-00	3 months	10-Aug-00	98	Auction	400	1200	3.0	4.010	4.010
02-May-00	6 months	26-Oct-00	175	Auction	365	660	1.8	4.180	4.160
02-May-00	12 months	12-Apr-01	343	Auction	261	560	2.1	4.430	4.430
09-May-00	3 months	10-Aug-00	91	Auction	398	1673	4.2	4.180	4.180
09-May-00	6 months	26-Oct-00	168	Auction	255	1425	5.6	4.330	4.330

(Continued)

Date	Term	Matures	Days	Format	Sold	Bid	Bid/cover	Stop rate	Average rate
09-May-00	12 months	10-May-01	364	Auction	523	1300	2.5	4.630	4.630
16-May-00	3 months	10-Aug-00	84	Auction	397	1323	3.3	4.200	4.200
16-May-00	6 months	26-Oct-00	161	Auction	390	940	2.4	4.380	4.370
16-May-00	12 months	10-May-01	357	Auction	225	1125	5.0	4.730	4.720
23-May-00	3 months	24-Aug-00	91	Auction	297	1410	4.7	4.340	4.330
23-May-00	6 months	23-Nov-00	182	Auction	400	700	1.8	4.540	4.530
23-May-00	12 months	10-May-01	350	Auction	320	1380	4.3	4.840	4.830
30-May-00	3 months	24-Aug-00	84	Auction	477	1827	3.8	4.260	4.260
30-May-00	6 months	23-Nov-00	175	Auction	300	1370	4.6	4.460	4.460
30-May-00	12 months	10-May-01	343	Auction	300	1600	5.3	4.750	4.750
06-Jun-00	3 months	07-Sep-00	91	Auction	338	938	2.8	4.320	4.320
06-Jun-00	6 months	23-Nov-00	168	Auction	297	800	2.7	4.490	4.480
06-Jun-00	12 months	07-Jun-01	364	Auction	425	1250	2.9	4.770	4.770
13-Jun-00	3 months	07-Sep-00	84	Auction	332	1877	5.7	4.420	4.400
13-Jun-00	6 months	23-Nov-00	161	Auction	336	1945	5.8	4.590	4.580
13-Jun-00	12 months	07-Jun-01	357	Auction	350	1845	5.3	4.900	4.900
20-Jun-00	3 months	21-Sep-00	91	Auction	320	1517	4.7	4.410	4.380
20-Jun-00	6 months	21-Dec-00	182	Auction	500	1410	2.8	4.560	4.550
20-Jun-00	12 months	07-Jun-01	350	Auction	250	1660	6.6	4.810	4.810
27-Jun-00	3 months	21-Sep-00	84	Auction	678	1143	1.7	4.430	4.420
27-Jun-00	6 months	21-Dec-00	175	Auction	350	1460	4.2	4.590	4.590
27-Jun-00	12 months	07-Jun-01	343	Auction	460	1290	2.8	4.890	4.890
04-Jul-00	3 months	12-Oct-00	98	Auction	700	3660	5.2	4.420	4.420
04-Jul-00	6 months	21-Dec-00	168	Auction	396	2425	6.1	4.600	4.590
04-Jul-00	12 months	07-Jun-01	336	Auction	198	1980	10.0	4.900	4.890
11-Jul-00	3 months	12-Oct-00	91	Auction	514	1604	3.1	4.400	4.400
11-Jul-00	6 months	21-Dec-00	161	Auction	320	2170	6.8	4.590	4.590
11-Jul-00	12 months	12-Jul-01	364	Auction	370	1810	4.9	4.930	4.930
18-Jul-00	3 months	12-Oct-00	84	Auction	495	1815	3.7	4.430	4.420
18-Jul-00	6 months	25-Jan-01	189	Auction	396	1110	2.8	4.720	4.710
18-Jul-00	12 months	12-Jul-01	357	Auction	200	960	4.8	5.000	5.000
25-Jul-00	3 months	26-Oct-00	91	Auction	750	1485	2.0	4.470	4.460
25-Jul-00	6 months	25-Jan-01	182	Auction	297	1035	3.5	4.760	4.750
25-Jul-00	12 months	12-Jul-01	350	Auction	119	1210	10.2	5.030	5.020

Millions of euros
Source: Belgian Treasury and authors

5
The Finnish Government Bond Market

5.1 INTRODUCTION

The Finnish State Treasury Finance Unit is responsible for the management of government borrowing, as well as for the administration and performance of operations relating to the public debt (in both local and foreign currencies), risk management and the custody of assets in issue. The Treasury itself also manages the government's daily liquidity requirements.

The three fundamental principles governing the Finnish State's financing system are:

1. flexibility of borrowing
2. transparency in debt issuance and management
3. ensuring that assets in issue enjoy sufficient liquidity.

The ultimate aim is to secure the widest demand for public debt among the greatest possible investor audience, in other words the liquidity and breadth of Finnish Treasury holdings.

Finland's economy suffered a deep recession in the early 1990s, which swelled its public debt ratio to almost 70% of GDP, doubled the volume of its debt issuance and ushered in a radical reconfiguring of public debt structure (Treasury bonds make up 70% of the total outstanding balance). In contrast, the current size of the Finnish government debt market is predicated on the State's minimal recourse to external funding, translating as a decline in the public debt/GDP ratio to approximately 60% in 1999. These changes were due in no small measure to the deployment of the government's Stability Programme and its success in bringing public accounts fully into balance. As a result, year-2000 borrowing requirements are restricted to the service of debt already in issue.

The exchange risk attached to Finnish public debt has been allayed by a sharp decrease in foreign-currency borrowings. The reduction in exchange-rate exposure over the past 10 years

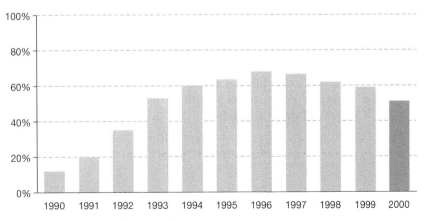

Source: Finnish State Treasury and authors

Figure 5.1 Finnish public debt/GDP and estimate for 2000

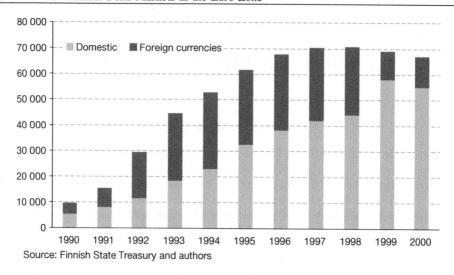

Source: Finnish State Treasury and authors

Figure 5.2   Finnish debt in domestic (euros) and foreign (euro equiv.) currencies

has been achieved despite the impact of restating eurocurrency debt as domestic debt. As can be seen from Figure 5.2, the proportion of central government debt drawn up in foreign currencies has consistently lost ground to euro issues (or issues in euro-legacy currencies).

5.2   ASSETS ISSUED BY THE FINNISH TREASURY

5.2.1   Treasury Bills (VVSs)

Finland's Treasury Bills or VVSs are tradeable money-market assets, represented by book entries, issued at discount and maturing between 1 and 364 days (the average term is three months).

The Treasury has two options for VVS issuance: the traditional auction system, or tap placement. The latter format (favoured in the new T-bill issuance programme) allows issues to be tailored to individual investor needs as regards debt maturity and currency denomination. Recent underbidding at auctions by comparison with tap issues has led the Finnish Treasury increasingly to favour the latter, using a panel of financial institutions. Thus, seven months into its new VVS programme, tap placements account for over 90% of issuance.

Despite the large volume of Finnish Treasury VVS issues, money-market trading is still dominated by the deposit certificates issued by the Bank of Finland. As a result, secondary-market trading of VVSs suffers something of a liquidity deficit.

The yield of VVSs is calculated as follows:

$$P = \frac{100}{1 + r \times \dfrac{d}{360}}$$

where

P = weighted average price at auction, stated as a percentage of nominal value
d = number of days between payment or value date and the bill's maturity
r = weighted average rate at auction (IRR)

The basis Current/360 has been in use since 1 January 1999, against the previous Current/365.

5.2.2 Serial Bonds

Serial Bonds are tradeable fixed-rate instruments with a range of maturities from 1 to 30 years. They pay an annual coupon, are redeemable upon maturity (bullet bonds), and may be represented by book entries (80%) or bearer certificates (20%) with a face value of 100 000 euros. As the most prized instrument in the Treasury's financing armoury, they are the assets with the greatest weight in the Finnish public debt market.

Although Serial Bonds have a wide range of maturities, the Treasury is seeking to consolidate issues into a small number of lines, to secure the most liquid possible benchmark references. Since 1999, issues have been primarily concentrated in the 3- and 10-year terms. The treasury has also started up a debt exchange programme, to buy back references nearing maturity or with coupons appreciably higher than market rates and to replace them with either bonds or cash (cash or bond reverse auctions). It has likewise stated its ambition to make the Finnish 10-year benchmark the cheapest to deliver (CTD) of the futures basket specified in the contract on the *Notionnel* traded on the French futures market MATIF.

To attain benchmark status, Serial Bonds must meet a series of requirements regarding investor distribution and market liquidity. The responsibility for this falls to a group of primary dealers or market makers, which undertake with the Treasury to ensure a sufficiently active level of secondary-market trading in the selected references, in exchange for privileges which are detailed below (section 6.8). Bonds automatically lose their benchmark status when they have less than 12 months left to run.

Serial bonds are issued at 'Dutch' auctions or through banking syndicates via the tap-issue format. Investors then place their orders through market makers.

The yield formula for Finnish bonds is as follows:

$$P + Cc = \sum_{t=1}^{t=N} \frac{F(t)}{(1 + R)^t}$$

where

$F(t)$ = cash flow on the bond in the year t
  R = yield (IRR)
  P = clean price in %
  Cc = accrued interest on a Current/Current basis (prior to the euro, Current/360)
  N = number of years to maturity

The Finnish public debt market currently has six bond lines accorded benchmark status.

5.2.3 Yield Bonds (Retail Investors)

These are fixed-rate bullet bonds geared to the retail investor, with nominal values of 1000, 2000 and 10 000 euros, issued at par and maturing from 2 to 4 years. In order to reach the widest possible retail audience, they are sold directly through banks, post offices and at the Treasury itself over three-week subscription periods. Yield Bonds are tradeable

Table 5.1 Finnish public debt market benchmarks

Line	Coupon	Matures	Outstanding
1994 I Serial Bond	10.00%	15/09/2001	5 252
1998 III Serial Bond	3.75%	12/11/2003	5 203
1993 I Serial Bond	9.50%	15/03/2004	8 392
1996 I Serial Bond	7.25%	16/04/2006	6 080
1997 I Serial Bond	6.00%	18/04/2008	4 024
1998 II Serial Bond	5.00%	25/04/2009	5 921
2000 I Serial Bond	5.75%	23/02/2011	4 218
Total			39 090

Figures as of May 2000
Millions of euros
Source: Finnish State Treasury and authors

Table 5.2 Yield Bonds to June 2000

Line	Coupon	Matures	Outstanding
VI	3.40%	07/09/2000	207.7
XV	4.50%	07/10/2000	143.6
VII	3.10%	19/10/2000	45.2
XVII	4.30%	02/12/2000	102.5
III	3.60%	23/03/2001	48.9
X	4.10%	04/08/2001	2.9
XII	4.30%	01/09/2001	41.8
XIV	4.50%	29/09/2001	26.2
XVI	4.70%	27/10/2001	23.3
XVI	4.60%	04/11/2001	76.5
III	4.50%	02/01/2002	111.2
I	2.90%	18/01/2002	81.2
II	4.00%	16/02/2002	85.2
V	4.30%	24/02/2002	53.0
V	4.00%	27/04/2002	28.0
X	6.30%	20/05/2002	67.4
XII	6.00%	05/08/2002	120.8
XIV	5.80%	09/09/2002	283.8
VIII	3.25%	19/10/2002	18.1
Total			1567.4

Figures as of 21 June 2000
Millions of euros
Source: Finnish State Treasury and authors

on the Helsinki Stock Exchange. Their yield formula and interest basis is as stated for Serial Bonds.

The sharp fall in interest rates since the onset of stage three of EMU has robbed this product of much of its attractiveness. The retail investors making up its target audience have largely abandoned its use in favour of higher-yielding assets, despite the greater risk attached. The Treasury responded to the slump in demand by scaling down its 1999 issuance volumes, and is trying to devise new instruments for raising finance from this investor group. The outstanding balance of Yield Bonds as of June 2000 was approximately 1.57 billion euros.

Table 5.3   Finnish central government debt

	Amount	%/total
VVSs	1 397	2.1%
Serial Bonds	41 364	61.0%
Housing Bonds	2 207	3.3%
Yield Bonds	1 955	2.9%
Others	9 865	14.6%
Foreign-currency debt	11 006	16.2%
Total	67 794	

Figures as of May 2000
Millions of euros
Source: State Treasury and authors

5.3   OVERVIEW OF THE FINNISH PUBLIC DEBT MARKET

The outstanding balance of Finnish debt, as of 31 July 2000, was 71.12 billion euros, with almost 84% drawn up in euros and Finnish markka. The remaining 16% is represented by

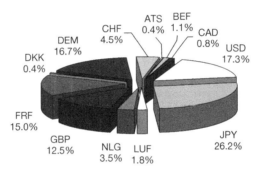

Source: Bloomberg and authors

Figure 5.3   International issues by currency as of July 2000

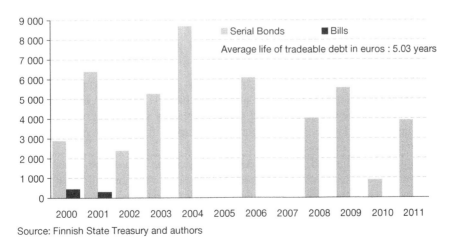

Source: Finnish State Treasury and authors

Figure 5.4   Maturities curve of Finnish debt as of July 2000 (domestic issues, in millions of euros)

issues conducted in other currencies, predominantly the dollar, yen and pound sterling, with over 4% each.

The total average life of Finnish debt (domestic and foreign-currency issues) was 4.67 years in May 2000, while that of domestic debt alone (VVSs, Serial Bonds, Housing Bonds and Yield Bonds) stood at 5.03 years. Both figures come out slightly below the average for other euro-zone countries. Of domestic debt, 73% of the outstanding total is bunched in issues dated under 6 years.

Finally, note that the Finnish public debt market is one of the six within the euro zone accorded a maximum credit rating by leading international agencies. The other markets sharing this distinction are Germany, France, Austria, Ireland and the Netherlands.

5.4   THE PRIMARY MARKET

The Finnish Treasury issues its main securities by three methods: (1) auctions— 'American' for VVSs or bills and 'Dutch' for Serial Bonds, (2) tap issues via financial institutions (only VVSs to date, under the new continuous bill issuance programme adopted in January 1999), and (3) bank syndicates (Serial Bonds exclusively and only on rare occasions).

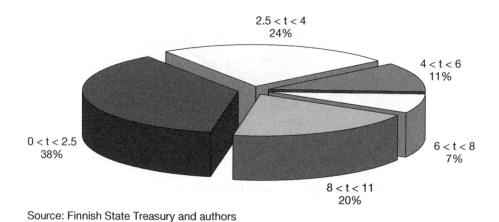

Source: Finnish State Treasury and authors

Figure 5.5   Finnish public debt by term (domestic issues, in millions of euros)

Since early 1999, the tap placement of bills has increasingly taken over from the 'American' auction system, such that the latter now channels more than twice the volume. So successful has the new system proved that the Treasury is thinking of switching over entirely to tap issues. Finally, Yield Bonds—earmarked for retail investors—are sold directly through banks and post offices or at the Treasury itself.

The healthy state of Finland's public accounts has led the Treasury to scale down bond issues to just one day a month, on the second Thursday. Auctions of Serial Bonds are announced on a twice-yearly basis at the close of each semester in a calendar published on the Treasury's Reuters page (SUVB). The progress of each quarter's issues is tracked in the monthly reports issued by the Treasury, alongside the results of all issues conducted since the start of the year. The Monday before auctions, the Treasury gives details of the securities to be issued. Bill issuance, on the otherhand, does not follow a pre-set calendar, since placement can be via either auction or tap issue and is, in any case, continuous.

Among the 1999 innovations in the Finnish public debt market was the switch from the old bid presentation and confirmation system, via telephone and fax respectively, to the electronic BAS system, supported by Bloomberg terminals. This new system was inaugurated with the bond exchange auction held on 10 June 1999.

5.4.1 VVS Auctions

VVS or bill auctions use the 'American', i.e. multi-price, system. Institutions wishing to subscribe the issue submit their competitive bids to the Treasury, specifying rates and volumes for each, in the case of more than one bid. Bids are then sorted in ascending order of yield, and the Treasury fixes the maximum rate (minimum price) it is willing to concede, i.e. its cut-off or stop-out rate. Allocation is at the rate specified in the bid, provided this is at or below the stop-out rate, while all bids at higher rates are automatically discarded. Minutes after resolution, the Treasury publishes the results, including stop-out and average rates (in terms of nominal value), the lowest rate bid, the total volume of submitted bids and the final amount accepted, as well as the outstanding balance of bills post-issue.

5.4.2 Serial Bond Auctions

The dates and details of Serial Bond auctions are announced by the Treasury on the preceding Monday. Auctions are held over two rounds: a first, competitive round using the 'Dutch' or single-price system, in which institutions can present one or more competitive bids; and a second round in which the Treasury announces the amount to be issued—in no case more than 30% of that allotted in first-round proceedings—and the issue price. Only primary dealers may participate in this second subscription stage.

Competitive bidding works as follows. Institutions submit their bids to the Treasury, specifying volume and price to two decimal places. They are then sorted in ascending order of price to determine the minimum accepted or stop-out price. All bids specifying a higher price are accepted, with the option of pro rata allocation if the resulting volume exceeds the Treasury's target, while all those below the stop-out are rejected. The Treasury subsequently notifies the marginal price and rate, the total bids submitted and the coverage resulting, as well as the new outstanding balance of the references concerned and the amount available for non-competitive subscription.

In the second round, the price at which the Treasury allots to market makers must be equal to or higher than the stop-out price set in competitive bidding.

5.4.3 Continuous Daily Posting (Tap Issue)

The Treasury timed its switch to the tap-issue format to coincide with the launch of its new VVS programme. Tap placements are channelled though private investment banks (in 1999, Goldman Sachs International and Merita Bank): the Treasury posts a daily price for its assets, which the banks then place in accordance with investor buy orders.

5.4.4 Characteristics of VVS and Serial Bond Issues

VVSs

- *Auction announcement*: bill auctions are held on a continuous basis, without a pre-set calendar.
- *Issue procedure*: 'American' auction via the continuous daily posting system established under the VVS issuance programme.
- *Auction participants*: only primary dealers (market makers) are eligible to bid at auctions. They subsequently place the securities among other bidders.
- *Minimum denomination*: 10 000 euros.
- *Presentation of competitive bids*: bids specifying the rate and amount sought can be submitted up to 13.00 local time on the auction resolution date (T − 0).
- *Minimum amount of bids*: 100 000 euros.
- *Auction results*: the Bank of Finland posts results on the Reuters SUVA page from 13.30 local time.
- *Value/payment date*: two working days after the auction (T + 2).
- *Admission to secondary-market trading*: paid-up securities can be traded on the Helsinki Stock Exchange (HEX).
- *Calculation basis*: Current/360.

Table 5.4 Announcement of VVS auction, 21/6/99

Number of days	183	364
Maturity	23/12/99	21/6/00
Value/payment date	23/6/99	23/6/99
Maximum amount to be issued	100 million euros	
Presentation of bids	Before 13.00 on 21/6/99	
Announcement of results	After 13.30	

Source: authors

Table 5.5 Resolution of VVS auction, 21/6/99

	3 months	12 months
Weighted average rate	—	2.71%
Stop-out rate	—	2.71%
Minimum rate	—	2.71%
Number of bids presented	1	1
Number of bids accepted	0	1
Amount allotted	0	100 m euros
Volume of bids	100 m euros	100 m euros
VVSs outstanding at 23/6/99	3740 m euros	—

Source: authors

Serial Bonds

- *Auction announcement*: three working days (T − 3) in advance, with details of the main characteristics of the bonds to be issued.
- *Auction procedure*: 'Dutch' auction (alternatively through a banking syndicate, though this option is little used).

- *Presentation of bids*: bids, specifying price and volume, may only be placed by primary dealers. The deadline for submission (via the Bloomberg BAS system) is 13.00 local time on the date set for the auction, and the Treasury confirms reception, also via Bloomberg, at 13.05 local time. When the syndication option is used, bids are placed through syndicate members.
- *Interest payment*: fixed annual coupon.
- *Minimum denomination*: 100 000 euros.
- *Presentation of competitive bids*: bids must be placed on auction day (T – 0) by 13.00 local time.
- *Minimum amount of bids*: 2 000 000 euros.
- *Auction results*: the Bank of Finland posts auction results on its REUTERS page (SUVA) minutes after auction resolution (about 13.30 local time).
- *Value/payment date*: three working days after the auction (T + 3).
- *Admission to secondary-market trading*: the securities are admitted to trading on the Helsinki Stock Exchange (HEX) as of the corresponding payment date (T + 3).
- *Interest calculation basis*: Current/Current.

An example of a Serial Bond issue is given in Table 5.6.

Table 5.6   Issue (4/8/99) of 3.75% bond maturing November 2003

Maturity	12/11/2003
Stop-out price	101.88%
Amount issued	206.5 m euros
Volume of bids	638.5 m euros
Number of bids	26
Accepted bids	5
Outstanding balance of reference	3068 m euros

Source: authors

Debt Exchanges (Bond or Cash Exchange Auctions)

The Finnish Treasury offers investors the chance voluntarily to exchange bonds nearing maturity for 'on-the-run' securities or the corresponding cash sum. Exchanges are effected through specific programmes announced on the Treasury's Reuters page, SUVQ. Investors must place their bids through primary dealers, specifying in each case the volume of the old bonds they wish to exchange, in multiples of 1 million euros, and the price they are seeking, to three decimal places. The Treasury sorts bids in ascending order of price and sets a stop-out price for the exchange or payment of the bonds to be withdrawn. In the event of overbidding at the stop-out price, allocation may be on a pro rata basis. Bids must be submitted to the Treasury before 13.00 local time on the day the exchange auction is held (T – 0), and participants are notified of the results from 13.30 onwards, with a statement of the price at which the exchange went through and the volume to be exchanged.

Table 5.7 gives as an example the 10/6/99 exchange of the 'on-the-run' Serial Bond, coupon 5%, maturing on 25 April 2009, for the 4% Serial Bond maturing on 21 June 2000 or the corresponding cash amount.

Table 5.7   Serial Bond exchange 10/6/99

	Bond withdrawn	Option 1	Option 2
	Serial 2000	Serial 2009	Cash
Maturity	21/6/2000	25/4/2009	—
Coupon	4.00%	5.00%	—
Conversion ratio	2.71%	4.56%	2.71%
Conversion price	101.276	103.417	101.276
Amount accepted (of bond to be withdrawn)	645.3 m euros	223.6 m euros	421.7 m euros
Total volume of bids	998 m euros	—	—
Outstanding balance post-exchange	1879 m euros	5311 m euros	—

Source: authors

5.5   THE SECONDARY MARKET

Secondary-market trading in Finnish public debt takes place on the Helsinki Stock Exchange (HEX), with business hours from 9.30 to 17.00 local time. The most important members are the 10 market-making entities appointed by the Treasury. Though a number of brokers are also active in the market, their trading volumes are relatively muted.

Average monthly turnover contracted sharply in the first half of 1999: just 39.70 billion euros, against the 53.38 billion of the year before, due largely to the reduction in the outstanding debt balance. The bid/ask spread is currently running at an average of 2–3 basis points, on a par with comparably sized markets of similar liquidity. One distinguishing feature of Finland's market is that yields are quoted to two decimal places, as opposed to the clean price quoted on the other European markets.

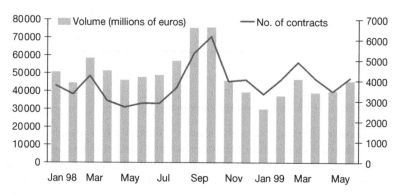

Source: Finnish State Treasury and authors

Figure 5.6   Trading of Serial Bonds on the Finnish market

5.5.1   The Strips Market

There is no strips market in Finnish government debt.

5.5.2   The Repo Market

Finland's OTC repo market, once extremely narrow and short on liquidity, has expanded significantly since the Treasury's 1998 decision to change the calculation format governing transactions. Nevertheless, trading volumes continue relatively subdued (rising from 24 contracts over January–April 1998, to 1024 over the same months of 1999). The change referred to was the Treasury's undertaking to remunerate the deposits posted by market makers (at 1.5%), provided they acquired the bonds prior to 11.00 local time (otherwise, the interest is zero). Another spur to development was the alignment of trading hours with those of the other repo markets. However, high transaction costs and liquidity shortcomings—virtually no activity beyond that conducted by the Treasury itself—have tended to dissuade investors from entering the market.

5.5.3   The Futures Market

The futures contract on the Finnish bond was introduced in 1994. This market has the peculiarity that debt futures are traded not on the basis of a notional bond (as elsewhere in Europe), but on a real bond transacted on the markets. As a result, there is no requirement either to post margin or to mark to market on a daily basis. The future on the Finnish bond is quoted identically to the bond itself, that is, in yield stated to two decimal places. For this reason, the contract more closely resembles a traditional forward contract—on the corresponding bond—than a future per se.

Trading in debt futures takes place on the Helsinki Stock Exchange. Three contracts are currently negotiated, on the 2-, 5- and 10-year benchmark bonds. Contracts are for a nominal value of 100 000 euros and have a roll-over of two maturities. A total of 76 100 contracts were traded to June 1999, an average of 304 a day. The three most actively traded debt-futures contracts are shown in Table 5.8.

Table 5.8   Most actively traded debt-futures contracts

Future	Settlement	Underlying asset
2001 Sep	15-Sep-2001	Serial 10.0% 2001
2004 Sep	15-Sep-2004	Serial 9.5% 2004
2009 Sep	15-Sep-2009	Serial 5.0% 2009

Source: authors

5.6   CLEARING AND SETTLEMENT

VVSs are settled on $T + 2$ and Serial Bonds on $T + 3$. Domestic operations can be cleared through the book-entry system and international operations through CEDEL or EUROCLEAR. Since 1997, the Finnish Central Securities Depository (FCSD) has taken on the centralised clearing and settlement of all bill and bond operations transacted on the Helsinki Stock Exchange.

Investors wishing to transact in book-entry Finnish debt securities must do so through the FCSD, opening a securities account at any of the Depository's member institutions. These institutions, which include the majority of Finland's commercial banks, several securities broker–dealers, the Helsingin Arvo-osuukeskus association, the Finnish State and the Bank of Finland, channel most of their operations through the FCSD via own-name accounts.

Futures transactions on Finnish bonds are cleared and settled on the futures market itself (HEX).

The legal and supervisory framework of the Finnish debt market is fully compliant with EU requirements. The Securities Market Act of 1994 regulates both public issues and trading practices for all other assets, whether fixed-income or equities. The Financial Supervision Office, under the Bank of Finland, plays a watchdog role with regard to the operation of the financial markets and their participating agents.

5.7   TAXATION

Foreign investors are exempt from any tax on interest earned on the holding of Finnish bonds. Nor are they liable for withholding tax on the income earned, whether through coupon payments or capital gains on bond transactions. Domestic investors pay a withholding tax of 28%.

5.8   MARKET MAKERS

The present market-maker or primary-dealer system was introduced in 1992, and has served since then to ensure sufficient depth and liquidity in the market. Only banks and savings banks are eligible for market-maker status, subject to authorisation from the National Debt Office, and all short-listed institutions must serve a six-month probationary period. Ten market makers currently operate in the Finnish debt market, including the most recent appointment, the French bank BNP.

Market-maker status entails the following obligations:

- active participation in auctions and tap issues, submitting bids compatible with current market conditions
- activity as a counterparty on the secondary market, quoting prices for all debt references and maintaining a permanent commitment to ensuring the maximum possible market liquidity
- The quoting of firm prices to the Bank of Finland, the Finnish Treasury and clients outside the Finnish system. The bid-ask spread quoted by primary dealers must in no case exceed 5 basis points of yield.
- the provision of information to the Bank of Finland on government bond market transactions and activity.

In return, market makers enjoy the following privileges:

- the exclusive right to participate in Serial Bond auctions
- the right to participate in the second round of bond auctions, held on T + 1
- the commercial benefits deriving from their role as a channel for investor bidding.

The following banks and broker–dealers are currently primary dealers in Finnish public debt:

Alfred Berg
Barclays Capital
Deutsche Bank AG
Salomon Smith Barney
Merita Bank PLC
Ökobank
Skandinaviska Eskilda Banken
Svenska Handelsbanken
Unibank
Banque Nationale de Paris (BNP)

ANNEXE: THE FINNISH PUBLIC DEBT MARKET

Outcome of Finnish Public Debt Issues, 2000

Date	Operation	Instrument	Coupon	Term	Settles	Matures	Sold	Bids	Bid/cover	Stop rate	Stop price
20-Jan-00	Exchange	Serial Bond 2003	3.75%	3 years	25-Jan-00	12-Nov-03	618	2004	3.24	5.050	95.580
15-Feb-00	Syndicate	Serial Bond 2011	5.75%	10 years	18-Feb-00	23-Feb-11	3000	3000	1.00	Bund + 30 bp	99.110
17-Feb-00	Exchange	Serial Bond 2003	3.75%	3 years	25-Feb-00	12-Nov-03	498	1199	2.41	5.110	95.470
16-Mar-00	Exchange	Serial Bond 2011	5.75%	10 years	21-Mar-00	23-Feb-11	417	467	1.12	5.560	101.499
13-Apr-00	Exchange	Serial Bond 2011	5.75%	10 years	18-Apr-00	23-Feb-11	301	451	1.50	5.440	102.504
11-May-00	Conversion	Serial Bond 2011	5.75%	10 years	14-May-00	23-Feb-11	171	321	1.88	5.595	101.200
08-Jun-00	Repurchase	Serial Bond 2001	10.00%	2 years	13-Jun-00	15-Sep-01	350	560	1.60	4.810	106.130
08-Jun-00	Repurchase	Serial Bond 2004	9.50%	5 years	13-Jun-00	15-Mar-04	145	922	6.36	5.060	114.806
24-Aug-00	Exchange	Serial Bond 2011	5.75%	10 years	29-Aug-00	23-Feb-11	134	427	3.19	5.440	102.420
21-Sep-00	Conversion	Serial Bond 2003	3.75%	3 years	26-Sep-00	12-Nov-03	450	961	2.14	5.214	95.860
21-Sep-00	Conversion	Serial Bond 2011	5.75%	10 years	26-Sep-00	23-Feb-11	284	349	1.23	5.501	101.900
12-Oct-00	Auction	Serial Bond 2003	3.75%	3 years	17-Oct-00	12-Nov-03	135	720	5.33	5.175	—
12-Oct-00	Auction	Serial Bond 2011	5.75%	10 years	17-Oct-00	23-Feb-11	345	606	1.76	5.436	—

Millions of euros
Source: Bloomberg, Reuters and authors

6
The French Government Bond Market

6.1 INTRODUCTION

France is Europe's third-largest public debt market after Italy and Germany (around 667 billion euros in June 2000, with 597 billion tradeable). By the measure of benchmark liquidity, however, the French market is not only ranked second in Europe but also one of the most highly regarded worldwide as a reference for private-sector issues. Specifically, over two-thirds of all euro-denominated 5-year corporate bond issues in 1999 and 2000 opted for the French BTAN as their reference asset.

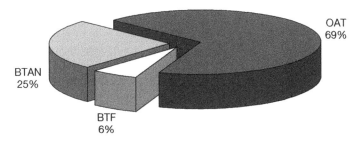

Source: French Treasury, Bloomberg and authors

Figure 6.1 Composition of French tradeable public debt (as of June 2000)

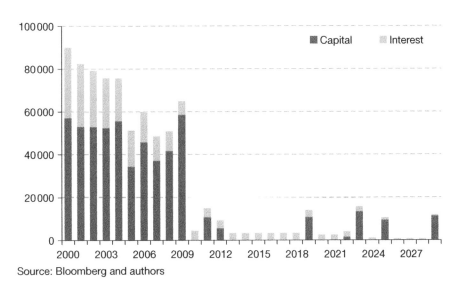

Source: Bloomberg and authors

Figure 6.2 The French debt maturities curve (OATs and BTANs) (in millions of euros)

This above-par liquidity is largely due to the full fungibility of asset lines, which are issued with uniform characteristics. The Treasury's goal at all times is to secure large outstanding balances of BTANs and OATs, the assets most actively traded on secondary markets, in a small number of issues. Another key factor is the existence of a market-maker group (SVTs or *Spécialistes en Valeurs du Trésor*) whose role is to assure the primary-market take-up of Treasury issues and procure the maximum liquidity in their secondary-market trading. At the time of writing, trading and therefore liquidity are keenly concentrated in the 10-year segment of the curve. Market transparency is additionally favoured by an issuance policy based on competitive bids.

The Treasury publishes advance information on its mid- and long-term borrowing requirements at the start of every year, alongside the corresponding issuance schedule. Issues follow a regular pattern and the Treasury is constantly releasing new information on central government debt issues and management through a wide variety of channels.

6.2   ASSETS ISSUED BY THE FRENCH TREASURY

The French Treasury has the widest range of public debt instruments of the 11 euro-zone countries. The money-market side is covered by Treasury bills or BTFs, and the medium and long terms by 2- or 5-year BTANs and OATs, with maturities running from 10 to 30 years.

The range of OATs has broadened in tandem with the modernisation of the French public debt market. As well as the fixed-coupon OAT lines geared to wholesale investors, the Treasury has also folded in Constant Maturity OATs (TEC 10), launched in 1996, and, since 1998, the inflation-indexed product OATi. Issuance of certain lines has also been discontinued, specifically the floating-rate OATs linked to a variety of benchmarks. Finally, in a bid to secure the widest possible investor base, a given volume of regularly-issued OAT lines is directed at the retail public.

The following sections provide a detailed description of BTFs (bills), BTANs and OATs (bonds), and the latter's variants: the inflation-linked OATi and Constant Maturity OAT or TEC 10.

6.2.1   *Bons du Trésor à Taux fixe et à Intérêt Précompté* (BTFs)

BTFs are tradeable fixed-rate bills issued at discount with standard maturities of 13 weeks (3 months), 27 weeks (6 months) and 48 weeks (12 months), though the Treasury has the option of slotting in 4- or 7-week terms where necessary. All securities in the same line are fully fungible.

BTFs are the Treasury's main instrument for the short-term management (under 1 year) of the government borrowing requirement. They are issued each Monday, according to an annual calendar which specifies issue, payment and maturity dates.

The net price payable at BTF issues is calculated as follows:

$$P = \frac{N}{\left(1 + R \times \dfrac{n}{360}\right)}$$

where

n = number of days between issue and maturity (on a Current/360 basis)
R = yield as defined at auction
N = nominal value
P = net price payable

6.2.2 *Bons du Trésor à Taux fixe et à Intérêt Annuel* (BTANs)

BTANs are Treasury bonds paying annual fixed-rate coupons and redeemable upon maturity. Lines are fully fungible and dated 2 or 5 years at issue.

Sixteen lines were in issue as of January 2000, with remaining terms falling between April 2000 and July 2005. Coupons on outstanding lines range from 7.75% to 3%, and their residual life stands at around 2 years on average. BTANs account for over 27% (150 billion euros) of the total outstanding balance of French public debt tradeable on secondary markets.

BTAN sales prices are determined by the following formula:

$$P + Cc = \frac{100}{\left(1 + \dfrac{TA}{100}\right)^{\left(A - \frac{n}{365}\right)}} + \sum \frac{100}{\left(1 + \dfrac{TA}{100}\right)^{\left(i - \frac{n}{365}\right)}}$$

where

P = price as a percentage of nominal value
Cc = accrued interest, as a percentage of nominal value
TA = yield calculated on a Current/Current basis
CN = nominal coupon, as % of nominal value
A = maturity in years
n = number of days between transaction and value date, on a Current/Current basis
(365 or 366 in leap years)

The accrued interest Cc is calculated as follows:

$$Cc = CN \times \frac{n}{365}$$

6.2.3 *Obligations Assimilables du Trésor* (OATs)

OATs are Treasury bonds which may be at a fixed, variable, floating or inflation-indexed rate. Fixed-rate OATs are fully fungible, pay fixed annual coupons and are issued for terms ranging from 10 to 30 years. As standard, however, the Treasury issues two 10-year lines per year (one each semester).

6.2.4 Inflation-Indexed OATs (OATi)

OATi are Treasury bonds similar to fixed-rate OATs except that cash flows (interest and principal on maturity) are multiplied by a ratio based on price-index variations between the baseline date and the date of coupon payment. The reference index is the French

CPI. Provided market conditions are right, these bonds are issued on the same dates as fixed-rate OATs.

6.2.5 Floating-Rate OATs

These are Treasury bonds paying annual coupons (quarterly in the case of the OAT TEC 10) indexed to the reference rates of other assets. Component classes are:

- *OAT TMB*: the reference rate (TMB) is the arithmetical average of the monthly yields of 3-month BTFs (bills) over the year prior to payment.
- *OAT TRB*: the reference rate (TRB) is a quarterly-adjusted rate based on the yield of 3-month BTFs at the auction prior to coupon payment.
- *OAT TRA*: the reference rate (TRA) is a long-term rate adjusted in line with the monthly average yields of *Emprunts d'État* (bonds whose issuance has been discontinued and which are only traded on the secondary market) maturing in 7 years or longer.
- *OAT TME*: the reference rate (TME) is the secondary-market yield of a selection of *Emprunts d'État*, i.e. the monthly average rate of long-term bonds over the 12 months prior to coupon payment.
- *OAT TEC 10*: paying quarterly coupons linked to the TEC 10 index tracking the average yield of OATs with a constant 10-year maturity.

6.3 OVERVIEW OF THE FRENCH PUBLIC DEBT MARKET

France, like the other euro-zone government issuers, has moved to a major restructuring of its debt position. Specifically, the reduction in its recourse to short-term as opposed to longer-dated assets (OATs) has lengthened the average life of tradeable public debt from 5.47 years in 1990 to 6.35 years by the end of 2000—within the 6 to 6.5 years set by the Treasury as its target range.

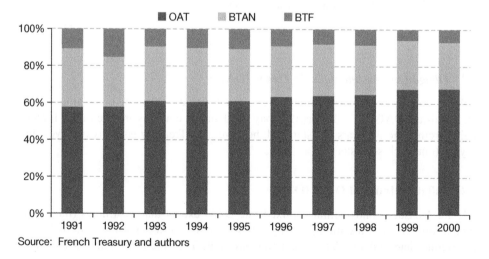

Source: French Treasury and authors

Figure 6.3 Composition of French tradeable public debt

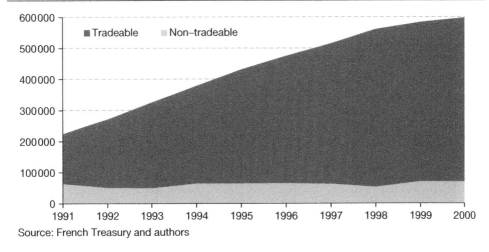

Source: French Treasury and authors

Figure 6.4 French public debt (1991–2000) (in millions of euros)

France's entry to the third stage of EMU has entailed the maintenance of convergence discipline and the formulation of a stability programme (envisaging GDP growth in the next three years between 2.5% and 3%). Programme commitments include a public debt/GDP ratio of 57.5% on the back of a reduction in the general government deficit from 2.1% in 1999 to 0.4% in 2003.

The wave of debt portfolio diversification that followed the euro's launch was felt particularly keenly in the French market. The result is that non-resident holdings of BTFs, BTANs and OATs had advanced to 24.9% of tradeable debt outstanding by March 2000.

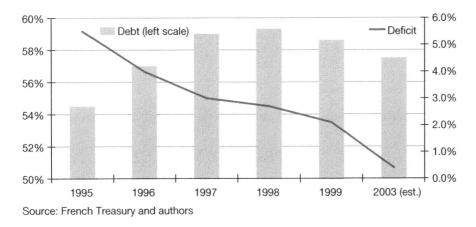

Source: French Treasury and authors

Figure 6.5 Public debt and the public deficit (% of GDP)

As to the composition of French medium- and long-term debt, the dominant instruments are BTANs and fixed-rate OATs, with more than 93% between them of the tradeable debt total and around 83% of all public debt.

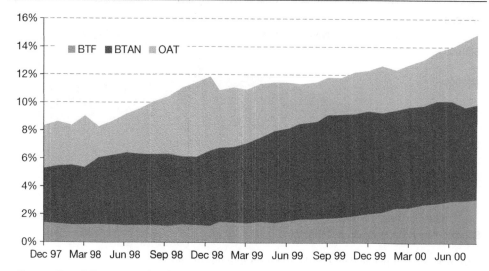

Source: French Treasury and authors

Figure 6.6   Proportion of outstanding balance held by non-residents

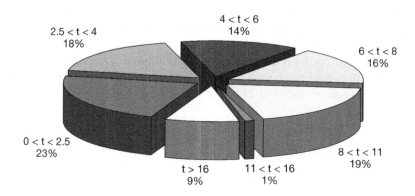

Source: Bloomberg and authors

Figure 6.7   Outstanding balance of OATs and BTANs (as of August 2000, in millions of euros)

6.4   THE PRIMARY MARKET

6.4.1   Issuance Procedures

- *'American' auction*: The French Treasury favours this auction format for its securities issuance. Assets are allotted at bid prices (rates in the case of BTANs): bids seeking a lower yield are allotted first; the Treasury then works down the scale until its target volume is reached. Thus auction participants pay different prices depending on their bid specifications. Bids at OAT and BTF auctions are stated as a percentage of ex-coupon nominal value to two decimal places, while BTAN bids must specify the yields sought to three decimal places $(+/-0.005\%)$.

- *Syndicated placement among market makers*: The syndication option is also used, though less frequently.

6.4.2 Description of Issue using the 'American' Auction Format

Bidders must be members of the French central clearing and settlement system (Sicovam) and account holders at the Bank of France. Take-up, for the moment, is primarily by market makers (SVTs). Entities not affiliated to Sicovam must place their bids through SVTs (a full list of these given in section 6.8 below).

The Treasury announces the procedure to be followed two working days in advance, after due consultation with the SVTs, specifying the issue amount in the case of BTFs or the upper and lower limits in the case of BTANs and OATs, as well as other features of the lines to be issued. As stated above, all bids are allotted at the price or rate specified, rather than at the corresponding average. Bids may be submitted to the Bank of France up to 10 minutes before the auction. The Bank then sorts them in ascending order of rates (BTFs) or descending order of price (BTANs and OATs). The Treasury decides how much of each line it will sell, depending on the prices and quantities sought by bidders. In the case of BTANs and OATs, the total volume will be within the pre-set limits; in the case of BTFs, it will be at the target announced, rounded off as necessary. The Treasury also has the option of making a pro rata allocation at the auction's stop-out price to ensure a better match between issue volume and bids received.

Auctions are organised by the Bank of France, which forwards SVT bids to the Treasury on a real-time basis. The Treasury then decides on the final issue volume (between the pre-set limits) and the lines to be allotted. Bids can be submitted by any institution holding an account with Sicovam, RGV (see section 6.6) or the Bank of France. Over 90% of securities issued at auction are bought by the SVT group. Participants can either submit their bids direct to the Bank of France or use the remote-access system TELSAT, installed at their own desks. TELSAT's main function is to shorten auction resolution time, an increasingly important factor in today's volatile markets.

Auction results are posted within 20 minutes of the bidding deadline on all the main financial information screens (AFP, Bridge, Reuters, Telerate, Bloomberg), with details of bid volumes, amounts sold, stop-out prices per asset (stop-out rate in the case of BTFs) and the weighted average rate of the securities allotted.

6.4.3 Characteristics of BTF, BTAN and OAT Issues

BTFs

- *Issue procedure*: 'American' auction.
- *Auction dates*: every Monday (or the working day before or after in the event of a public holiday) at 15.00 local time. The exceptionally high frequency of BTF issuance reflects their use by the Treasury as a monetary-policy tool.
- *Issue maturities*: 3-month BTFs alternating with 6- and 12-month BTFs.
- *Announcement*: the Thursday before the auction $(T-2)$, with notice of the exact amount to be issued per term.
- *Formulation of bids*: in terms of interest rate rather than price, to three decimal places $(+/-0.005\%)$ and on a Current/360 basis.
- *Payment*: the first Thursday after the auction $(T+3)$.

Table 6.1 Examples of a BTF auction

13-week (3-month) BTF	
Maturity	17 June 1999
Average rate	2.906%
Amount allotted	1605 million euros
Volume of bids	5170 million euros
Stop-out rate	2.910%
Allotted at stop-out	45.80%
48-week (12-month) BTF	
Maturity	17 February 2000
Average rate	2.915%
Amount allotted	604 million euros
Volume of bids	2870 million euros
Stop-out rate	2.920%
Allotted at stop-out	37.30%

Source: authors

- *Second rounds*: resolved the Wednesday after the auction. The Treasury allots a given amount at the average price fetched in competitive bidding.
- *Grey-market trading*: authorised from the announcement date of weekly auctions up to payment or settlement date. The value date for grey-market transactions coincides with the auction's payment date, and conventions are exactly the same (yields, to three decimal places). Accrued interest is calculated with reference to the payment or settlement date.

BTANs

- *Issue procedure*: usually an 'American' auction.
- *Auction date*: the third Thursday of each month at 11.00 local time.
- *Announcement of issue target*: two days before the auction (T − 2) (at times coinciding with the issue of other medium-term securities, principally OATs, and new BTAN lines) the Treasury announces the upper and lower limits of the volumes envisaged and the lines to be placed including, at the very least, a 2- or 5-year BTAN.
- *Formulation of bids*: banks state their bids as a percentage of clean nominal value to two decimal places.
- *Payment*: value date is T + 7 (or the following day if this is a public holiday).
- *Interest basis*: Current/Current.
- *Payment of principal and interest*: on the 12th day of the corresponding month.
- *Grey-market trading*: authorised as of the auction announcement up to payment or settlement date. The value date for grey-market transactions coincides with the auction's payment date and the accrued interest is calculated with reference to the same (payment or settlement) date.

OATs

- *Auction date*: the first Thursday of each month at 11.00 local time.
- *Announcement of issue target*: two days before the auction (or at least a week in the case of OATi or floating-rate OATs), the Treasury announces the lines to be issued and

Table 6.2 Example of a BTAN auction: BTAN 3%, July 2001

Auction date	18 March 1999
Maturity	12 July 2001
Average rate	3.0%
Amount allotted	11 080 million euros
Volume of bids	3477 million euros
Stop-out price	99.98%

Source: authors

Table 6.3 OAT 4% auction, April 2009

Maturity	25 April 2009
Average rate	4.260%
Amount allotted	3494 million euros
Volume of bids	5909 million euros
Stop-out price	97.85%
Allotted at stop-out	60%

Source: authors

sets its upper and lower placement limits. Monthly issues must include at least one 10-year OAT line (normally one new line per semester) and, when the Treasury deems necessary on account of changed market conditions, an issue of 30-year fixed-interest OATs, or floating-rate OATs and OATi. Also, when the Treasury opts to slot in OAT TEC 10 or OATi issues, it must give at least one week's notice of its target.

- *Formulation of bids*: as a percentage of clean nominal value to two decimal places.
- *Payment*: the Thursday after the auction (or one day earlier/later in the event of a public holiday).
- *Interest basis*: Current/Current.
- *Grey-market trading*: OATs can be traded on the primary market between two and five days before the monthly auction and up to the corresponding payment or settlement date; the settlement date is also the value date for grey-market transactions and the baseline for calculating accrued interest.
- *Secondary-market trading*: settlement of secondary-market transactions (coupon and principal payment) is on $T + 3$. OATs are traded via the screens of market makers or authorised dealers (SVTs).

6.5   THE SECONDARY MARKET

The secondary market in French public debt is one of the most liquid worldwide behind its US and, in certain tranches, German equivalents. Recently, however, the overwhelming concentration of hedging operations in futures contracts on the German *Bund*, and the resulting strong demand for the underlying assets (solely German sovereign debt issues), has caused some loss of liquidity. Even so, OATs, BTANs and BTFs remain among the most actively traded of all euro-zone assets.

Ten-year OATs are the most keenly traded of France's public debt assets, making this the most liquid segment of the yield curve. Panning out to euro-zone level, the 5-year BTAN leads in liquidity across the corresponding curve segment, as evidenced by the high concentration of corporate issues choosing it as their sovereign debt reference (almost 66% of private fixed-rate issues are referenced to BTAN yields).

Data furnished by the Sicovam clearing and settlement system, which channels over 80% of trading in French Treasury securities, show a sharp rise in total (OAT, BTF and BTAN) turnover over first half 2000, to a level well ahead of pre-euro levels (see Figure 6.8).

This advance, however, does not take in all the securities issued by the French Treasury. As Figures 6.9 and 6.10 show, while turnover in BTANs has effectively boomed—for the reasons given above—OAT turnover stands only slightly higher than its pre-euro levels.

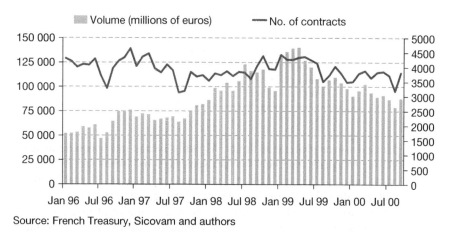

Source: French Treasury, Sicovam and authors

Figure 6.8   Total turnover and transaction numbers (OATs, BTANs and BTFs)

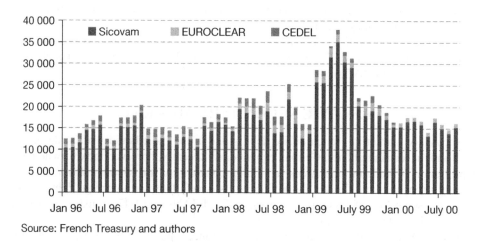

Source: French Treasury and authors

Figure 6.9   Daily turnover in OATs (monthly average of the five most actively traded lines, in millions of euros)

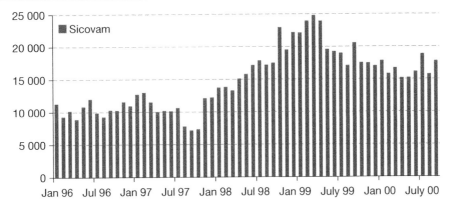

Source: French Treasury, Sicovam and authors

Figure 6.10 Daily turnover in BTANs (monthly average of the five most actively traded lines, in millions of euros)

6.5.1 The Repo Market

The success of a repo market is measured by the liquidity gained in spot trading. Repos provide investors with new ways to finance their positions or earn returns from temporarily assigning their debt security holdings. Other prominent uses of repo trading include the temporary purchase or sale of securities to cover the refinancing needs of an investment portfolio, and the opportunity for investors to lock in a fixed return by lending over a short period (normally less than 12 months).

Transaction volumes in the French public-debt repo market have gone from strength to strength since 1994. This was a watershed year for the market, in which repo trading was endowed with a legal, regulatory and tax framework and a new specialist market-maker group was brought into being (SPVTs or *Spécialistes de la Pension sur Valeurs du Trésor*), with the task of greatly enlarging the market's liquidity. On 12 July 1994, legislation was enacted to govern the obligations and rights of this new group, which was merged in February 1996 with the original SVTs.

The role of SVTs is to ensure the maximum liquidity of repo trading. Members are required to quote reference rates on request for fixed-interest repo transactions on open-access screens, i.e. in conditions of transparency vis-à-vis other market agents. This obligation also extends to maintaining minimum transaction volumes for repo operations on BTFs, BTANs and OATs, as follows:

- one-day repos, 100 million euros
- one-week repos, 100 million euros
- one-month repos, 50 million euros
- three-month repos, 20 million euros.

Turnover soared in consequence from a monthly 60 billion euros in July 1994 to over 300 billion in July 1997 (see Figure 6.11). At the time of writing, however, volumes have receded somewhat to a monthly average of around 150 billion euros.

This step-up in trading was accompanied by greater transparency in the repo segment. Market makers quote prices continuously for standardised amounts and terms, while the Bank of France, in turn, publishes daily reference rates based on market-maker prices. Agents thus have up-to-date information on the prevailing market conditions. The result is that the fixed rate of repo transactions on Treasury securities has become, as in other markets with extensive repo trading, a benchmark rate for the money market (as defining the depo-repo spread).

By transaction terms (see Figure 6.12), the 1–3 day range accounts for 60% of turnover, though increasingly rivalled in recent years by the 4–11 and 12–35 day ranges. Finally, as in most other euro-zone repo markets, transactions dated one month or more are lower on liquidity and trading volumes.

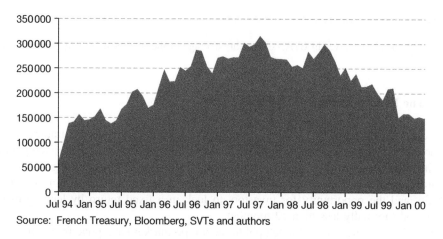

Source: French Treasury, Bloomberg, SVTs and authors

Figure 6.11   Outstanding month-end balance of repo transactions (in millions of euros)

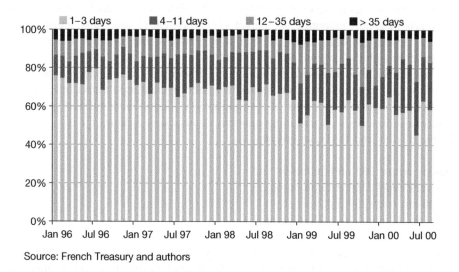

Source: French Treasury and authors

Figure 6.12   Monthly repo turnover by term

6.5.2   The Strips Market in OATs

Created in June 1991, the French strips market now ranks beside its US equivalent as the largest and most efficient worldwide. The market was brought into being by Sicovam and the SVTs, which continue to oversee stripping and unstripping operations. The stripping of bonds into principal only (PO) and interest only (IO) works basically as follows: any SVT holding strippable OATs (as authorised by the Treasury) can approach Sicovam to exchange them for tradeable securities representing a zero-coupon rate at a range of maturities (coupons) together with a capital to maturity (principal). From the SVT's standpoint, this is recorded as the sale of a strippable OAT and simultaneous purchase of a series of assets, i.e. giving rise to two identical entries (in respect of the sale amount and the sum of the values of the asset series). The process can also be reversed at any time by reconstituting the stripped bond, i.e. re-affixing its component assets.

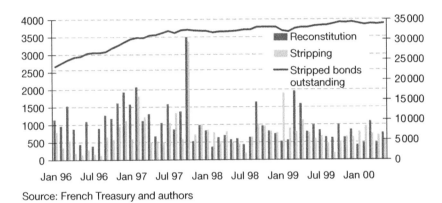

Source: French Treasury and authors

Figure 6.13   Stripping activity in French public debt (in millions of euros)

The SVTs undertake to conduct market-making functions for OAT strips. In addition, coupons are quoted on the Paris Stock Exchange on a Current/Current yield basis. The price is calculated as a percentage of nominal value. The settlement of strips transactions takes place on T + 3, through Sicovam, CEDEL or EUROCLEAR.

The advantages of the strips market are firstly that final investors can enhance bond portfolio returns, since strips are more sensitive to interest-rate variations and, as such, offer greater leverage than conventional OATs. Secondly, and by the same token, as zero-coupon bonds they are free of the interest-rate risk attached to reinvesting conventional bond coupons, though their exposure to interest-rate movements (sensitivity) is greater than that of bonds with a cash flow or intermediate coupons.

6.5.3   The Futures Market in OATs

France's MATIF offers 2-, 5-, 10- and 30-year contracts on French government debt securities. Liquidity is primarily concentrated in the 10-year contract.

A particularly attractive characteristic of French futures trading is the inclusion of public debt references from other European markets (German 2-, 5- and 10-year bonds, Dutch

30-year DSLs) in the basket of deliverable securities on its notional bond. All such assets must meet certain requirements regarding residual life and volumes in issue.

Contract	Deliverable securities and notional bond coupon
E-Note (2 years)	German/French references with residual life between 1.5 and 2.5 years Coupon 3.5%
Euro 5 (5 years)	German/French references with residual life between 4 and 5.5 years Coupon 3.5%
Euro Notional (10 years)	German/French references with residual life between 8.5 and 10.5 years Coupon 3.5%
E-Bond (30 years)	German/French/Dutch references with residual life between 25 and 30 years Coupon 5.5%

The Euro Notional (10-year) contract has the following features:

Underlying asset	Notional bond denominated in euros and issued in the EMU, with residual life between 8.5 and 10.5 years and a coupon of 3.5%
Nominal or face value	1 00 000 euros
Quotation	Percentage of nominal to two decimal places
Tick	0.01% of nominal value, or 10 euros
Maturity	March, June, September and December
Deliverables	Debt references of the seller's choice from a basket of French and German bonds with residual life between 8.5 and 10.5 years, a minimum outstanding balance of 6 billion euros and payable one month before the contract's settlement

6.6   CLEARING AND SETTLEMENT OF BTFs, BTANs AND OATs

The French Treasury uses a new system, RGV (*Relit Grande Vitesse*), for the gross-term clearing and settlement of public debt transactions. RGV supports real-time settlement of operations and their payment in national currencies, and offers intra-day connection capabilities with the Bank of France's TBF system (local branch of TARGET). In addition, the collateral system in place provides enhanced flexibility for participants and aids them in optimising position management by facilitating total or partial use of the securities held in their accounts to guarantee purchase or sale operations. RGV is thus the Treasury's main tool for monetary policy implementation and the management of intra-day liquidity in euros. Participating agents also enjoy a watertight framework for their cash and securities transactions with all EU institutions.

Clearing and settlement procedures for each class of French Treasury securities are as described below.

6.6.1   BTFs and BTANs

- *Transactions between residents*: through Sicovam using the RGV (*Relit Grande Vitesse*) system.
- *International transactions*: the combination of instant irrevocability and real-time order processing allows BTF and BTAN transactions in the primary and secondary markets to be settled via RGV, Clearstream and EUROCLEAR with the same accounting date. Counterparties with safe custody at Clearstream or EUROCLEAR can use these entities' RGV accounts under the following conditions:

  (a)   Members of Clearstream or EUROCLEAR must specify the RGV account of the custodian used by the resident buyer or seller.
  (b)   The RGV member must specify the account (with EUROCLEAR or Clearstream) of the non-resident subscribing or selling the securities.

6.6.2   OATs

- *Transactions between residents*: through Sicovam using the RGV (*Relit Grande Vitesse*) system, either via SLAB (bilateral agreement delivery system), working on a delivery-against-payment basis, or via a combination of fund transfer from the Bank of France and securities transfer from Sicovam.
- *International transactions*: transactions involving an international counterparty can be settled through EUROCLEAR or Clearstream, or directly via their respective connections with Sicovam.

Secondary-market settlement of BTF and BTAN transactions is on T + 1 for domestic operations and T + 3 for operations with non-resident investors. OATs are settled on T + 3.

6.7   TAXATION

6.7.1   Non-residents

The interest earned on OAT, BTAN and BTF holdings is exempt from withholding tax. Where the investor's country of residence has a tax accord with France, the individual's word suffices as proof of non-resident status, duly renewed on any change of tax address.

In the absence of tax agreements, non-residence status must be demonstrated each time interest is collected.

Non-resident operations on futures and option markets—essentially MATIF—are not subject to withholdings or any other French tax, unless transactions are concluded with liable institutions.

6.7.2 Residents

Resident individuals liable for tax on income, interest and redemption premiums (the last of which are exempt from withholding tax) can choose one of the following options:

- a fixed withholding tax of 25% (including 10% in respect of social security contributions)
- progressive income tax (paying a 10% increment in respect of social security contributions).

Capital gains on securities sales transacted after 1 January 1998 are taxed at 26% if the amount earned exceeds 50 000 French francs. The redemption premiums linked to bonds issued after 1 January 1992, or which have been stripped, are tax exempt, provided the premium does not exceed 5% of the asset's nominal value.

Non-profit organisations holding bonds issued before 1 January 1987 pay no tax on the interest earned. For bonds issued later, a 10% rate is applied. Such organisations are also exempt from tax on their capital gains from security disposals.

Corporate taxpayers pay the standard 33.33% rate on interest, premiums and capital gains; this may be subject to an exceptional 10% increment or a temporary increment of 15% when a company's turnover exceeds 50 million French francs. In both cases, the interest earned on OAT holdings is taxed on an accrual basis.

6.8   MARKET MAKERS

The function of these institutions is to optimise the placement of Treasury securities at the lowest possible cost. The current market-maker group, selected in April 1998, is a fairly heterogeneous mix of 10 French and 10 non-resident institutions. The selection process privileges institutions with a commitment to public-debt management and liquidity, and the list itself reflects the broad diversity of debt-market participants. Aware that the current merger wave in France may erode counterparty numbers, the Treasury has joined forces with MATIF, among others, to attract and retain financial institutions.

The current list of market makers is as follows:

ABN AMRO Fixed Income France	Crédit Lyonnais
Banque CPR	Deutsche Bank France, SA
Banque d'Escompte	Dresdner Kleinwort Benson
Banque Lehman Brothers SA	Goldman Sachs Paris Inc. & Cie
Banque Nationale de Paris Finance	HSBC Markets
Banque Paribas	J.P. Morgan & Cie, SA
Barclays Capital France SA	Merrill Lynch Finance, SA
CDC Marchés	Morgan Stanley, SA
Crédit Agricole Indosuez	Société Générale
Crédit Commercial de France	Union Européenne

ANNEXE: THE FRENCH PUBLIC DEBT MARKET

Outcome of BTAN Issues in 2000 (as of August 2000)

Date	Instrument	Coupon	Term	Target	Settles	Matures	Sold	Bids	Bid/sold	Stop rate	Average rate
20-Jan-00	BTAN	5.00%	5 years	3600–4100	27-Jan-00	12-Jul-05	4017	12 067	3.00	99.170	5.170
17-Feb-00	BTAN	4.00%	2 years	3000–3500	22-Feb-00	12-Jan-02	1829	5 707	3.12	99.140	4.470
17-Feb-00	BTAN	5.00%	5 years	3000–3500	22-Feb-00	12-Jul-05	1518	5 718	3.77	98.910	5.230
16-Mar-00	BTAN	4.00%	2 years	2800–3300	22-Feb-00	12-Jan-02	1590	6 358	4.00	99.110	4.510
16-Mar-00	BTAN	5.00%	5 years	2800–3300	22-Feb-00	12-Jul-05	1502	6 660	4.43	99.620	5.080
20-Apr-00	BTAN	4.00%	2 years	3000–3500	26-Apr-00	12-Jan-02	1530	6 290	4.11	99.220	4.460
20-Apr-00	BTAN	5.00%	5 years	3000–3500	26-Apr-00	12-Jul-05	1711	6 101	3.57	99.880	5.020
18-May-00	BTAN	4.00%	2 years	2900–3400	23-May-00	12-Jan-02	1346	5 618	4.17	98.390	5.030
18-May-00	BTAN	5.00%	5 years	2900–3400	23-May-00	12-Jul-05	1785	5 600	3.14	98.230	5.400
22-Jun-00	BTAN	4.00%	2 years	3200–3700	27-Jun-00	12-Jan-02	1345	4 835	3.59	95.510	5.000
22-Jun-00	BTAN	4.50%	2 years	3200–3700	27-Jun-00	12-Jul-02	1258	5 070	4.03	99.030	5.000
22-Jun-00	BTAN	5.00%	5 years	3200–3700	27-Jun-00	12-Jul-05	1053	4 651	4.42	99.250	5.170

Millions of euros

Source: Bloomberg, Reuters and authors

Outcome of OAT Issues in 2000 (as of August 2000)

Date	Instrument	Coupon	Term	Target	Settles	Matures	Format	Sold	Bids	Bid/sold	Stop price	Avge rate
06-Jan-00	OAT	4.00%	10 years	3300–3700	13-Jan-00	25-Oct-09	Auction	2732	5817	2.13	87.620	5.680
06-Jan-00	OAT	5.50%	30 years	3300–3700	13-Jan-00	25-Apr-29	Auction	730	1845	2.53	91.300	6.140
03-Feb-00	OAT	5.50%	10 years	3700–4200	08-Feb-00	25-Apr-10	Auction	4156	11350	2.73	99.030	5.620
03-Feb-00	OATi	3.00%	10 years	400–600	08-Feb-00	27-Jul-09	Auction	551	1788	3.25	93.300	3.850
02-Mar-00	OAT	8.50%	8 years	3500–4000	07-Mar-00	25-Oct-08	Auction	530	2225	4.20	120.050	5.510
02-Mar-00	OAT	5.50%	10 years	3500–4000	07-Mar-00	25-Apr-10	Auction	2333	8689	3.72	98.840	5.650
02-Mar-00	OAT	5.50%	30 years	3500–4000	07-Mar-00	25-Apr-29	Auction	653	1523	2.33	93.550	5.970
02-Mar-00	TEC 10	CMT	10 years	400–600	07-Mar-00	25-Jan-09	Auction	425	1470	3.46	97.450	—
06-Apr-00	OAT	8.50%	8 years	3100–3600	11-Apr-00	25-Oct-08	Auction	555	2215	3.99	122.290	5.190
06-Apr-00	OAT	5.50%	10 years	3100–3600	11-Apr-00	25-Apr-10	Auction	2424	8710	3.59	101.450	5.310
06-Apr-00	OAT	5.50%	30 years	3100–3600	11-Apr-00	25-Apr-29	Auction	533	1466	2.75	97.250	5.690
06-Apr-00	OATi	3.40%	30 years	200–400	11-Apr-00	25-Jul-29	Auction	253	718	2.84	94.200	3.720
04-May-00	OAT	7.25%	6 years	3100–3600	10-May-00	25-Apr-06	Auction	425	1440	3.39	109.800	5.290
04-May-00	OAT	5.50%	10 years	3100–3600	10-May-00	25-Apr-10	Auction	2135	7385	3.46	99.310	5.590
04-May-00	OAT	5.50%	30 years	3100–3600	10-May-00	25-Apr-29	Auction	695	1587	2.28	94.900	5.860
04-May-00	OATi	3.00%	10 years	400–600	10-May-00	25-Jul-09	Auction	259	844	3.26	94.420	3.720
04-May-00	OATi	3.40%	30 years	400–600	10-May-00	24-Jul-29	Auction	162	556	3.43	94.350	3.710
08-Jun-00	OAT	7.25%	6 years	2400–2900	14-Jun-00	25-Apr-06	Auction	689	1850	2.69	111.050	5.020
08-Jun-00	OAT	5.50%	10 years	2400–2900	14-Jun-00	25-Apr-10	Auction	945	5339	5.65	101.510	5.290
08-Jun-00	OAT	6.50%	11 years	2400–2900	14-Jun-00	25-Apr-11	Auction	795	2375	2.99	109.550	5.320
08-Jun-00	TEC 10	CMT	10 years	2400–2900	14-Jun-00	25-Jan-09	Auction	235	730	3.11	96.000	—

Millions of euros

Source: Bloomberg, Reuters and authors

Outcome of BTF Issues in 2000 (as of August 2000)

Date	Instrument	Term	Target	Matures	Days	Settles	Format	Sold	Bids	Bid/cover	Stop rate	Avge rate
03-Jan-00	BTF	3 months	800	06-Apr-00	91	06-Jan-00	Auction	806	2545	3.2	3.100	3.097
03-Jan-00	BTF	6 months	500	29-Jun-00	175	06-Jan-00	Auction	504	2155	4.3	3.420	3.417
11-Jan-00	BTF	3 months	1000	13-Apr-00	91	13-Jan-00	Auction	1004	3585	3.6	3.080	3.079
11-Jan-00	BTF	12 months	800	11-Jan-01	364	13-Jan-00	Auction	802	3020	3.8	3.770	3.758
17-Jan-00	BTF	3 months	1100	20-Apr-00	91	20-Jan-00	Auction	1104	4220	3.8	3.100	3.098
17-Jan-00	BTF	12 months	700	11-Jan-01	357	20-Jan-00	Auction	701	2180	3.1	3.775	3.758
24-Jan-00	BTF	3 months	600	27-Apr-00	91	27-Jan-00	Auction	610	3470	5.7	3.125	3.118
24-Jan-00	BTF	6 months	800	17-Aug-00	203	27-Jan-00	Auction	802	2050	2.6	3.480	3.466
31-Jan-00	BTF	3 months	1000	04-May-00	91	03-Feb-00	Auction	1004	3495	3.5	3.290	3.280
31-Jan-00	BTF	12 months	600	11-Jan-01	343	03-Feb-00	Auction	603	2340	3.9	3.920	3.917
07-Feb-00	BTF	3 months	1000	11-May-00	91	10-Feb-00	Auction	1006	4095	4.1	3.280	3.280
07-Feb-00	BTF	6 months	600	17-Aug-00	189	10-Feb-00	Auction	603	2385	4.0	3.570	3.570
14-Feb-00	BTF	3 months	800	18-May-00	91	17-Feb-00	Auction	865	4365	5.0	3.260	3.258
14-Feb-00	BTF	12 months	800	15-Feb-01	364	17-Feb-00	Auction	820	3070	3.7	3.965	3.959
21-Feb-00	BTF	3 months	1000	25-May-00	91	24-Feb-00	Auction	1005	4190	4.2	3.370	3.365
21-Feb-00	BTF	6 months	600	17-Aug-00	175	24-Feb-00	Auction	604	2050	3.4	3.680	3.678
28-Feb-00	BTF	3 months	1000	31-May-00	90	02-Mar-00	Auction	1003	4205	4.2	3.370	3.369
28-Feb-00	BTF	12 months	600	15-Feb-01	350	02-Mar-00	Auction	604	3245	5.4	3.980	3.974
06-Mar-00	BTF	3 months	1000	08-Jun-00	91	09-Mar-00	Auction	1000	4680	4.7	3.385	3.382
06-Mar-00	BTF	6 months	800	28-Sep-00	203	09-Mar-00	Auction	800	3100	3.9	3.760	3.756
13-Mar-00	BTF	3 months	1000	15-Jun-00	91	16-Mar-00	Auction	1004	3207	3.2	3.485	3.480
13-Mar-00	BTF	12 months	600	15-Feb-01	336	16-Mar-00	Auction	602	2215	3.7	4.115	4.106

Date	Instrument	Term	Target	Matures	Days	Settles	Format	Sold	Bids	Bid/cover	Stop rate	Avge rate
20-Mar-00	BTF	3 months	1000	22-Jun-00	91	23-Mar-00	Auction	1003	4165	4.2	3.520	3.520
20-Mar-00	BTF	6 months	600	28-Sep-00	189	23-Mar-00	Auction	601	3125	5.2	3.805	3.799
27-Mar-00	BTF	3 months	800	29-Jun-00	91	30-Mar-00	Auction	885	4775	5.4	3.525	3.520
27-Mar-00	BTF	12 months	800	29-Mar-01	364	30-Mar-00	Auction	845	2378	2.8	4.180	4.174
03-Apr-00	BTF	3 months	1200	06-Jul-00	91	06-Apr-00	Auction	1201	3060	2.5	3.545	3.540
03-Apr-00	BTF	12 months	1000	29-Mar-01	357	06-Apr-00	Auction	1000	4125	4.1	4.170	4.167
10-Apr-00	BTF	3 months	1100	13-Jul-00	91	13-Apr-00	Auction	1105	4195	3.8	3.595	3.930
10-Apr-00	BTF	6 months	800	02-Nov-00	203	13-Apr-00	Auction	803	3235	4.0	3.591	3.927
17-Apr-00	BTF	45 days	500	31-May-00	41	20-Apr-00	Auction	500	1495	3.0	3.560	3.550
17-Apr-00	BTF	3 months	1400	20-Jul-00	91	20-Apr-00	Auction	1403	3275	2.3	3.630	3.627
17-Apr-00	BTF	12 months	1000	29-Mar-01	343	20-Apr-00	Auction	1000	3160	3.2	4.175	4.168
25-Apr-00	BTF	45 days	500	08-Jun-00	41	28-Apr-00	Auction	500	1275	2.6	3.720	3.698
25-Apr-00	BTF	3 months	1200	27-Jul-00	90	28-Apr-00	Auction	1207	2925	2.4	3.790	3.782
25-Apr-00	BTF	6 months	800	02-Nov-00	188	28-Apr-00	Auction	802	2510	3.1	4.040	4.032
02-May-00	BTF	3 months	1200	03-Aug-00	91	04-May-00	Auction	1204	4120	3.4	3.935	3.930
02-May-00	BTF	12 months	1000	03-May-01	364	04-May-00	Auction	1005	2615	2.6	4.500	4.481
09-May-00	BTF	3 months	1000	10-Aug-00	91	11-May-00	Auction	1008	3190	3.2	4.090	4.084
09-May-00	BTF	6 months	700	02-Nov-00	175	11-May-00	Auction	700	1800	2.6	4.295	4.282
15-May-00	BTF	3 months	1000	17-Aug-00	91	18-May-00	Auction	1008	3571	3.5	4.090	4.088

15-May-00	BTF	6 months	1000	07-Dec-00	175	18-May-00	Auction	1003	2530	2.5	4.400	4.388
22-May-00	BTF	3 months	1000	24-Aug-00	91	25-May-00	Auction	1003	3725	3.7	4.220	4.214
22-May-00	BTF	12 months	800	03-May-01	343	25-May-00	Auction	804	2395	3.0	4.820	4.815
29-May-00	BTF	3 months	900	31-Aug-00	91	01-Jun-00	Auction	910	3485	3.8	4.140	4.140
29-May-00	BTF	6 months	600	07-Dec-00	189	01-Jun-00	Auction	603	2320	3.8	4.440	4.437
05-Jun-00	BTF	1 month	500	06-Jul-00	28	08-Jun-00	Auction	502	1400	2.8	—	4.034
05-Jun-00	BTF	3 months	1200	07-Sep-00	91	08-Jun-00	Auction	1203	3665	3.0	—	4.149
05-Jun-00	BTF	12 months	800	03-May-01	329	08-Jun-00	Auction	802	1980	2.5	—	4.665
12-Jun-00	BTF	3 months	1000	14-Sep-00	91	15-Jun-00	Auction	1007	3320	3.3	4.270	4.269
12-Jun-00	BTF	6 months	700	07-Dec-00	175	15-Jun-00	Auction	702	1705	2.4	4.540	4.537
19-Jun-00	BTF	3 months	700	21-Sep-00	91	22-Jun-00	Auction	703	2915	4.1	4.235	4.231
19-Jun-00	BTF	12 months	1000	21-Jun-01	364	22-Jun-00	Auction	1004	2090	2.1	4.770	4.760
26-Jun-00	BTF	3 months	700	28-Sep-00	91	29-Jun-00	Auction	703	2915	4.1	4.235	4.231
26-Jun-00	BTF	6 months	900	18-Jan-01	203	29-Jun-00	Auction	1004	2090	2.1	4.770	4.760

Millions of euros
Source: Bloomberg, Reuters and authors

The Dutch Government Bond Market

7.1 INTRODUCTION

The Dutch State Treasury Agency (DSTA) is the debt manager of the central government of the Netherlands. It acts on behalf of the Ministry of Finance, the institution legally empowered to borrow in the government's name, and is a division of the Ministry of Finance Treasury General. It conducts the sale or placement of assets issued by the Treasury—DTCs or bills and DSLs or bonds—and accounts for coupon payments and debt redemption. The DSTA is thus responsible for managing the liquid funds of the central government, to which end it maintains a target daily balance of 25 million euros in the government's account at the Dutch National Bank (DNB), depositing or investing any surplus to this threshold amount, or financing any deficit on the money market through instruments like DTCs.

The economic boom enjoyed by the Netherlands over recent years has facilitated reduction of the public deficit from 4.2% of GDP in 1995 to a 0.25% surplus. In tandem with this reduction, the public debt/GDP ratio has been reined back from 77.2% in 1995 to 63.5% at end-1999. The Dutch government was aiming at a 60% ratio in 2000, which would bring it within the limit set by the Maastricht Treaty.

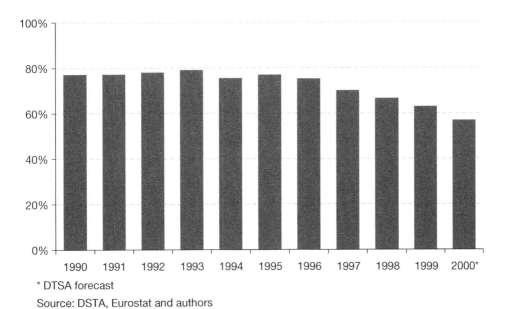

* DTSA forecast

Source: DSTA, Eurostat and authors

Figure 7.1 Dutch public debt/GDP (1990–2000)

Despite a lighter 2000 redemptions calendar, the probable upward revision of budgetary surplus targets in the course of that year and the windfall proceeds from UMTS (mobile

Table 7.1 Dutch central government borrowing requirement

	1999	2000
Budget deficit	4 900	7 600
Redemptions	19 500	18 300
Early redemptions	2 300	—
Borrowing requirement	26 700	26 000
In capital markets	25 900	26 000
Others	800	—

Millions of euros
Source: DSTA and authors

telecommunications) licence awards, there were at the time of writing no plans for the DSTA to scale down its envisaged issuance volumes (amounting to 26 billion euros).

Finally, note that the Dutch Treasury, alone of euro-zone finance departments, discontinued foreign-currency issues in 1975. The long-standing links between the Dutch florin and the deutschmark have effectively obviated the need for foreign-currency issuance, as in the German public debt market itself.

7.2   ASSETS ISSUED BY THE DUTCH TREASURY

7.2.1   Dutch State Certificates (DTCs or Bills)

DTCs have been the preferred instrument for government intervention in money markets since the abandonment on 1 January 1999 (euro launch date) of Netherlands Bank Certificates (NBCs). DTCs figure among the Tier 1 assets of the ECB, and on the general collateral list kept by the International Securities Market Association (ISMA).

DTCs are tradeable money-market instruments represented by book entries and issued at a discount. Issuance is conducted via regular auctions using the 'Dutch' system, held on a twice-monthly basis since January 2000. This replaces the tap-issue system previously in use, whereby DTCs were placed directly among market makers. Under the old system, issuance was via lines maturing in 3, 6 and 12 months. Each month, as an outstanding line expired (on the last working day), the subscription period for a new line was opened (two days prior to the old one's maturity). There were thus always five lines in issue at the same time, up to a maximum volume per line of 6 billion euros. Under the new system, two lines are issued at each regular auction (3- and 12-month DTCs on the first Monday of the month and 3- and 6-month DTCs on the third Monday).

This change in issuance procedures was a response to the growing importance of DTCs as a government financing instrument, and was only the last in a series of measures to enhance their market appeal. In 1999, for instance, the DSTA introduced cash settlements of transactions on T + 2, in a move directly addressing international investors. Firstly, it aligns settlement practices with those of other euro-zone treasuries and, secondly, date conventions now coincide with those governing swap-market transactions. The next step was to raise the maximum permissible volume of each line outstanding to 7.50 billion euros. These measures have combined to improve the transparency, depth and liquidity of this public debt market segment.

The yield of DTCs is calculated on a discount basis, as follows:

$$P = \frac{N}{1 + \dfrac{(d \times R)}{360 \times 100}}$$

where

N = nominal
d = exact number of days
R = yield at time of issue
P = amount payable

On 31 May 2000, 3-month DTCs in issue (15.06 billion euros) accounted for almost 70% of bills outstanding—naturally enough, considering that they are issued twice-monthly against the monthly interval of 6- and 12-month assets.

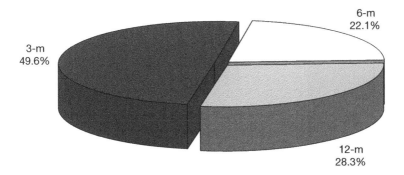

Figure 7.2   Outstanding balance of DTCs as of August 2000

7.2.2   Dutch State Loans (DSLs or Bonds)

DSLs are medium- and long-term tradeable securities represented by book entries, paying annual coupons and redeemable on maturity. Placement is on a tap basis, i.e. direct placement among market makers.

The 1999 issuance programme, privileging 3-, 10- and 30-year bonds, combines continuity in the use of the longer-dated instruments with the novelty of the 3-year term. Lines issued are regularly reopened in volumes of 2–5 billion euros a time, until the maximum outstanding amount targeted, currently 10 billion euros, is reached. The DSTA announces the asset lines to be issued at the start of each quarter, together with the main features of each.

On 31 May 2000, the outstanding balance of DSLs was spread fairly evenly across the spectrum of maturities. As with most euro-zone treasuries, assets with a remaining term of less than 6 years account for the bulk (59%) of the balance outstanding. The term up to 2.5 years is, however, considerably under-represented compared to neighbouring markets because of the government debt restructuring drive begun in 1999.

DSLs are quoted at a clean price (ex-coupon) calculated on the following basis:

$$P + Cc = \sum_{t=1}^{t=N} \frac{F(t)}{(1+R)^t}$$

where

$F(t)$ = cash flow on the bond in year t
    R = yield to maturity
    P = clean price
  Cc = accrued interest*
    N = years remaining to maturity

* Accrued interest is calculated differently according to the type of DSL:

• DSLs issued since 1/1/99: Current/Current.
• DSLs redenominated in euros on 1/1/99: Current/Current since the 1999 coupon payment date. Taking the example of a bond paying a coupon in October 1999, accrued interest for the period October 1989 to October 1999 is on the basis Current/365, but switches thereafter to a Current/Current basis.

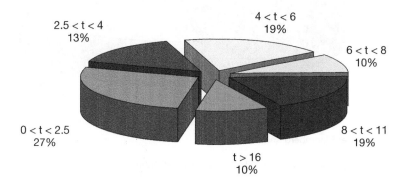

Source: Bloomberg and authors

Figure 7.3   Dutch medium- and long-term debt as of August 2000

7.3   OVERVIEW OF THE DUTCH PUBLIC DEBT MARKET

The DSTA, as the government's agency, will persist in the strategy lines mapped out in 1999, within an overall context of more muted borrowing requirements. What this means, essentially, is pursuing the greater promotion, transparency and liquidity of the public debt market as a route to maximum efficiency in the management of refinancing risk.

Achievement of these objectives requires both the restructuring of outstanding debt and steps to rationalise future issuance. Success hangs, in no small measure, on the liquidity and tradeability of the assets issued on the secondary market. The measures taken adopt a two-pronged approach:

1. First, the streamlining of outstanding debt into a small number of highly liquid references offering greater investor attraction.
2. Second, adequately laying the groundwork to ensure maximum breadth, depth and transparency in secondary-market trading. The DTSA has made far-reaching changes in this respect, such as the creation of a market-making system in early 1999 and the admission of several DSL lines to trading on the electronic market EuroMTS (the four benchmark references), as well as the creation of MTS Amsterdam—in partnership with MTS Italy and DSL market makers—for trading in all the most liquid DSL lines. This last measure is discussed in greater detail under the secondary market in section 7.5.

7.3.1   The 1999–2000 Exchange and Repurchase Programme

In July 1999, the DSTA began work on streamlining debt in issue via a programme of exchange and early redemption (the repurchase of the outstanding balance of lines not exchanged in full at the close of exchange operations).

The last exchange, on 16 March 2000, marked the close of this first phase of the restructuring programme. A total of six exchanges took place, spanning all segments of the Dutch government securities curve up to 10 years. In the process, over 30 billion euros were 'switched' out of illiquid into large-volume benchmark issues. As a result, of the 176 billion euros outstanding on 17 March 2000, over 75% (136.91 billion euros) was bunched in fourteen lines with an average outstanding balance of nearly 10 billion euros (see Table 7.2).

As the Spanish case shows, exchange facilities as an issue type can become as important as, or more so than, standard auction or tap placements. They are also more costly, however, due to the higher financial costs entailed in the year of their realisation. Of

Table 7.2   DSL market distribution

DSL reference	Outstanding	Benchmark
DSL 9000 1-2001	6 106.3	—
DSL 3000 2-2002	13 999.3	***
DSL 5750 9-2002	7 487.4	—
DSL 6500 4-2003	11 200.0	***
DSL 5750 1-2004	7 487.4	—
DSL 7250 10-2004	7 260.5	—
DSL 7750 3-2005	10 950.0	***
DSL 6000 1-2006	12 329.0	—
DSL 5750 2-2007	13 637.2	—
DSL 5250 7-2008	11 118.0	—
DSL 3750 7-2009	12 088.0	***
DSL 5500 7-2010	6 142.0	***
DSL 7500 1-2023	8 241.5	—
DSL 5500 1-2028	8 863.8	***
Total 14 references	**136 910.3**	—
Total DSL outstanding balance	**175 396.3**	—
Percentage of the market	**78.1%**	—

Millions of euros
Source: DSTA and authors

the 52.2 billion euros issued by the DSTA in 1999, 29.1 billion (over 55.7% of the total) resulted from the four exchange operations conducted between 15 July and 11 November. So important have these operations become that that they channelled more of the government's 1999 issuance than the normal tap placements. Finally, note that, after the two year-2000 exchanges on 10 February and 16 March (with a combined value of 3.2 billion euros), the total issued across the six facilities comes to more than 32 billion euros. The nominal cost of the programme, taken as the difference between the amount of 'old' bonds withdrawn and 'liquid' bonds issued, stands at 2 billion euros (the 32.2 billion issued less

Table 7.3   Summary of DSTA exchange operations 1999–2000

Lines withdrawn	Date	Withdrawal	Outstanding Pre-exch.	Outstanding Post-exch.	Total
DSL 8.25% 15-Feb-2002	15-Jul-99	2 800	4 500	1 700	2 800
DSL 8.25% 15-Jun-2002	15-Jul-99	1 500	5 200	3 700	—
DSL 8.25% 15-Jun-2002	14-Oct-99	1 500	3 700	2 200	—
DSL 8.25% 15-Jun-2002	16-Mar-00	200	2 200	2 000	3 200
DSL 7.00% 15-Feb-2003	14-Oct-99	2 800	5 300	2 500	—
DSL 7.00% 15-feb-2003	16-Mar-00	500	2 500	2 000	3 300
DSL 7.00% 15-Jun-2005	15-Jul-99	2 800	4 900	2 100	—
DSL 7.00% 15-Jun-2005	14-Oct-99	700	2 100	1 400	3 500
DSL 6.75% 15-Nov-2005	15-Jul-99	2 000	4 500	2 500	—
DSL 6.75% 15-Nov-2005	16-Sep-99	1 200	2 500	1 300	—
DSL 6.75% 15-Nov-2005	14-Oct-99	100	1 300	1 200	3 300
DSL 8.50% 1-Jun-2006	16-Sep-99	2 900	4 500	1 600	—
DSL 8.50% 1-Jun-2006	11-Nov-99	300	1 600	1 300	3 200
DSL 8.75% 15-Jan-2007	16-Sep-99	200	500	300	200
DSL 8.25% 15-Feb-2007	16-Sep-99	4 100	5 600	1 500	—
DSL 8.25% 15-Feb-2007	11-Nov-99	300	1 500	1 200	4 400
DSL 8.25% 15-Sep-2007	16-Sep-99	2 600	5 200	2 600	—
DSL 8.25% 15-Sep-2007	11-Nov-99	1 400	2 600	1 200	4 000
DSL 7.50% 15-Apr-2010	10-Feb-00	2 100	3 400	1 300	2 100
—	—	**30 000**	—	—	**30 000**

Lines issued	Date	Withdrawal	Outstanding Pre-exch.	Outstanding Post-exch.	Total
DSL 3.00% 15-Feb-2002	15-Jul-99	4 900	7 000	11 900	4 900
DSL 4.75% 15-Feb-2003	16-Mar-00	700	2 000	2 700	700
DSL 6.50% 15-Apr-2003	14-Oct-99	4 400	6 800	11 200	4 400
DSL 6.00% 15-Jan-2006	16-Sep-99	4 600	7 350	11 950	—
DSL 6.00% 15-Jan-2006	11-Nov-99	400	11 900	12 300	4 950
DSL 7.75% 01-Mar-2005	15-Jul-99	4 600	5 700	10 300	—
DSL 7.75% 01-Mar-2005	14-Oct-99	700	10 250	10 950	5 250
DSL 5.75% 15-Feb-2007	16-Sep-99	8 000	5 600	13 600	8 000
DSL 5.25% 15-Jul-2008	11-Nov-99	1 500	9 450	10 950	1 500
DSL 5.50% 15-Jul-2010	10-Feb-00	2 500	2 000	4 500	2 500
—	—	—	—	—	**32 200**

Source: DSTA and authors

the 30 billion withdrawn). It was precisely for this reason that the end-1999 ratio of public debt to GDP stuck at 60% rather than the lower proportion targeted by government.

The target for the 2000 close was to have 80% of the outstanding balance lodged in 16 DSL lines, with an average amount in issue of 10 billion per line. And this is precisely where the second plank of the programme came in, namely the repurchase of the remaining balances of exchanged DSL lines (around 13.8 billion euros) and the creation of a repo facility on these lines. The purpose of this programme was to boost the liquidity of the designated lines, which had fallen even lower since the earlier exchange cycle. The first DSL repurchase, on 20 June 2000, concluded in the withdrawal of a total of 1 billion euros in 5 references.

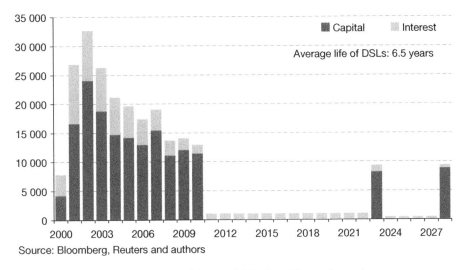

Source: Bloomberg, Reuters and authors

Figure 7.4 DSL maturities curve as of August 2000 (in millions of euros)

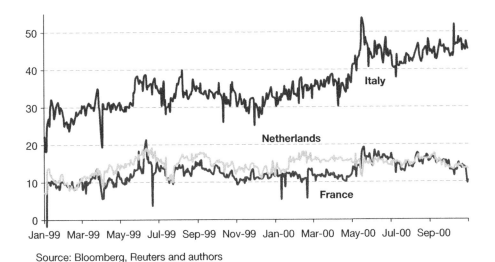

Source: Bloomberg, Reuters and authors

Figure 7.5 Ten-year bond spread vs. Germany (in basis points)

These advances have secured a considerable improvement in both the maturities curve of the DSL segment and the traditional spread between DSL and *Bund* yields. To give another instance, the spread between the OAT and the DSL, over many years consistently in favour of the former (by between 2 and 4 bp), is now in favour of the Dutch bond.

7.4   THE PRIMARY MARKET

7.4.1   Issuance Procedures

The DSTA has three methods at its disposal for the primary-market issuance of government debt, the most common of which is the tap issue, i.e. securities placement among market makers. Set out below is a brief description of each method.

- *Tap issue*: the DSTA announces its asking price for the debt securities to be issued on the dates set for subscription. Interested institutions can then phone in the nominal amount they will subscribe at this price. The DSTA may reject bids or reduce the amount to be issued at its own discretion. It is also empowered to modify or withdraw the price given whenever it so decides. The agency notifies bidders by fax of all orders accepted. This issuance procedure is used for DSL sales and was also applied as standard for DTCs up to January 2000.
- *Ordinary auction or tender issue*: in this case, the DSTA announces the maturities and characteristics of the securities to be issued, and invites eligible institutions (market makers) to communicate the amounts they wish to subscribe and the price they are willing to pay. The DSTA sets a single price for allocation, based on the bids received. Bids below this amount are rejected; bids at the price set are allotted wholly or in part, and bids specifying higher prices are allotted in their entirety—this procedure is known as a 'Dutch' auction. All DTCs have been issued by this method since 17 January 2000.
- *Issue portfolio*: the DSTA may acquire up to 20% of tap-issue volumes for its issue portfolio, reserving this amount for post-tap placement. The take-up or otherwise of this option depends on the Treasury's financing needs at a given time, and is quite independent of budgetary implementation. The procedure, in fact, resembles a 'covert' second round in which, by withholding paper from the market over a certain length of time, the government secures greater issuance flexibility. The volume of securities to be placed via the portfolio is announced immediately after the original tap issue, by posting on the DSTA screens, and their sale takes place over the next few weeks, depending on demand and market conditions. Prospective buyers of these securities should phone in their orders to the DSTA, which will apply the same conditions as in the first placement round. The DSTA offers weekly updates on its 'issue portfolio' position.

7.4.2   Issuance Characteristics of DTCs and DSLs

DTCs

- *Issuance procedure*: tap issue up to December 1999; currently single-price auctions conducted according to the 'Dutch' system.
- *Announcement*: the DSTA publishes an orientative calendar at the start of each year. Auctions are held on a regular basis on the first (3- and 12-month) and third

Mondays (3- and 6-month) of each month. The DSTA also pre-posts the lines to be issued and indicative volumes on Reuters DSTA 09 and Bloomberg DSTA9 five working days before the auction.

- *Issue programmes or lines*: a new DTC line or programme is opened each month according to a pre-set pattern: four 6- and 12-month DTC lines are created each year (in alternate months), and four lines of 3-month DTCs in the remaining four months; 6- and 12-month lines are thus reopened on several occasions, and 3-month series once only. Each line has a maximum volume of 7 billion euros.
- *Presentation of bids*: each investor can submit more than one competitive bid (indicating the rate and amount sought). These are registered bids, so potential investors must enter their names beforehand (once only) in the DTC register kept by the DSTA.
- *Minimum amount of bids*: 10 million euros each.
- *Resolution*: once all bids are in, the DTSA sorts them in ascending order interest rate, then begins at the bottom (lowest rate = highest price) and works up to its target issue volume. The marginal rate for allocation is then calculated on the basis of all accepted bids. The DSTA reserves the right to limit the amount allotted to each bidder to 40% of total issuance, to prevent overconcentration in the hands of particular investors.
- *Amounts payable*: equal to the principal discounted at the interest rate at issue, on a Current/360 basis.
- *Payment*: on a trade-for-trade basis, i.e. settling and paying each operation the moment it is concluded (as opposed to the netting system, whereby all operations are cleared at the end of the day). The DSTA accounts to be credited are:

Account no. 60.01.12.098 with the National Bank of the Netherlands, before 15.00 hours local time
Account no. 97 449 with EUROCLEAR
Account no. 82 913 with CEDEL.

- *Repurchase facility*: the DSTA is empowered to repurchase previously issued securities whenever it so decides.

Table 7.4 DTC auction: issue of 3- and 6-month DTCs 19/6/2000

	6-month DTC	12-month DTC
Maturity	29/9/00	29/6/01
Issue target	750–1 250 m euros	500–1 000 m euros
Marginal rate	4.41%	4.79%
Amount allotted	767 m euros	495 m euros
Total bids	2175 m euros	1915 m euros
Allotted at marginal rate	20%	100%

Source: authors

DSLs

- *Issuance procedure*: tap issue among primary dealers or market makers.
- *Announcement*: the DSTA posts the initial issue price on its Reuters screen (DSTA 08). The agency reserves the right to modify such prices at its own discretion or to withdraw the offer unilaterally.

Table 7.5   DSL 3.75% 15/7/2009

Announcement	
Announcement date	5 March 1999
Type of issue	Tap
Auction date	9 March 1999, between 10.00 and 17.00 local time or until target volumes are met
Coupon payment	15 July 2000
Accrual of interest	As of 19 January 1999
Payment	16 March (56 days' accrued interest)
Minimum bid	25 million euros
Issuance volume	2000–2500 million euros
Resolution 9/3/99	
Maturity	15 July 2009
Average price	96.42
Average yield	4.176%
Amount allotted	2300 million euros

Source: authors

- *Presentation of bids*: authorised counterparties may place their buying orders as of the issue announcement date up to the presentation deadline. Orders must be received is between 10.00 and 17.00 local time, save notification to the contrary or modification of target amounts, on Amsterdam Stock Exchange (AEX) trading days.
- *Minimum amount of orders and allocation*: securities are allotted at the price set by the DSTA, in nominal amounts starting from a minimum per operation of 25 million euros. The total volume placed at the issue's close is published in the Official State Gazette (*Staatscourant*).
- *Amounts payable*: equal to the issue price multiplied by the nominal amount allotted plus accumulated interest.
- *Calculation of interest rates*: according to the formulae set out in the *Reglement Afwikkeling van Effectentransacties* of the Amsterdam Stock Exchange. This is no different from the standard ISMA method, and the basis used is Current/Current. Any changes in interest-calculation methods between the payment dates of two coupons will not be enforced until the following coupon begins to accrue.
- *Redemption of principal*: the principal of the bond is repaid at par on the date of maturity.
- *Payment*: on a trade-for-trade basis, i.e. the moment the operation is concluded, and payment is deposited in the accounts designated by the DSTA.
- *Coupon*: annual; in the case of the old 10-year benchmark, the coupon falls due on 15 July and collection began on 15 July 2000. Interest started to accrue on 19 January 1999.

7.5   THE SECONDARY MARKET

Though DSL and DTC trading remains concentrated on the Amsterdam Exchanges (AEX), part of the EURONEXT alliance, the newly created electronic platforms will undoubtedly rise to prominence in the next few years and are therefore the focus of this section.

In early 1999, only German and Italian government debt securities were traded on electronic platforms. Since then, however, the format has spread to most of the public debt markets in the euro zone (France, Spain, Belgium and the Netherlands). Over 30% of trading in euro-zone benchmark bonds is currently channelled through EuroMTS, the market run by private-sector banks using the trading system and software developed by MTS Italia SpA.

Neither the Dutch government nor the DSTA have any direct involvement in the DSL secondary market, yet the efficiency, liquidity and transparency of secondary-market trading provides vital assurance that future refinancing needs can be adequately covered.

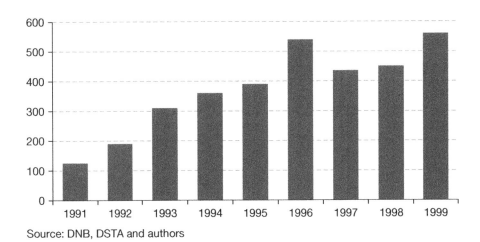

Source: DNB, DSTA and authors

Figure 7.6 Turnover of Dutch government securities on the AEX (in billions of euros)

Table 7.6 Lines traded on MTS Amsterdam

Benchmark lines	Balance
NE 3000 2-2002	13 999.3
NE 5250 7-2008	11 118.0
NE 3750 7-2009	12 088.0
NE 5500 7-2010	10 227.0
NE 5500 1-2028	8 863.8

'Liquid' lines	Balance
NE 8750 9-2001	6 012.6
NE 5750 9-2002	7 487.4
NE 6500 4-2003	11 200.0
NE 5750 1-2004	7 487.4
NE 7250 10-2004	7 260.5
NE 7750 3-2005	10 950.0
NE 6000 1-2006	12 329.0
NE 5750 2-2007	13 637.2
NE 7500 1-2023	8 241.5

Millions of euros
Source: DSTA and authors

Proof of its interest is the small ownership stake taken by the Dutch State in the MTS Amsterdam electronic trading platform, established in September 1999. The shareholder structure of the new market is as follows: MTS Italia 30%, the thirteen public debt market makers designated by the DSTA 5% each, and the above-mentioned 5% held by the Dutch government. This ownership breakdown mirrors that of other markets where the MTS system has been adopted.

MTS Amsterdam is an electronic interdealer broker system, but with one key difference from traditional blind markets: that of being price- rather than order-led. Primary dealers in DSLs (market makers in MTS Amsterdam) undertake to quote prices for all specified references (benchmarks and liquid DSLs) over at least five hours a day. Investors, as such, may transact directly at these prices.

Thirteen lines are currently traded (the four benchmarks also traded on EuroMTS and the nine references deemed to be the most liquid in the Dutch market). The liquidity of the DSL lines quoted has grown exponentially since market start-up. As Figure 7.7 shows, the total turnover on MTS Amsterdam and EuroMTS has also picked up sharply.

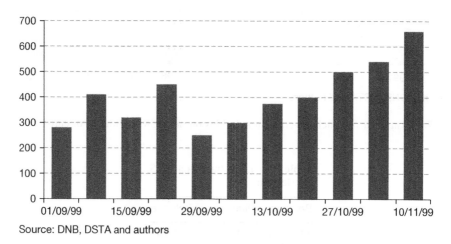

Source: DNB, DSTA and authors

Figure 7.7 Average weekly turnover in DSLs on EuroMTS and MTS Amsterdam from 1/9/99 (in millions of euros)

Another key characteristic of MTS Amsterdam is the openness of trading: its 13 market makers are joined by a group of market takers or 'Market dealers', 10 at the time of writing, whose admission requires the prior approval of their respective boards of directors. Eligibility is restricted to financial institutions meeting certain standards of capitalisation and levels of DSL trading, among other membership conditions.

7.5.1 Repo Transactions in DSLs

The Dutch repo market centres mainly on DSLs or bonds, though there is some trading in Eurobonds drawn up in florins. Weekly repo turnover in these assets is appreciably higher than traditional bond trading. This is therefore a vitally important market for the whole structure of DSL trading and derivatives market transactions. Thanks to the short-selling option and the temporary bond purchases facilitated by the repo system, the liquidity of the bond market is greatly enhanced.

Repo trading is via standard contracts, which may be modified or added to as each country's law requires. The Dutch repo contract has recently been amended to comply with the specifications of the standard ISMA contract.

Dutch law envisages a specific alternative to the standard repo (a single transaction whose associated interest is at the repo rate), consisting of a blocked or 'Spanish' repo. Such operations involve two simultaneous and independent transactions whereby ownership of a bond is transferred and reacquired. The Dutch repo market thus has the same trading structure as Spain's. The DSTA regularly stands as counterparty in this type of operation, which is primarily associated with the mutual funds segment of the money market.

7.5.2   The Strips Market in DSLs

Since February 1993, the DSTA has made certain DSL lines strippable, such that coupons (CO or Coupon Only) and principal (PO or Principal Only) can be separately traded. As in other markets running a strips segment, the two may also be rejoined or unstripped to recreate the original DSL.

All lines issued since January 1999 are automatically strippable. Strips are not issued as such; instead, the DSTA, upon the request of a market maker, repurchases the original DSL and turns it into strips. The agency can also purchase strips and deliver the original reconstituted asset, again at a market maker's request. Four DSLs had been stripped as of 31 March 2000, totalling a stripped amount of no more than 211 million euros, equivalent to just 0.69% of the total strippable volume outstanding.

Fund code	Characteristics of loan	Stripped amount	Amount in issue	%
10231	5.5% DSL 1991 maturing 15/01/2028	8 863	40.8	0.46%
10207	7.5% DSL 1993 maturing 15/01/2023	8 241	149.2	1.81%
10214	5.75% DSL 1994 maturing 15/01/2004	7 487	17.9	0.24%
10190	9.0% DSL 1991 maturing 15/01/2001	6 106	4.3	0.07%
Total		30 699	211.6	0.69%

Millions of euros

Strips are traded on the Amsterdam Exchange (AEX) and their prices quoted on its Official Price List. Principal and coupons may also be traded directly via the screens of market members.

Strip-market transactions are settled through the clearing house of the Dutch National Bank. Transactions on the AEX are settled via Effectenclearing BV and the depository institution NIEC. CEDEL and EUROCLEAR may also settle strip operations through special designated accounts.

7.5.3   The Derivatives Market in DSLs

Relatively little use is made of DSLs as notional bonds for derivative transactions, and attempts to launch a futures contract have met with little or no success. Most hedging operations, therefore, have recourse to the German futures market, despite the fact that only German Federal Government bonds are deliverable. Options on DSLs can, however, be negotiated on the AEX or directly with counterparties on OTC markets, though trading volumes are somewhat subdued.

The DSTA is currently pressing for the inclusion of DSLs in the deliverables baskets of German futures contracts, which would enormously enhance the attractiveness of the Dutch bond and would put the Dutch government on a good competitive footing with other euro-zone government issuers.

7.6   CLEARING AND SETTLEMENT OF DTCs AND DSLs

Both DTCs and DSLs can be made available on the day of settlement. There are three alternative methods for clearing and settlement:

- *Domestic operations*, through Necigef (the Dutch clearing institute). The paying agent is the Dutch National Bank (DNB).
- *Directly though EUROCLEAR*, or via Necigef with ABN AMRO as cash correspondent and depository.
- *Directly via CEDEL*, or via Necigef with RABOBANK as cash correspondent and Kas-Asociatie and ABN AMRO as depositories of DSLs and DTCs respectively.

All primary- and secondary-market transactions are settled on a trade-for-trade basis (as opposed to the end-of-day netting system) in the accounts designated by the DSTA.

EUROCLEAR, CEDEL and the DSTA invariably use the ISIN code, as a permanent reference for the clearing and settlement of primary market transactions, in preference to the temporary AEX ISIN.

Clearing system account numbers are:

	Necigef	EUROCLEAR	CEDEL
DSL primary settlement	555.ISS1	25003	82929
Other DSL transactions	556.NEC	97449	82913
DTCs	555.ISS2	97449	82913

(The DSTA's account at the Dutch National Bank is number 60.01.12.098.)

7.7 TAXATION

The information given here relates to personal income tax, so is only relevant to the individual investor.

7.7.1 Non-residents

Non-residents holding bonds issued by the Dutch Treasury are not taxed at source, i.e. in the Netherlands, on the interest earned.

7.7.2 Residents

Interest is considered income for tax purposes, whatever its source, since the same treatment is assigned to all assets generating income in the form of interest. Gains on the sale of securities are treated as capital gains on an income source and are not subject to personal income tax. By the same token, losses on the sale of securities are not tax-deductible. Thus the buyer of a bond paying annual interest will be taxed on all interest earned. If the acquisition price includes accrued interest, this can be used to offset subsequent interest payments. Conversely, the interest accruing to a bond seller is up to the disposal date treated as income, and is therefore subject to tax.

In the case of strips, investors (individuals) holding the bond principal (PO) must make an annual return, for tax purposes, setting out the notional interest on the nominal value of the bond. The interest earned by coupon (CO) holders is subject to income tax. Sale of the PO is not liable on tax, but the price received on the sale of COs is treated as interest and taxed accordingly.

7.8 MARKET MAKERS

The DSTA has been using a market-maker system for the distribution of DSLs since 1 January 1999. These entities (also known as primary dealers) are at the same time shareholders and market makers in MTS Amsterdam NV, the electronic trading platform sponsored by the DSTA.

According to the evaluation criteria applied during the first six months of 2000, the ranking of market makers stood as follows:

Deutsche Bank
ABN AMRO
ING Barings / BBL
Fortis Bank
NIB Capital Bank
Crédit Suisse First Boston
Société Générale
Salomon Smith Barney
BNP Paribas
Rabobank International
J.P. Morgan
Banca d'Intermediazione Mobiliare IMI
BBVA

ANNEXE: THE DUTCH PUBLIC DEBT MARKET

DSL Lines in Issue at 31/5/00 and Summary of Exchange Operations in 2000

Reference	Current balance	Strippable	Lines withdrawn		Lines issued	
			Included	Withdrawn	Included	Issued
NE 8750 5-2000	1 278.9	—	—	—	—	—
NE 9000 5-2000	4 356.3	—	—	—	—	—
NE 9000 7-2000	1 251.1	—	—	—	—	—
NE 9000 10-2000	1 951.3	—	—	—	—	—
NE 9250 11-2000	2 268.9	—	—	—	—	—
NE 9000 1-2001	6 106.3	***	—	—	—	—
NE 8500 3-2001	4 537.8	—	—	—	—	—
NE 8750 9-2001	6 012.6	—	—	—	—	—
NE 8250 2-2002	1 704.6	—	***	2 800	—	—
NE 3000 2-2002	**13 999.3**	—	—	—	***	4 900
NE 8250 6-2002	2 035.0	—	***	3 200	—	—
NE 5750 9-2002	7 487.4	—	—	—	—	—
NE 7000 2-2003	1 992.0	—	***	3 300	—	—
NE 4750 2-2003	2 700.0	—	—	—	***	700
NE 6500 4-2003	**11 200.0**	—	—	—	***	4 400
NE 5750 1-2004	**7 487.4**	***	—	—	—	—
NE 7250 10-2004	7 260.5	—	—	—	—	—
NE 7750 3-2005	**10 950.0**	—	—	—	***	5 250
NE 7000 6-2005	1 400.0	—	***	3 500	—	—
NE 6750 11-2005	1 200.0	—	***	3 300	—	—
NE 6000 1-2006	12 329.0	—	—	—	***	4 950
NE 8500 6-2006	1 300.0	—	***	3 200	—	—
NE 8750 1-2007	270.6	—	***	200	—	—
NE 8250 2-2007	1 300.0	—	***	4 200	—	—
NE 5750 2-2007	**13 637.2**	—	—	—	***	8 000
NE 8250 9-2007	1 600.0	—	***	4 000	—	—
NE 5250 7-2008	11 118.0	—	—	—	***	1 500
NE 3750 7-2009	**12 088.0**	—	—	—	—	—
NE 7500 4-2010	1 327.0	—	***	2 100	—	—
NE 5500 7-2010	**6 142.0**	—	—	—	***	2 500
NE 7500 1-2023	8 241.5	***	—	—	—	—
NE 5500 1-2028	**8 863.8**	***	—	—	—	—
Total	**175 396.3**	—	—	29 800	—	32 200

Millions of euros

Benchmark lines in bold type

Source: DSTA and authors

DSL Issuance Calendar 2000

Auction	Issuer	Instru-ment	Coupon	Term	Target	Cur-rency	Settles	Matures	Format
11-Jan-00	Netherlands	DSL	5.50%	10 years	1500–2000	EUR	14-Jan-00	15-Jul-10	Tap issue
08-Feb-00	Netherlands	DSL	4.75%	3 years	1500–2000	EUR	11-Feb-00	15-Feb-03	Tap issue
10-Feb-00	Netherlands	DSL	5.50%	10 years	—	EUR	15-Feb-00	15-Jul-10	Exchange
14-Mar-00	Netherlands	DSL	5.5%	10 years	1500–2000	EUR	17-Mar-00	15-Jul-10	Tap issue
16-Mar-00	Netherlands	DSL	4.75%	3 years	—	EUR	21-Mar-00	15-Feb-03	Exchange
11-Apr-00	Netherlands	DSL	4.75%	3 years	1500–2000	EUR	14-Apr-00	15-Feb-03	Tap issue
09-May-00	Netherlands	DSL	4.75%	3 years	1500–2000	EUR	12-May-00	15-Feb-03	Tap issue
13-Jun-00	Netherlands	DSL	5.50%	10 years	1500–2000	EUR	16-Jun-00	15-Jul-10	Tap issue
20-Jun-00	Netherlands	DSL	8.25%	3 years	—	EUR	23-Jun-00	15-Feb-02	Repurchase
20-Jun-00	Netherlands	DSL	8.25%	3 years	—	EUR	23-Jun-00	15-Jun-02	Repurchase
20-Jun-00	Netherlands	DSL	7.00%	3 years	—	EUR	23-Jun-00	15-Feb-03	Repurchase
20-Jun-00	Netherlands	DSL	6.75%	5 years	—	EUR	23-Jun-00	15-Nov-05	Repurchase
20-Jun-00	Netherlands	DSL	8.25%	7 years	—	EUR	23-Jun-00	15-Feb-07	Repurchase
11-Jul-00	Netherlands	DSL	—	—	—	EUR	14-Jul-00	—	Tap issue
12-Sep-00	Netherlands	DSL	—	—	—	EUR	15-Sep-00	—	Tap issue
10-Oct-00	Netherlands	DSL	—	—	—	EUR	13-Oct-00	—	Tap issue
14-Nov-00	Netherlands	DSL	—	—	—	EUR	17-Nov-00	—	Tap issue
12-Dec-00	Netherlands	DSL	—	—	—	EUR	15-Dec-00	—	Tap issue

Millions of euros
Source: DSTA and authors

DTC Issuance Calendar 2000

Auction	Issuer	Instru-ment	Term	Target	Cur-rency	Matures	Days	Settles	Format
05-Jun-00	Netherlands	DTC	3 months	—	EUR	31-Aug-00	85	07-Jun-00	Auction
05-Jun-00	Netherlands	DTC	2 months	—	EUR	29-Dec-00	205	07-Jun-00	Auction
19-Jun-00	Netherlands	DTC	3 months	—	EUR	29-Sep-00	100	21-Jun-00	Auction
19-Jun-00	Netherlands	DTC	6 months	—	EUR	29-Dec-00	191	21-Jun-00	Auction
19-Jun-00	Netherlands	DTC	2 months	—	EUR	29-Jun-01	373	21-Jun-00	Auction
03-Jul-00	Netherlands	DTC	3 months	—	EUR	29-Sep-00	86	05-Jul-00	Auction
03-Jul-00	Netherlands	DTC	2 months	—	EUR	29-Jun-01	359	05-Jul-00	Auction
17-Jul-00	Netherlands	DTC	3 months	—	EUR	31-Oct-00	104	19-Jul-00	Auction
17-Jul-00	Netherlands	DTC	6 months	—	EUR	29-Dec-00	163	19-Jul-00	Auction
07-Aug-00	Netherlands	DTC	3 months	—	EUR	31-Oct-00	83	09-Aug-00	Auction
07-Aug-00	Netherlands	DTC	2 months	—	EUR	29-Jun-01	324	09-Aug-00	Auction
21-Aug-00	Netherlands	DTC	3 months	—	EUR	30-Nov-00	99	23-Aug-00	Auction
21-Aug-00	Netherlands	DTC	6 months	—	EUR	29-Dec-00	128	23-Aug-00	Auction
04-Sep-00	Netherlands	DTC	3 months	—	EUR	30-Nov-00	85	06-Sep-00	Auction
04-Sep-00	Netherlands	DTC	2 months	—	EUR	29-Jun-01	296	06-Sep-00	Auction
18-Sep-00	Netherlands	DTC	3 months	—	EUR	29-Dec-00	100	20-Sep-00	Auction
18-Sep-00	Netherlands	DTC	6 months	—	EUR	30-Mar-01	191	20-Sep-00	Auction
02-Oct-00	Netherlands	DTC	3 months	—	EUR	29 Dec 00	86	04 Oct 00	Auction
02-Oct-00	Netherlands	DTC	2 months	—	EUR	29-Jun-01	268	04-Oct-00	Auction
16-Oct-00	Netherlands	DTC	3 months	—	EUR	31-Jan-01	105	18-Oct-00	Auction
16-Oct-00	Netherlands	DTC	6 months	—	EUR	30-Mar-01	163	18-Oct-00	Auction
06-Nov-00	Netherlands	DTC	3 months	—	EUR	31-Jan-01	84	08-Nov-00	Auction
06-Nov-00	Netherlands	DTC	2 months	—	EUR	29-Jun-01	233	08-Nov-00	Auction

Source: DSTA and authors

Outcome of DSL Issues in 2000

Operation	Date	Instru-ment	Coupon	Term	Issue	Matures	Sold	Bids	Bid/cover	Stop rate	Stop price	Avge rate	Avge price
Tap issue	11-Jan-00	DSL	5.50%	10 years	14-Jan-00	15-Jul-10	2025	—	—	—	—	5.620	98.970
Tap issue	08-Feb-00	DSL	4.75%	3 years	11-Feb-00	15-Feb-03	2000	—	—	—	—	4.890	99.620
Exchange	10-Feb-00	DSL	5.50%	10 years	15-Feb-00	15-Jul-10	2500	—	—	5.690	98.400	—	—
Tap issue	14-Mar-00	DSL	5.50%	10 years	17-Mar-00	15-Jul-10	1580	—	—	—	—	5.490	99.940
Exchange	16-Mar-00	DSL	4.75%	3 years	21-Mar-00	15-Feb-03	670	—	—	4.880	99.640	—	—
Tap issue	11-Apr-00	DSL	4.75%	3 years	14-Apr-00	15-Feb-03	1500	—	—	—	—	4.670	100.180
Tap issue	09-May-00	DSL	4.75%	3 years	12-May-00	15-Feb-03	1610	—	—	—	—	5.070	99.170
Tap issue	13-Jun-00	DSL	5.50%	10 years	16-Jun-00	15-Jul-10	1680	7802	4.64	—	—	5.290	101.440
Repurchase	20-Jun-00	DSL	8.25%	3 years	23-Jun-00	15-Feb-02	218	—	—	—	—	—	105.130
Repurchase	20-Jun-00	DSL	8.25%	3 years	23-Jun-00	15-Jun-02	94	—	—	—	—	—	106.020
Repurchase	20-Jun-00	DSL	7.00%	3 years	23-Jun-00	15-Feb-03	192	—	—	—	—	—	104.700
Repurchase	20-Jun-00	DSL	6.75%	5 years	23-Jun-00	15-Nov-05	267	—	—	—	—	—	107.150
Repurchase	20-Jun-00	DSL	8.25%	7 years	23-Jun-00	15-Feb-07	302	—	—	—	—	—	116.460

Millions of euros
Source: DSTA and authors

Outcome of DTC Issues in 2000

Auction	Instru-ment	Term	Target	Matures	Days	Issue	Sold	Bids	Bid/cover	Stop rate
17-Jan-00	DTC	3 months	1250–1750	28-Apr-00	100	19-Jan-00	1395	3650	2.6	3.190
17-Jan-00	DTC	6 months	750–1250	30-Jun-00	163	19-Jan-00	1015	5465	5.4	3.370
07-Feb-00	DTC	3 months	1750–2250	28-Apr-00	79	09-Feb-00	1850	3430	1.9	3.330
07-Feb-00	DTC	12 months	500–1000	29-Dec-00	324	09-Feb-00	870	2940	3.4	3.890
21-Feb-00	DTC	3 months	1250–1750	31-May-00	98	23-Feb-00	1290	1650	1.3	3.590
21-Feb-00	DTC	6 months	400–600	30-Jun-00	128	23-Feb-00	498	1870	3.8	3.640
06-Mar-00	DTC	3 months	1250–1750	31-May-00	84	08-Mar-00	1254	3500	2.8	3.570
06-Mar-00	DTC	12 months	250–500	29-Dec-00	296	08-Mar-00	301	2615	8.7	4.000
20-Mar-00	DTC	3 months	1000–1500	30-Jun-00	100	22-Mar-00	1220	3315	2.7	3.690
20-Mar-00	DTC	6 months	750–1250	29-Sep-00	191	22-Mar-00	895	2255	2.5	3.880
03-Apr-00	DTC	3 months	1000–1500	30-Jun-00	86	05-Apr-00	1248	3780	3.0	3.740
03-Apr-00	DTC	12 months	250–500	29-Dec-00	268	05-Apr-00	350	2945	8.4	4.060
17-Apr-00	DTC	3 months	1000–1500	31-Jul-00	103	19-Apr-00	1075	2565	2.4	3.850
17-Apr-00	DTC	6 months	350–650	29-Sep-00	163	19-Apr-00	400	2070	5.2	3.940
02-May-00	DTC	3 months	1000–1500	31-Jul-00	88	04-May-00	1100	1650	1.5	4.030
02-May-00	DTC	12 months	250–500	29-Dec-00	239	04-May-00	366	1630	4.5	4.300
15-May-00	DTC	3 months	1000–1500	31-Aug-00	105	18-May-00	1258	2265	1.8	4.260
15-May-00	DTC	6 months	250–500	29-Sep-00	134	18-May-00	460	2015	4.4	4.300
05-Jun-00	DTC	3 months	1000–1500	31-Aug-00	85	07-Jun-00	1150	2050	1.8	4.300
05-Jun-00	DTC	12 months	350–650	29-Dec-00	205	07-Jun-00	510	1985	3.9	4.530
19-Jun-00	DTC	3 months	750–1250	29-Sep-00	100	21-Jun-00	767	2175	2.8	4.410
19-Jun-00	DTC	6 months	350–650	29-Dec-00	191	21-Jun-00	425	1297	3.1	4.550
19-Jun-00	DTC	12 months	500–1000	29-Jun-01	373	21-Jun-00	495	1915	3.9	4.790

Millions of euros
Source: DSTA and authors

8
The Irish Government Bond Market

8.1 INTRODUCTION

The Irish public debt market represents only 1% of total euro-zone government debt, and Ireland is one of the six member states in receipt of the maximum short- (A1+) and long-term (AAA) credit rating. The government agency entrusted with issuance and management of Irish government public debt is the National Treasury Management Agency (NTMA). This agency was created on 3 December 1990 to manage Ireland's National Debt, by order and under the supervision of the Finance Ministry. All rights or obligations accepted by the NTMA are therefore understood as having been undertaken by the Ministry.

Ireland has one of the lowest public debt/GDP ratios in the euro zone, currently 47%. This percentage would have been lower still, possibly the second lowest after Luxembourg, save for the Securities Exchange Programme (SEP) implemented in May 1999 in order to provide the market with greater liquidity. The Irish Treasury was able to deploy this strategy thanks to the exceptional growth of the preceding decade, with GDP growth rates exceeding 8%, and the resultant fiscal surpluses. At the time of writing, gross issuance requirements amount to slightly over 1.8 billion euros, on a par with the previous year's and coinciding with the interest on outstanding debt.

Here as elsewhere, the advent of the single currency in January 1999 spurred a root-and-branch transformation to align the public debt market with its euro-zone counterparts. Furthermore, the small size of the Irish market and the below-par liquidity of its issues called for new measures to offer larger-volume issues on the one hand, and more liquid secondary-market trading on the other.

The changes introduced, primarily a successful exchange programme and the extension of the Irish Treasury's repo activity, have completely transformed the country's debt market. Foreign-currency denominated issues have practically disappeared (except for pound-sterling bonds in issue, equivalent to 6% of total public debt), and the outstanding balance has been consolidated in four references to enhance secondary-market liquidity. From a technical point of view, Ireland's break with its British market heritage and conventions has marked the definitive step in its alignment with the other euro-zone markets (annual coupon, Current/Current interest-rate basis, elimination of the ex-dividend rule, etc.).

8.2 ASSETS ISSUED BY THE IRISH TREASURY

Although the Irish Treasury issues many different government debt instruments, trading is largely concentrated in Irish Government Bonds (IGBs) and Exchequer Notes (ENs).

8.2.1 Irish Government Bonds (IGBs or Bonds)

IGBs are euro-denominated securities paying a fixed (annual or semiannual) or floating (quarterly) coupon. They are tradeable on the Irish Stock Exchange (ISE) and represented by entries in the Central Bank of Ireland Book-Entry System.

Before the launch of the euro, practically all bonds in the Irish public debt market paid semiannually (fixed-coupon bonds) or quarterly (floating-coupon bonds) and the applicable interest-rate basis was 30/360. In 1999, IGBs began to be issued with annual coupons only and interest calculated on a Current/Current basis. All existing debt was redenominated in euros. Nevertheless, issues prior to 1999 retain their original characteristics (semiannual coupon on a 30E/360 basis). With the introduction of the euro, the ex-dividend rule, whereby bonds stopped accruing interest as of the tenth working day prior to payment date, was finally abolished. This rule gave rise to negative accrued interest if the value date fell between the ex-dividend date (exclusive) and the coupon payment date (inclusive).

As of March 2000, the Treasury has 24 IGB lines in issue, of which 13 have fixed-rate semiannual coupons, 10 pay a fixed annual coupon and only one has a variable rate and floating coupon. Following the NTMA's May exchange programme, in which older series were replaced with four new lines, liquidity and trading were consolidated in eight lines paying a fixed annual coupon (which market makers are obliged to quote), whereas future issuance will be restricted solely to the new 3-, 5-, 10- and 15-year bonds. Furthermore, the four new IGB lines must be compulsorily quoted by Irish public debt market makers under pre-set spread and volume conditions.

Table 8.1 Benchmark bonds in the Irish government bond market

Benchmark references	Maturity	Outstanding balance at 31/3/00
IGB 2.75%*	18/10/2002	3031
IGB 3.50%*	18/10/2005	4774
IGB 4.00%*	18/04/2010	6176
IGB 4.60%*	18/04/2016	3612

*'on-the-run' in 2000
Millions of euros
Source: authors

The price formula applied to fixed annual-coupon IGBs issued since 1 January 1999, and therefore calculated on a Current/Current basis, is as follows:

$$P_0 + Cc = \sum_{t=1}^{t=T} \frac{100}{\left(1 + \dfrac{R}{100}\right)^{n_j}}$$

where n_j is the number of years, on a Current/Current basis, between the value date and each coupon payment date.

The formula for semiannual-coupon IGBs issued prior to January 1999, and therefore calculated on a 30E/360 basis, is as follows:

$$P + Cc = \frac{C_1}{(1 + r_{sa})^{d_1/180}} + \sum_{i=2}^{n} \frac{C_i}{(1 + r_{sa})^{d_2/180}} + \frac{100}{(1 + r_{sa})^{d_n/180}}$$

where $d_1, d_2, \ldots, d_n$ express the days between value date and coupon payment date, on a 30E/360 basis, as per the following calculation:

$$\text{no. of days} = d = 360 \times (\text{years}) + 30 \times (\text{months}) + 1 \times (\text{days})$$

Annualised yield, accordingly, corresponds to the following formula:

$$R = \left[(1 + R_{sa})^2 - 1 \right] \times 100$$

8.2.2 Exchequer Notes (ENs)

ENs are money-market assets issued at a discount, represented by book entries and trade-able on the Irish Stock Exchange (ISE). Maturities range from 7 to 365 days. They are thus comparable to the Treasury bills issued by any other euro-zone government. Their importance in the public debt armoury is now marginal only, as evidenced by an outstanding balance at July 1999 of just 1 billion euros. At present, the NTMA issues these securities upon request with maturities of one week and 1, 2, 3, 6, 9 and 12 months. Indicative prices for transactions of less than 15 million euros are posted on the NTMA pages, but investors must contact the agency directly to establish a firm transaction price.

Like IGBs, ENs issued from 1 January 1999 onwards use the calculation conventions drawn up by the now defunct European Monetary Institute, and are quoted on a Current/360 basis (previously Current/365).

The Treasury's price is calculated as follows:

$$P_0 = \frac{100}{\left(1 + \dfrac{R}{100} \times \dfrac{d}{b} \right)}$$

where d represents the exact number of days between the payment or value date and the maturity date of the note, and b indicates the calculation basis employed: 365 days for securities issued after 1 January 1999.

8.2.3 Section 69 Multicurrency Notes

These are notes maturing in under one year, created by the government in 1985 to attract portfolio investment from multinational companies established in Ireland. Their main selling point is that interest accrued is not subject to any taxation. Companies can acquire them at any time, either directly from the NTMA or from the group of banks designated for this purpose (market makers). The only take-up requirement for this tax-privileged investment is the subscription of an amount equivalent to 100 000 euros or more. The credit rating of these assets is the same as that of other Irish government securities, i.e. the maximum allowable.

8.2.4 Commercial Paper (CP) Programmes

These programmes provide funding at rates lower than euribid, and are used primarily to cover exceptional liquidity needs and to secure bridge financing for the replacement of long-term debt holdings or issues. The Irish government has three facilities open at the time of writing:

- a 2 billion euro-denominated CP based in Frankfurt
- a US$ 1 billion multicurrency Euro Commercial Paper (ECP) based in London
- a US$ 1 billion CP based in New York.

8.2.5 MTN Programmes

The Irish government currently runs two programmes of medium-term notes drawn up in a range of currencies (a US$ 2 billion EMTN programme and a US$ 500 million MTN programme), which are placed through a syndicate. Table 8.2 below sets out all the EMTNs and MTNs in issue:

Table 8.2 EMTNs and MTNs in issue

Reference	Maturity	Currency	Rating	Volume issued
EMTN 7.50%	5/06/2001	GRD	AAA	10 000
EMTN variable	5/02/2003	DEM	AAA	50
EMTN 4.25%	22/06/2004	JPY	AAA	20 000
EMTN 4.80%	5/01/2005	JPY	AAA	30 000
EMTN 4.50%	5/04/2005	JPY	AAA	15 000
EMTN variable	21/12/2015	JPY	AAA	10 000
MTN 7.64%	2/01/2002	USD	AAA	50

Millions, local currency
Source: NTMA and authors

8.3   OVERVIEW OF THE IRISH PUBLIC DEBT MARKET

The market's limited volume, lack of depth and relative shortage of participating agents requires a hands-on approach by the NTMA to ensure its efficiency and competitiveness within the euro zone.

Specifically, to prevent the differential between the Irish and other European debt markets with the same credit rating being aggravated by an illiquidity premium (higher than normal since Ireland is a peripheral market), the NTMA has taken radical steps to transform market structure, involving (1) the practical elimination of foreign-currency debt, (2) the streamlining of the outstanding balance into a small number of issues, and (3) the redenomination in euros of existing debt and the harmonisation of calculation conventions with euro-zone standards.

8.3.1   Elimination of Foreign-Currency Debt

The NMTA has gone beyond the mere redenomination of euro-legacy currency issues, and has proceeded to swap many others drawn up in Japanese yen and US dollars. The aim of this reduction is to minimise exposure to foreign-exchange market movements. Traditionally, the narrowness of Ireland's market had forced frequent recourse to international markets, particularly in foreign currencies (40% of the public debt total in 1993). But the explosive growth of the country's GDP and the improvement in public finances have effectively reversed this trend. At present, only 6% of the Republic of Ireland's sovereign debt is in a foreign currency, exclusively pounds sterling.

8.3.2   Debt Consolidation

At the beginning of 1999, the average balance of IGB lines in issue was less than 2.5 billion euros. In view of this, and anticipating the introduction of the single currency and the onset of competition from other euro-zone markets, the NTMA designed a

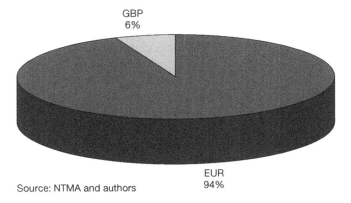

Source: NTMA and authors

Figure 8.1 Composition of Irish public debt as of 31 December 1999

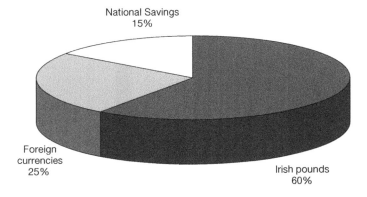

Source: NTMA and authors

Figure 8.2 Composition of Irish public debt as of 31 December 1998 (after swaps)

debt-exchange programme aimed at concentrating over 80% of trading in four bond lines (2.75% 2002, 3.5% 2005, 4% 2010 and 4.6% 2016). These benchmarks would have an average outstanding balance of approximately 3–5 billion euros (currently 4.4 billion) and coupons in tune with investor demand. As a sweetener, the Irish government decided to exempt from taxation any capital gains arising from the exchange, due to the high price of the old references—which had a much higher coupon than the new issues. The programme has proved an exceptional success, with over 91% of the old bonds withdrawn in exchange for the four new lines.

Despite these measures, IGB trading on secondary markets contracted from a total of 155 billion euros in 1995 to slightly over 90 billion euros in 1998. The deceptive 110.92 billion euros recorded in August 1999 was due to the huge turnover spike of the previous May (67 billion euros), coinciding with the above-mentioned exchange operations. Average daily turnover dropped from 364 million euros in 1998 to 236 million in 1999 (excluding May) and to slightly over 150 million in March 2000. The culprit is mainly portfolio diversification by large Irish institutional investors, who have stepped up investment in other euro-zone government bonds to the detriment of their IGB holdings—now only 1.3% of domestic fund-manager holdings.

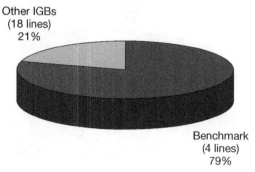

Source: Bloomberg and authors

Figure 8.3 Structure of outstanding balance of IGBs as of 31 July 2000

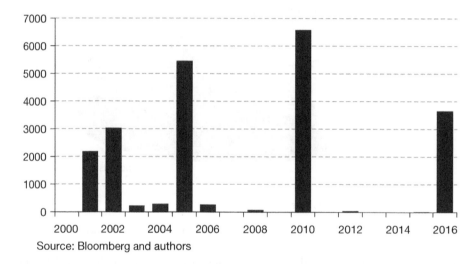

Source: Bloomberg and authors

Figure 8.4 Irish public debt maturities curve as of 31 July 2000 (in millions of euros)

Table 8.3 Outcome of debt-exchange programme

Exchangeable bonds	Amount withdrawn	% of initial balance
Treasury 6.5% 2001	895.3	30%
Capital 9.25% 2003	1 270	81%
Treasury 6.25% 2004	1 906	83%
Treasury 8% 2006	2 672	94%
Treasury 6% 2008	1 909	93%
Treasury 8.75% 2012	1 236	96%
Treasury 8.25% 2015	2 366	98%
Total	12 257	Average = 91%

Millions of euros
Source: authors

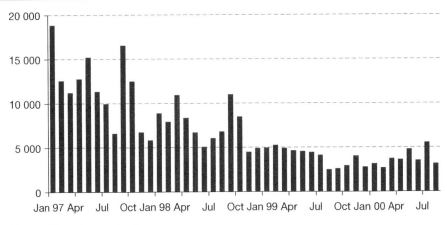

Source: Bloomberg and authors

Figure 8.5 Monthly turnover in IGBs (except May 99) in millions of euros

8.3.3 Redenomination into Euros

The 'idiosyncrasies' of the Irish public debt market (including the semiannual coupon, a 30E/360 basis for bonds and a Current/365 basis for money-market securities) were the first sacrifice to the new euro environment. The principal changes made were as follows:

- the switch to a Current/360 interest-rate basis for money-market assets and Current/Current for bond issues subsequent to 1 January 1999
- the redenomination of existing debt into euros
- the alignment of value dates with European standards: T + 3 for bonds
- international settlement through EUROCLEAR and CEDEL, with the possibility of a same-day value date
- the change to annual coupons for bond issues conducted from 1 January 1999 onwards
- abolition of the ex-dividend rule.

8.4   THE PRIMARY MARKET

The NTMA is in charge of conducting all public debt issues in Ireland. The agency uses three issuance procedures, depending on the instrument: one for Exchequer Notes, based on (i) direct sale to investors through the NTMA, and two for IGBs, comprising (ii) multi-price or 'American' auctions and (iii) tap placements (tap issuance was important in the past, but since 1997 the auction system has increasingly prevailed and is now the standard format for all issues).

8.4.1   EN and IGB Issuance Procedures

Direct Sale of Exchequer Notes

The NTMA publishes daily ask prices for Exchequer Notes at various maturities and in volumes of under 15 million euros on its Reuters (QNTMA-K) and Bloomberg (NTMA) pages. These prices are indicative only, since the issue price is set by the NTMA on a sale-by-sale basis. The price of transactions exceeding 15 million euros is contracted bilaterally by the agency and interested parties.

IGB Auctions

The NTMA publishes its IGB auction calendar at the close of each year, normally specifying a monthly auction on the third Thursday each month, except for January and December. Two working days prior to the auction (T − 2), at 9.00 GMT, the NMTA posts details of the lines to be issued (maturity, coupon and issue target) on the Reuters NTMB or Bloomberg NTMA pages.

The auction itself comprises two tranches or rounds, one competitive and the other non-competitive. The first round uses the 'American' or multi-price format. After receiving subscriber bids, the agency determines the stop-out price above which bids will be allotted at the price specified. If the volume of bids at this stop-out (marginal) price exceeds the target volume stated, bids are allotted on a pro rata basis. The weighted average price applicable at the second, non-competitive stage is determined in this first, auction round, calculated as the average of allocation prices weighted for the amount allotted at each. In the second round, held immediately after the competitive auction, the NTMA allots all market-maker subscriptions at this weighted average price. The volume issued in the second round may in no case exceed 20% of the nominal amount allotted in competitive bidding.

IGB Tap Issues

The tap-issue system, used extensively up to 1997, has fallen into disuse and seems unlikely to be revived. Its main advantage for treasuries is that they can opt to issue at any time, giving just a few minutes' notice to market makers.

The procedure followed by the Irish Treasury is as follows: at either 8.45 or 14.00 local time, the Treasury announces its intention on the Reuters NTMB screen with details of the reference and volume to be issued. Five minutes later, it notifies the placement price exclusively to market makers (note that, contrary to standard euro-zone practice, this price is not made public). These entities then phone in the volumes they wish to acquire at the stated price. Once the Treasury has completed the tap (i.e. allotted its target volume), the amount issued and the issue price are posted on the Reuters NTMB screen.

8.4.2   IGB Issuance Characteristics

- *Issuance procedure:* a two-round auction system with a first multi-price or 'American' round and a second non-competitive stage, restricted to market makers only, resolved at the weighted average price of the bids allotted in the first round.
- *Auction participants:* only the six market makers appointed by the NTMA may participate.
- *Presentation of competitive bids:* up to 10.00 local time on the day the auction is resolved (T − 0).
- *Minimum denomination:* one euro cent (0.01 euros).
- *Minimum bid amount:* 100 000 euros.
- *Announcement of issue volume:* two working days before the auction (T − 2).

- *Auction results:* posted minutes after resolution on the Reuters NTMB and Bloomberg NTMA screens.
- *Payment/value date:* three working days after auction resolution (T + 3).
- *Trading on the secondary market:* admission to secondary-market trading (i.e. on the Irish Stock Exchange) coincides with the value date or T + 3.
- *Interest-rate basis:* Current/Current since 1999.
- *Second rounds:* immediately following the competitive tranche, restricted to market makers and resolved at the weighted average price of the first round. Market makers may present an unlimited number of non-competitive bids (amount only).

Table 8.4   IGB auction calendar

First half 2000	Second half 2000
17 February	20 July
16 March	17 August
20 April	21 September
18 May	19 October
15 June	16 November

Source: authors

Table 8.5   IGB issue 20/4/2000

IGB 4% 18/10/2010	
Volume allotted	150 million euros
Bid volume	785 million euros
Marginal interest rate (stop rate)	5.49%
Stop-out price	88.78
Weighted average rate	5.49%
Weighted average price	88.78
Pro rata at marginal rate	100%
Volume allotted in second round	0 million euros

Source: authors

8.5   THE SECONDARY MARKET

8.5.1   General Characteristics

The secondary market in Irish public debt is composed of two tiers or trading segments: a *first tier* between market makers and a *second tier* of retail trading on the Irish Stock Exchange (ISE). First-tier or market-maker trading is conducted anonymously on Inter-dealer Broker (IDB) screens and is thus similar to the Spanish 'blind market' system.

This secondary-market segment is of crucial importance for the liquidity of the Irish public debt market. Its institutional structure centres on the primary dealers, or market makers, who make up the market's core (almost 95% of turnover), and a group of brokers acting as mere intermediaries, i.e. who execute orders on their clients' behalf.

As to trading features, the standard size of IGB transactions is 10 million euros, with a bid/ask spread that varies by maturity:

- 5 basis points for terms of around 5 years
- 10 basis points for terms of around 10 years
- 20 basis points for terms of around 20 years.

As of March 2000, IGB trading on the Irish Stock Exchange (ISE) privileged bonds with maturities of between 7 and 12 years, accounting for over 46% of total turnover, at a daily average of 79 million euros.

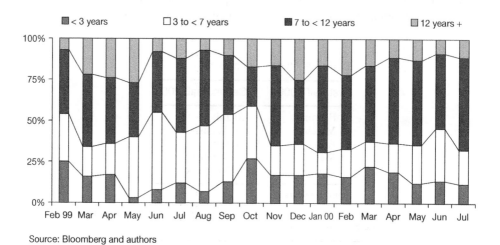

Source: Bloomberg and authors

Figure 8.6 IGB turnover on the Irish Stock Exchange (as a percentage of monthly total)

Ireland's secondary trading is also coloured by the NTMA's dominant role, aimed at endowing the greatest possible liquidity on the market as a whole. The importance of its role is evidenced by the fact that almost 15% of spot and repo transactions can be traced directly to the Treasury. This degree of intervention—unique within the euro zone—is exemplified by three primary-dealer facilities:

1. A continuous back-stop bidding facility, providing an escape mechanism to undo bond positions in extreme market situations. This mechanism is intended to prevent an excessive liquidity drain during severe market pullbacks.
2. The IGB bond-switching facility whereby the NTMA regularly offers to exchange bonds of similar maturity or duration. This facility is most often applied immediately post-issue, to boost the trading liquidity of the reference in question.
3. An emergency repo window for market-management operations, again to give the market additional liquidity.

8.5.2   The Repo Market

Repo activity in Irish government securities generates almost five times the volume of the spot equivalent, reflecting the Treasury's keen involvement as a guarantor of market liquidity and depth.

8.5.3   The Futures Market

Ireland has no debt-futures market at the present time, so hedging of IGB positions is usually conducted through contracts on the German *Bund*.

8.5.4   The Strips Market

There is no strips market in Ireland, nor any plans to establish one, given the limited importance of the Irish market within the euro zone.

8.6   CLEARING AND SETTLEMENT

IGB transactions between residents (domestic operations) are settled through the Central Bank of Ireland Securities Settlement Office on a delivery-against-payment basis and with value date at $T + 3$.

Settlement of IGB international transactions (between non-residents or between a resident institution and a non-resident institution) is carried out through CEDEL and EURO-CLEAR with value date at $T + 3$. Same-day settlement of IGB transactions included in the Exchange Programme (i.e. the new benchmarks) is also possible through CEDEL and EUROCLEAR.

8.7   TAXATION

Non-resident investors (as in the rest of the euro-zone public debt market) are not liable for taxation at source in Irish public debt instrument transactions. Coupons are paid in full with no amounts withheld.

8.8   MARKET MAKERS

The market-maker system was first introduced in 1995. At the time of writing, there were six market-maker entities, appointed by the NTMA subject to prior approval by the Central Bank of Ireland.

Eligibility requirements can be summarised as follows:

- experience and excellence in management tasks, proven trading capacity and a wide geographical reach
- minimum capital requirements and the wherewithal to support the Treasury in its debt policy.

Appointed market makers must fulfil a series of obligations:

- the obligation to quote firm bid and ask prices, upon client request, at a maximum spread and in pre-set amounts for those debt references specified by the NTMA
- an undertaking to remain a market maker for at least three years
- the earmarking of part of their capital resources (between 6.5 and 7 million euros) for the conduct of market-making activity in Irish public debt.

In return, market makers are accorded the following privileges in the Irish public debt market:

- exclusive access to auctions and other fixed-income security issuance conducted by the NTMA
- access to the facilities created by the NTMA: (i) continuous back-stop bidding, (ii) bond switching after auctions, and (iii) the emergency repo window
- exclusive access to the second (non-competitive) rounds of IGB auctions at the average price resulting from the first round.

As of March 2000, the six market makers in Irish public debt were:

ABN AMRO, Dublin
AIB Capital Markets, Dublin
Crédit Agricole Indosuez, Paris
Davy Stockbrokers (Bank of Ireland), Dublin
Deutsche Bank AG, Frankfurt
NCB Stockbrokers (Ulster Bank/Natwest), Dublin

ANNEXE: THE IRISH PUBLIC DEBT MARKET

IGB Issuance Calendar 2000

Auction	Issuer	Instrument	Coupon	Term	Target	Currency	Settles	Matures	Format
17-Feb-00	Ireland	IGB	4.60%	15 years	125	EUR	22-Feb-00	18-Apr-16	Auction
16-Mar-00	Ireland	IGB	4.00%	10 years	150	EUR	07-Mar-00	18-Apr-10	Auction
20-Apr-00	Ireland	IGB	4.00%	10 years	150	EUR	21-Mar-00	18-Apr-10	Auction
18-May-00	Ireland	IGB	3.50%	5 years	200	EUR	09-May-00	18-Oct-05	Auction
15-Jun-00	Ireland	IGB	—	—	—	EUR	06-Jun-00	—	Auction
20-Jul-00	Ireland	IGB	—	—	—	EUR	11-Jul-00	—	Auction
17-Aug-00	Ireland	IGB	—	—	—	EUR	08-Aug-00	—	Auction
21-Sep-00	Ireland	IGB	—	—	—	EUR	12-Sep-00	—	Auction
19-Oct-00	Ireland	IGB	—	—	—	EUR	10-Oct-00	—	Auction
16-Nov-00	Ireland	IGB	—	—	—	EUR	10-Oct-00	—	Auction

Millions of euros
Source: Bloomberg, Reuters and authors

Outcome of IGB Issues in 2000

Auction	Instrument	Coupon	Term	Format	Matures	Sold	Bids	Bid/cover	Stop r.	Avge r.
17-Feb-00	IGB	4.60%	15 years	Auction	18-Apr-16	148	424	3.39	5.941	5.938
16-Mar-00	IGB	4.00%	10 years	Auction	18-Apr-10	182	683	4.50	5.572	5.569
20-Apr-00	IGB	4.00%	10 years	Auction	18-Apr-10	150	785	5.23	5.490	5.490
18-May-00	IGB	3.50%	5 years	Auction	18-Oct-05	240	628	2.62	5.516	5.510

Millions of euros
Source: Bloomberg, Reuters and authors

9

The Italian Government Bond Market

9.1 INTRODUCTION

Italy's public debt market ranks third in the world by outstanding balance, after only the USA and Japan. Its size is a product of the heavy borrowing requirements incurred by the Italian government in the 1970s and 1980s, which gave rise to capital markets with an overwhelming preponderance of public issues (basically by the Italian Treasury) at the expense of private securities placements, which have traditionally played a marginal role.

However, recent years have seen a gradual awakening of private and corporate issuance, thanks to the public deficit and public debt/GDP discipline imposed by the Maastricht convergence criteria and, in 1999, by the Stability Programme.

Other features of the Italian capital market which make it among the most attractive in the euro zone are:

- the existence to date of just one major issuer, the Italian Treasury
- the fact that the securities issued share common characteristics with those of the other euro-zone markets
- a minimum amount for debt securities bids that is within reach of any investor
- the sophistication of asset swaps and futures markets on debt instruments, though the former is only truly liquid for 'on-the-run' bonds, while the latter, in particular the contract on the 10-year bond, has lost much of its liquidity.

The euro has ushered in major changes in Italian public debt management:

1. The redenomination into euros of all lira issues starting 1 January 1999 and quotation in euros on both the retail market (MOT) and the wholesale market (MTS).
2. Compliance with the date conventions applied by TARGET.
3. Finally, tradeable securities were fully dematerialised by 1998, and the corresponding certificates subsequently withdrawn from the market. Since 1 January 1999, all government debt securities issued in Italy have been represented by book entries.

9.2 ASSETS ISSUED BY THE ITALIAN TREASURY

9.2.1 *Buoni Ordinari del Tesoro* (BOTs or bills)

BOTs or bills are securities issued at discount and maturing in 3, 6 or 12 months. Their yield is expressed as the difference between redemption price—at par—and acquisition price. Their issuance enables the Treasury to fund central government's current expenditure, and their relative importance is clearly on the wane.

In December 1998, the Italian Ministry of Finance launched a 5-billion-euro ECP (Euro Commercial Paper) programme co-ordinated between several international investment banks and tailored to the detected demand among international investors for euro-denominated assets in this maturity range. This facility will supplement the existing BOT programme for domestic-market issuance.

The yield of BOTs for non-resident investors (i.e. gross) is calculated as follows:

In simple capitalisation (Current/360):

$$r = \frac{100 - P}{P} \times \frac{360}{d}$$

And in compound terms (Current/360):

$$r = \left(\frac{100}{P}\right)^{\frac{360}{d}} - 1$$

where

P = weighted average price at auction
d = number of days between payment and asset maturity
r = gross yield, IRR

In the Italian domestic market, assets at discount are quoted on a Current/365 basis. For this reason, Bank of Italy communiqués of BOT auction results cite both ways of calculating gross yield.

9.2.2 Buoni Poliennali del Tesoro (BTPs or bonds)

These are generally dated 3, 5, 10 or 30 years, paying a fixed semiannual coupon and redeemed upon maturity at nominal value. The exception are BTPs issued prior to 1997, whose redemption is at nominal value less the appropriate issue premium. The gross redemption value of outstanding BTPs issued before 1997 can be checked on the Italian Treasury's Reuters page TESOROITALIA.

The calculation of BTP semiannual yield for non-resident investors (gross yield, as no withholding is applied) is as follows:

$$P + Cc = \frac{C_1}{(1 + r_{sa})^{d_1/b}} + \sum_{i=2}^{n} \frac{C_i}{(1 + r_{sa})^{d_2/b}} + \frac{100}{(1 + r_{sa})^{D/b}}$$

And for gross yield in annual terms (the yield at which bonds are quoted on the market):

$$r = \left[(1 + r_{sa})^2 - 1\right] \times 100$$

where

d_i = number of days between the security's value date and the payment date of the corresponding semiannual coupon
b = Current/365 or Current/Current* basis
D = number of days from the date interest begins to accrue up to bond maturity, on a 365 or Current* basis
C_i = semiannual coupon
r_{sa} = gross semiannual yield
r = gross annual yield
Cc = accrued interest on a Current/365 or Current/Current* basis

---

*Bonds paying coupons in July and issued before 1999 use a Current/365 basis. For all other bonds, i.e. paying coupons in months other than July or issued since January 1999, the calculation basis is Current/Current.

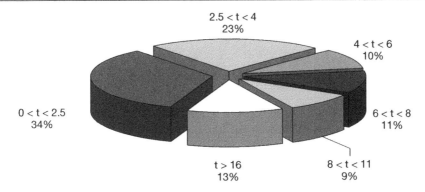

Source: Bloomberg and authors

Figure 9.1   Outstanding balance of BTPs as of August 2000 (in millions of euros)

9.2.3   *Certificati di Credito del Tesoro* (CCTs)

CCTs are bonds linked to the yield of 6- and 12-month BOTs, with a maturity of 7 years, paying semiannual coupons referenced to:

- the simple average of the yields of 12-month bills issued in the two months prior to the month before the date when interest of the corresponding coupon begins to accrue, plus a spread specified at issue
- the yield of the last 6-month bill issued prior to the date when the interest of the corresponding coupon begins to accrue, plus a spread specified at issue.

Issuance of the first group was discontinued in December 1994 and immediately replaced by the second. CCTs are redeemed upon maturity at nominal value, except those issued before 1997, which follow the same rules as BTPs. The fixed spread added to the reference rate, determined on issue date and valid throughout the asset's lifetime, currently stands at 15 bp.

These bonds formerly played a front-line role in the Treasury's issuance policy, and at one point accounted for more than 50% of the outstanding debt balance. Maturities have been streamlined from the former 5, 7 and 10 years into the 7-year certificate only (as of 1991, referenced to the yield of 6-month BOTs). There are various formulae for calculating CCT yield, depending on the issue date concerned.

CCTs Issued before December 1994

Yield in this case is referenced to the average yield of 12-month bills in the two months prior to the month before the date on which the interest of the corresponding coupon begins to accrue. Coupons and yield are calculated using the following date system:

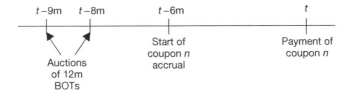

The yields (compound capitalisation) of each 12-month BOT issued in the two prior months correspond to the formula:

$$r = \left(\frac{100}{P}\right)^{\frac{360}{d}} - 1$$

The simple average of the annual effective yields of the 12-month bills issued in the two prior months (r_{t-9} and r_{t-8}) corresponds to the formula:

$$m = \frac{r_{t-9} + r_{t-8}}{2} \quad \text{or, on a semiannual basis,} \quad m_s = \left(\sqrt{1 + \frac{m}{100}} - 1\right) \times 100$$

The corresponding coupon (rounding to 0 or 5 in the second decimal place) thus comes out as:

$$C = m_s \times 100 + \text{spread}$$

And from this the yield can easily be calculated in the same way as for BTPs.

CCTs Issued since January 1995

In this case, yield is referenced to the last 6-month bill issued the month before the starting date of the coupon accrual period, while coupons are calculated as follows:

The yield of the reference 6-month BOT:

$$r_{\text{BOT6}m} = \frac{100 - P}{P} \times 100 \quad \text{where } P = \text{weighted average price}$$

The corresponding coupon (rounded to 0 or 5 in the second decimal place) comes out as:

$$C = r_{\text{BOT6}m} \times \text{spread}$$

Semiannual yield (r_{sa}) is obtained via the following formula ($P^1 = $ CCT issue price):

$$P^1 + Cc = \frac{C_1}{(1 + r_{sa})^{d_1/b}} + \sum_{i=2}^{n} \frac{C_i}{(1 + r_{sa})^{d_2/b}} + \frac{100}{(1 + r_{sa})^{D/b}}$$

where

$b = $ Current/365 or Current/Current* basis
$D = $ number of days from the starting date of the interest accrual period to the bond's maturity, on a 365 or Current* basis
$Cc = $ accrued interest on a Current/365 or Current/Current* basis

And annualised yield in %:

$$r = \left[(1 + r_{sa})^2 - 1\right] \times 100$$

---

*For bonds paying coupons in July, i.e. lines issued before 1999, the calculation basis is Current/365 (bond basis). For remaining bonds, paying coupons in months other than July or issued since January 1999, the basis used is Current/Current.

9.2.4   *Certificati del Tesoro Zero Coupon* (**CTZs or zero-coupon bonds**)

These are assets issued at discount maturing in 18 or 24 months and redeemable upon maturity at their nominal value. CTZs are issued across a series of tranches which make up a line, and are fully fungible. Issuance, at a fixed or marginal rate, is via fortnightly auctions coinciding with the auction dates of BOTs.

These instruments were first issued in 1995 with the retail investor in mind. This enabled the Treasury to enlarge the curve segment most widely invested in by households, where the dominant asset is the BOT.

Yield derives from the difference between nominal value (100) and issue price, and is calculated as follows:

$$r = \left[\left(\frac{100}{P} \right)^{\frac{b}{D}} - 1 \right] \times 100$$

where

P = issue price
D = number of days between payment and the asset's maturity (Current)
r = gross yield
b = year of 360 days

9.3   OVERVIEW OF THE ITALIAN PUBLIC DEBT MARKET

In recent years, Italy's Treasury Department has been re-engineering the structure of the outstanding debt balance and, with it, the interest-rate exposure of its debt portfolio. As Figure 9.4 shows, the percentage of debt issued at a variable rate has been reined back sharply in favour of fixed-rate issues. This change was unquestionably helped along by the macroeconomic environment, in the shape of downward-trending interest rates and the stability of monetary policy in the euro zone.

As a result, the composition of the outstanding debt balance (chiefly BOTs, CTZs, BTPs and CCTs) has radically shifted, as has the average life of debt in issue. Whereas in 1982 the dominant instruments were bills or BOTs (more than 60%), by the 1990s the reverse was true, namely a relentless advance of medium- and long-term assets, whether at fixed or floating rates (BTPs and CCTs respectively), and dwindling recourse to short-term funding (bills made up just 10.1% of the total in June 2000).

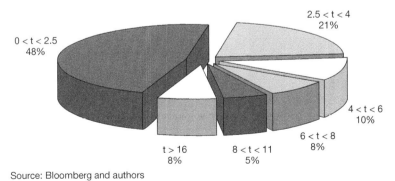

Source: Bloomberg and authors

Figure 9.2   Medium- and long-term Italian domestic public dept as of August 2000 (CTZs, CCTs, BTPs and CTEs)

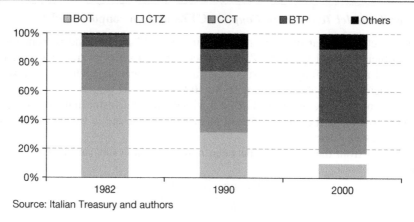

Source: Italian Treasury and authors

Figure 9.3 Composition of Italian domestic public debt (1982–2000)

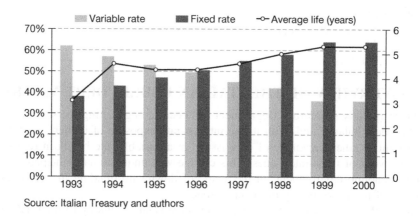

Source: Italian Treasury and authors

Figure 9.4 Changing structure of Italian public debt (1993–2000)

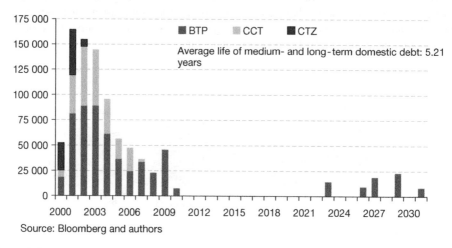

Source: Bloomberg and authors

Figure 9.5 Maturities as of August 2000 (domestic medium- and long-term debt in millions of euros)

The upshot is that the average life of Italian domestic debt lengthened from 1.13 years in 1982 to 2.57 years in 1990, and by June 2000 stood at 4.76 years. If international issues are built in, the overall average life of Italian public debt comes out at 5.30 years.

9.4   THE PRIMARY MARKET

9.4.1   Italian Government Debt Issuance Procedures

The Italian Treasury uses two issue formats:

- 'American' or multi-price auctions for BOTs
- 'Dutch' or single-price auctions for CCTs, BTPs and CTZs.

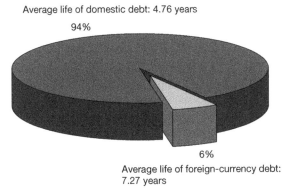

Average life of domestic debt: 4.76 years

94%

6%
Average life of foreign-currency debt:
7.27 years

Source: Bloomberg and authors

Figure 9.6   Italian public debt as of August 2000 (before swaps)

BOT Multi-Price Auctions

Under this system, each bid is allotted at the price specified, starting from the top and continuing down the price scale until the issue volume is used up.

To thwart purely speculative bidding, an exclusion price is set below which bids are automatically discarded. This exclusion price is calculated as follows:

- Bids are sorted in descending order of price.
- A weighted average price (w.a.p.) is worked out, corresponding to half the issue volume starting from the highest-priced bid.
- This w.a.p. is translated into yield terms.
- The exclusion yield is set on the basis of w.a.p. + 150 bp.
- The exclusion yield is translated back into price terms.

CTZ, CCT and BTP Single-Price Auctions

Allocation, in this case, is according to the prices of the bids received. Once bids have been sorted, the Treasury decides the minimum price (maximum rate) it is willing to concede for the securities in question, i.e. the stop-out price or rate. This price is reached by allotting bids in turn, starting with the top price, until supply and demand match up. The price of the last bid accepted sets the stop-out or marginal price at which all bids will be allotted (bids at higher-than-marginal price are allotted in their entirety, while bids at the stop-out set may be allotted wholly or partially, depending on whether or not a pro rata is necessary).

Here too an exclusion price is used, corresponding to the following more straightforward formula:

- Bids are sorted in descending order of price.
- A weighted average price is worked out, corresponding to half the issue volume starting from the highest-priced bid.
- Exclusion price: the above weighted average price less 200 bp.

Auctions of BTPs, CCTs and CTZs are conducted over two rounds. In the first, institutions can submit up to three competitive bids, while the second round, open exclusively to 'Central Government Securities Specialists' involves an additional quantity of securities subscribable at the stop-out price determined in competitive bidding. The quantity to be issued at this second stage is, in the case of new issues, up to 25% of the nominal amount offered in the first round and, in the case of old issues reopened, up to 10% of the nominal amount. The motive behind this dual system, introduced by the Treasury in May 1999, is to guarantee new issues the greatest possible liquidity from day one.

The Treasury publishes a provisional auction calendar for the following year (setting out announcement, resolution and payment dates) towards the end of December. The Bank of Italy also publishes a monthly issuance calendar on the last working day of the preceding month. This calendar includes the characteristics of scheduled issues: ISIN code, maturities, coupon, bid opening and closing dates, auction resolution date and the payment date corresponding.

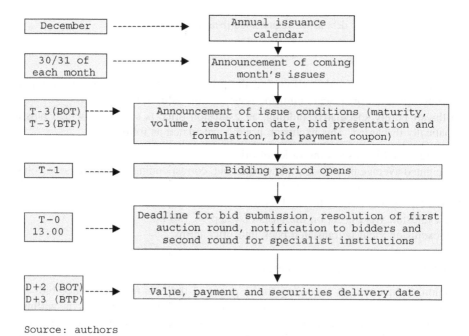

Source: authors

Figure 9.7   Standard time-frame for issuance

9.4.2   Standard Procedure for Government Securities Issuance

Figure 9.7 sets out the standard time-frame for BOT, CTZ, CCT and BTP issuance (the dates given for BTPs are also valid for CTZs and CCTs).

9.4.3   Characteristics of Italian Public Debt Issues

BOTs

- *Issue procedure*: 'American' auction.
- *Auction participants*: Italian, EU and non-EU banks, broker–dealers, insurance and pension companies and individual investors (through the banks). All these entities can bid on their own or others' behalf.
- *Minimum denomination*: 1000 euros.
- *Presentation of competitive bids*: from the day before the auction (T − 1) up to 13.00 local time on the auction date itself (T − 0). Bids must be sent to the Bank of Italy via the National Interbank Network.
- *Minimum amount of bids*: 1.5 million euros. The prices of the bids presented must have a minimum variation of 0.01 percentage points. Each participating operator or entity can place up to three bids.
- *Announcement of issue volume*: three working days before auction (T − 3), on the Italian Treasury's Reuters screens (TESA to TESZ).
- *Auction results*: the Bank of Italy posts the results on its Reuters pages (BITA to BITZ) minutes after resolution.
- *Payment/value date*: two working days after auction (T + 2).
- *Admission to secondary-market trading*: on value date (T + 2).
- *Interest basis*: Current/360.

CTZs

- *Issue procedure*: first round via 'Dutch' auction—with exclusion price—and second round reserved for 'Central Government Securities Specialists'.
- *Auction participants*: as described for BOTs.
- *Presentation of competitive bids*: as described for BOTs.

Table 9.1   6-month BOT issue (10/6/99)

Days to maturity	92 days
Amount offered	3500 million euros
Amount bid	13614 million euros
Amount allotted	3500 million euros
Weighted average price	99.35
Maximum price accepted	99.36
Minimum price accepted	99.34
Pro rata at minimum price	8.3%
Exclusion price	98.98
Gross yield (simple capitalisation) (Current/360)	2.56%
Outstanding as of 15/6/99	3500 million euros

Source: authors

- *Minimum denomination*: 1000 euros.
- *Minimum amount of bids*: Entities can place up to three competitive bids for a minimum amount of 500 000 euros and with a 0.01 euro variation in the bidding price.
- *Announcement of issue volume*: as described for BOTs.
- *Auction results*: as described for BOTs.
- *Second round*: held exclusively for 'Central Government Securities Specialists' at the end of the first. Allocation is a maximum 10% of the nominal amount offered in the first round at the price determined in the same.
- *Payment/value date*: two working days after auction (T + 2).
- *Admission to secondary-market trading*: on value date (T + 2).
- *Interest basis*: Current/360 (domestic Current/365).

As can be seen, 'Central Government Securities Specialists' are by no means obliged to cover the whole volume offered in second rounds.

Table 9.2   24-month CTZ issue (10/6/99)

Amount offered	1500 million euros
Amount bid	2593 million euros
Amount allotted	1500 million euros
Stop-out price	94.58
Pro rata	2.68%
Exclusion price	92.805
Gross yield (simple capitalisation) (Current/360)	2.95%
Amount offered in second round	150 million euros
Second-round demand	1 million euros
Amount allotted in second round	1 million euros

Source: authors

BTPs

- *Issue procedure*: first-round 'Dutch' auction—with exclusion price—and second round reserved for 'Central Government Securities Specialists'.
- *Auction participants*: as described for BOTs.
- *Presentation of competitive bids*: as described for BOTs.
- *Minimum denomination*: 1000 euros.
- *Minimum amount of bids*: Entities can place up to three competitive bids for a minimum amount of 500 000 euros and with a variation in the bidding price of 0.01 euros (3- and 5-year BTPs) or 0.05 euros (10- and 30-year BTPs).
- *Announcement of issue volume*: five working days before auction date (T − 5).
- *Auction results*: as described for BOTs.
- *Payment/value date*: three working days after auction (T + 3).
- *Admission to secondary-market trading*: on value date (T + 3).
- *Interest basis*: Current/Current.
- *Second round*: restricted to 'Central Government Securities Specialists'. Allocation is a maximum 10% to 25% of the volume offered in the first round, the percentage depending on whether the issue in question is new or reopened. The 25% assigned to new issues is to ensure their maximum possible liquidity.

Table 9.3   3-, 5- and 30-year BTP issues (10/6/99)

	3-year	5-year	30-year
Amount offered	2000 m euros	1250 m euros	750 m euros
Amount bid	4130 m euros	2477 m euros	1400 m euros
Amount allotted	2000 m euros	1250 m euros	750 m euros
Stop-out price	99.22	97.97	96.05
Pro rata	46.30%	70.00%	38.17%
Exclusion price	97.292	96.063	93.318
Gross yield (simple capitalisation) (Current/360)	3.29%	3.74%	5.59%
Amount offered in second round	500 m euros	125 m euros	75 m euros
Second-round demand	330 m euros	162 m euros	219 m euros
Amount allotted in second round	330 m euros	125 m euros	75 m euros

Source: authors

CCTs

- *Issue procedure*: first-round 'Dutch' auction—with exclusion price—and second round reserved for 'Central Government Securities Specialists'.
- *Auction participants*:as described for BOTs.
- *Presentation of competitive bids*: as described for BOTs.
- *Minimum amount of bids*: entities can make up to three competitive bids for a minimum amount of 500 000 euros and with a variation of 0.01 euros.
- *Announcement of issue volume*: five working days before auction (T − 5).
- *Auction results*: as described for BOTs.
- *Payment/value date*: two working days after auction (T + 2).
- *Admission to secondary-market trading*: on value date (T + 2).
- *Interest basis*: Current/Current.

Table 9.4   CCT issue (28/5/99)

Amount offered	1500 m euros
Amount bid	4875 m euros
Amount allotted	1500 m euros
Stop-out price	101.09
Pro rata	82.76%
Exclusion price	99.144
Gross yield simple capitalisation (Current/360)	2.75%
Coupon/spread	1.65%/15 bp
Amount offered in second round	150 m euros
Second-round demand	205 m euros
Amount allotted in second round	150 m euros

Source: authors

9.5   THE SECONDARY MARKET

9.5.1   *Mercato Telematico Secondario* or MTS

The secondary market in Italian public debt securities has two segments: the retail MOT and the wholesale MTS. As much as 98% of trading is conducted on the MTS or *Mercato Telematico Secondario*, while the MOT is gradually losing its little remaining liquidity.

The MTS was created in 1988 as an electronic or telematic trading market for Italian debt securities, and has since grown out of all recognition. A series of accords with Germany and France gave rise to EuroMTS, the platform which now centralises trading in the main European debt benchmarks (initially German, French and Italian, joined later by the Spanish, Dutch, Belgian, etc.). Trading, in consequence, has shot up from 23 billion euros in 1988 to more than 3 trillion euros in 1998. Table 9.5 sets out turnover figures on the MTS as of 1988.

Table 9.5   MTS turnover as of 1998

	Monthly volume	Annual volume
1988	—	23 244
1993	—	1 051 136
Avge 1998	269 158	3 229 896
Jan 99	184 113	—
Feb 99	204 828	—
Mar 99	196 278	—
Avge 1999	195 073	—

Millions of euros
Source: Italian Treasury and authors

Three types of institutions transact on the MTS: dealers, primary dealers and Central Government Securities Specialists ('Specialists'). Dealers operate at the prices set by the Specialists and primary dealers, which undertake to quote bid and ask prices continuously over market opening hours, from 08.00 to 17.10 local time. Specialists must also meet a series of conditions for participation in the primary and secondary markets (see section 9.8). Over 250 institutions are active on the MTS, counting both Italian and foreign operators.

MTS trading has the following characteristics:

- minimum lots of 2 500 000 euros, then multiples of the same
- a tick (minimum variation) of 1 bp in yield, i.e. approximately 5, 10 or 15 basis points in price, depending on the duration of the asset
- a transaction value date of T + 2, except for BOTs (T + 3)
- most actively traded Italian Treasury assets: BTPs, with almost 80% of the total, followed by floating-rate CCTs, with almost 14%.

The MTS has a grey-market segment for the trading of public debt securities due for issue. Investors can access grey-market quotations on Reuters <Q0#ITGREY = TT> via MTS pages <QIT/MTS1>.

9.5.2 *Mercato di Coupon Stripping* or MCS

The strips market in Italian public debt securities is a relative newcomer, dating back only to July 1998. The market's main features are:

- trading hours between 08.00 and 17.10 local time
- minimum lot of 2 500 000 euros and block trading of up to 5 lots
- market operators: all MTS market members
- non-disclosure of counterparties
- exclusive entitlement of Specialists to apply to the Treasury for bond stripping and subsequent reconstitution.

At the time of writing, strippable BTP lines were as follows:

BTP 1/11/2006 7.75%
BTP 1/11/2007 6.00%
BTP 1/05/2008 5.00%
BTP 1/11/2023 9.00%
BTP 1/11/2026 7.25%
BTP 1/11/2027 6.50%

Further information on MSC strip quotes can be found on Reuters <Q0#ITSTRIP=TTL>.

9.5.3 The Repo Market

The attractiveness of Italy's repo market lies in the liquidity of market trading in the underlying bonds. For many years, the Italian market had the distinctive trait of according special tax treatment to operations between residents and non-residents. Since the 1997 reform, however, this opportunity for tax arbitrage has disappeared.

The main features of the Italian repo market are as follows:

- trading hours from 08.00 to 18.35 local time
- buying and selling with a repurchase agreement
- minimum lots of 2 500 000 euros, then multiples of the same
- maturities most heavily traded: spot, week, month and three months
- the most active repo traders: non-resident institutions and Italian-based subsidiaries of foreign banks.

Italian repo market quotes are posted on Reuters <QIT/PCT1>.

9.5.4 The Derivatives Market in Italian Public Debt (MIF)

The most liquid futures and options on BTPs are those traded on the UK's LIFFE, but contracts are also actively traded on the MIF. This market came into being in 1992 and has functioned from the first as an electronic platform. Turnover has contracted sharply in recent years, most acutely in the contract on the 10-year BTP, due to the massive concentration of flows in Germany's EUREX market.

Two contracts on notional bonds are traded on the MIF:

- contract on the 10-year notional bond, yield of 6%, bond with maturity between 8 and 10 years on the contract date
- contract on the 30-year notional bond, yield of 5%, bond with maturity between 3.5 and 5 years on the contract date

Both contracts are traded with four expiry dates, in March, June, September and December.

9.6   CLEARING AND SETTLEMENT

As a rule, securities are settled on T + 2, except for BOTs and CTZs (T + 3).

9.6.1 Operations by Resident Investors (Domestic)

Operations conducted by resident investors are settled through the Bank of Italy clearing house. This institution runs six branches, all connected to the central clearing house.

9.6.2   Operations by Non-Resident Investors (International)

Operations between non-resident investors or between a resident and a non-resident can be settled in one of two ways:

- through accounts held with Italian 'agent banks'
- through CEDEL and EUROCLEAR.

9.7   TAXATION

A government decree published in April 1996 (D.L. 239/96) and implemented in January 1997 reformed the tax treatment of non-resident investors and of Italian companies liable for Local Corporate Tax. This legislative measure was intended to prepare the ground for the Europe of the euro, specifically the harmonisation of the withholding taxes applied to income raised from the public debt holdings of non-residents and national corporate taxpayers.

9.7.1   Taxation of Non-Resident Investors

Under the new tax system, the interest on Italian public debt holdings raised by resident and non-resident investors is in principle subject to withholding tax. However, a number of exceptions are made, in order to align the tax treatment of non-resident holdings with that applied elsewhere in the euro zone. Exemptions apply in the following cases:

(a)   If a double-taxation agreement is in force (for personal income tax) between Italy and the investor's country of residence and the said agreement contains an information-exchange clause.

(b)   If the assets giving rise to the income are deposited directly or indirectly with one of the following agents:

- banks or Italian investment companies resident in Italy
- the permanent establishments of non-resident banks or brokers connected electronically with the Italian Ministry of Finance
- non-resident companies or institutions holding accounts with centralised settlement systems (Cedelbank, Clearstream) directly connected with the Italian Ministry of Finance.

(c)   If the banks or brokers referred to in (b) are in receipt of a certificate from the tax authorities in their country of residence accrediting their resident status. Such certificates are valid up to 31 March of the year following their issue date.

(d)   If the above-mentioned banks and brokers have sufficient information to identify the non-resident beneficiary of the securities deposited, and are able to determine the amount of the interest to which the latter is entitled.

Non-resident investors unable to comply with any of the above conditions (a) to (d) are subject to a 12.5% withholding tax. So are all residents of territories classified by the Italian authorities as enjoying 'privileged tax regimes'—more simply, tax havens. A list of territories considered tax havens is set out in Decree 24/4/92 of the Finance Ministry.

Although trading in securities and the calculation of accrued interest are carried out in gross terms, all communications divulging auction results also detail the prices and yields applicable to investors liable for withholding tax.

9.7.2   Taxation of Resident Investors

In the case of resident investors and collective investment institutions, trading and interest accrual are in net terms, i.e. with the applicable withholding tax (12.5%) deducted at source.

9.8   DEALERS, PRIMARY DEALERS AND CENTRAL GOVERNMENT SECURITIES SPECIALISTS

Primary dealers or market makers in Italian public debt must make a series of undertakings relative to their primary- and secondary-market participation. This market-maker group also has a sub-group taking on primary market responsibilities of a higher order: the *Operatori Specialisti in Titoli di Stato* or Central Government Securities Specialists, known simply as Specialists. The third group, dealers, can transact in government securities without specific obligations.

9.8.1   *Operatori Specialisti in Titoli di Stato*

Eligibility requirements

The requirements for Central Government Securities Specialists are set out in Treasury Ministry decrees of 15/10/97 and the legislation of 23/7/96, which make particular reference to enhancing the efficiency of the public debt market and the need to compete effectively in the new euro setting.

At the same time, the regulatory framework governing the MTS Managing Company amended the selection guidelines for Specialist institutions, with reference to the following points:

- participation in the primary market
- secondary-market trading as regards both spot and forward transactions
- the need for the right structure and organisation to ensure the widest possible distribution of government debt securities among final investors
- the capacity to work alongside the Treasury in debt management and to propose new initiatives to the Treasury.

There are thus three distinct types of requirements, concerning primary-market activity, secondary-market activity, and organisational structure and capacity.

Obligations concerning primary-market activity
- Specialists must acquire an allotted amount equivalent to no less than 3% of the total securities issued yearly (a quota arrived at by weighting the amount of each asset subscribed for its term).
- The Treasury will also evaluate institutions' auction activity by such yardsticks as frequency of participation, allocations acquired and whether or not bid prices are effectively in line with secondary-market prices.

Obligations concerning secondary-market activity   The Treasury's goal in these trading fora is to lay the groundwork for their seamless, continuous and efficient functioning, in order to guarantee the liquidity of the public debt market at each and every level. Hence, the following indicators are particularly valued:

- a bid/ask spread of 1 basis point in benchmark bonds, and somewhat wider in other references
- the number and type of securities traded
- the continuity and scale of institutions' market activity.

Failure to comply with the above quotation requirement will meet with monetary sanctions imposed by the Bank of Italy.

Obligations concerning organisational structure and capacity   The Treasury will evaluate these entities by their capacity to place public debt securities with final investors in both the domestic and international markets. As a guide to evaluation, the Treasury makes regular soundings among final investor groups on the quality of the service provided by Specialist institutions.

Rights and Privileges

In return for the undertakings made, the Treasury confers the following rights and privileges on Specialist institutions:

- exclusive participation in second rounds at the price resulting from competitive bidding
- exclusive participation in debt-exchange auctions
- the exclusive right to strip and reconstitute government debt securities.

List of Operatori Specialisti in Titoli di Stato *for 2000*

Banca Commerciale Italiana
Banca d'Intermediazione Mobiliare IMI
Deutsche Bank
Banca Monte dei Paschi di Siena
Banca Nazionale del Lavoro
Bank of America NT & SA
Banco di Napoli
Banque Paribas
Caboto Holding SIM
Crédit Agricole Indosuez
Goldman Sachs International
ING Bank NV
J.P. Morgan Securities Ltd
Morgan Stanley & Co.
Salomon Brothers International Ltd
Unicredito Banca Mobiliare

9.8.2 Primary Dealers

Primary dealers, although free of specific primary-market obligations, are obliged to undertake market-making activities in the secondary market. Specifically, primary dealers must agree to quote a fixed number of references continuously, and to account for an annual 1% of total secondary-market operations.

ANNEXE: THE ITALIAN PUBLIC DEBT MARKET

BTP* and CCT Issuance Calendar 2000

Auction	Instrument	Coupon	Term	Issue	Format
14-Jun-00	BTP	—	3 years	19-Jun-00	Auction
14-Jun-00	BTP	—	5 years	19-Jun-00	Auction
14-Jun-00	BTP	—	30 years	19-Jun-00	Auction
28-Jun-00	CCT	Variable	7 years	03-Jul-00	Auction
28-Jun-00	BTP	—	10 years	03-Jul-00	Auction
30-Jun-00	BTP	—	3 years	05-Jul-00	Auction
30-Jun-00	BTP	—	5 years	05-Jul-00	Auction
13-Jul-00	BTP	—	3 years	18-Jul-00	Auction
13-Jul-00	BTP	—	5 years	18-Jul-00	Auction
13-Jul-00	BTP	—	30 years	18-Jul-00	Auction
28-Jul-00	CCT	Variable	7 years	02-Aug-00	Auction
28-Jul-00	BTP	—	10 years	02-Aug-00	Auction
31-Jul-00	BTP	—	3 years	03-Aug-00	Auction
31-Jul-00	BTP	—	5 years	03-Aug-00	Auction
16-Aug-00	BTP	—	3 years	21-Aug-00	Auction
16-Aug-00	BTP	—	5 years	21-Aug-00	Auction
16-Aug-00	BTP	—	30 years	21-Aug-00	Auction
30-Aug-00	CCT	Variable	7 years	04-Sep-00	Auction
30-Aug-00	BTP	—	10 years	04-Sep-00	Auction
31-Aug-00	BTP	—	3 years	05-Sep-00	Auction
31-Aug-00	BTP	—	5 years	05-Sep-00	Auction
13-Sep-00	BTP	—	3 years	18-Sep-00	Auction
13-Sep-00	BTP	—	5 years	18-Sep-00	Auction
13-Sep-00	BTP	—	30 years	18-Sep-00	Auction
28-Sep-00	CCT	Variable	7 years	03-Oct-00	Auction
28-Sep-00	BTP	—	10 years	03-Oct-00	Auction
29-Sep-00	BTP	—	3 years	04-Oct-00	Auction
29-Sep-00	BTP	—	5 years	04-Oct-00	Auction
11-Oct-00	BTP	—	3 years	16-Oct-00	Auction
11-Oct-00	BTP	—	5 years	16-Oct-00	Auction
11-Oct-00	BTP	—	30 years	16-Oct-00	Auction
30-Oct-00	CCT	Variable	7 years	02-Nov-00	Auction
30-Oct-00	BTP	—	10 years	02-Nov-00	Auction
31-Oct-00	BTP	—	3 years	03-Nov-00	Auction
31-Oct-00	BTP	—	5 years	03-Nov-00	Auction
15-Nov-00	BTP	—	3 years	20-Nov-00	Auction
15-Nov-00	BTP	—	5 years	20-Nov-00	Auction
15-Nov-00	BTP	—	30 years	20-Nov-00	Auction
29-Nov-00	CCT	Variable	7 years	04-Dec-00	Auction
29-Nov-00	BTP	—	10 years	04-Dec-00	Auction
30-Nov-00	BTP	—	3 years	05-Dec-00	Auction

(Continued)

Auction	Instrument	Coupon	Term	Issue	Format
30-Nov-00	BTP	—	5 years	05-Dec-00	Auction
14-Dec-00	BTP	—	3 years	19-Dec-00	Auction
14-Dec-00	BTP	—	5 years	19-Dec-00	Auction
14-Dec-00	BTP	—	30 years	19-Dec-00	Auction
28-Dec-00	CCT	Variable	7 years	02-Jan-01	Auction
28-Dec-00	BTP	—	10 years	02-Jan-01	Auction
29-Dec-00	BTP	—	3 years	03-Jan-01	Auction
29-Dec-00	BTP	—	5 years	03-Jan-01	Auction

*As of July 2000, the Treasury issues only one 5-year BTP line per month
Source: Italian Treasury

BOT and CTZ Issuance Calendar 2000

Auction	Instrument	Term	Matures	Days	Issue	Format
12-Jun-00	BOT	3 months	15-Sep-00	92	15-Jun-00	Auction
12-Jun-00	BOT	12 months	15-Jun-01	365	15-Jun-00	Auction
12-Jun-00	CTZ	24 months	—	—	—	Auction
27-Jun-00	BOT	6 months	29-Dec-00	182	30-Jun-00	Auction
27-Jun-00	CTZ	18 months	—	—	—	Auction
11-Jul-00	BOT	3 months	16-Oct-00	94	14-Jul-00	Auction
11-Jul-00	BOT	12 months	16-Jul-01	367	14-Jul-00	Auction
11-Jul-00	CTZ	24 months	—	—	—	Auction
26-Jul-00	BOT	6 months	31-Jan-01	184	31-Jul-00	Auction
26-Jul-00	CTZ	18 months	—	—	—	Auction
10-Aug-00	BOT	3 months	15-Nov-00	92	15-Aug-00	Auction
10-Aug-00	BOT	12 months	15-Aug-01	365	15-Aug-00	Auction
10-Aug-00	CTZ	24 months	—	—	—	Auction
28-Aug-00	BOT	6 months	28-Feb-01	181	31-Aug-00	Auction
28-Aug-00	CTZ	18 months	—	—	—	Auction
12-Sep-00	BOT	3 months	15-Dec-00	91	15-Sep-00	Auction
12-Sep-00	BOT	12 months	14-Sep-01	364	15-Sep-00	Auction
12-Sep-00	CTZ	24 months	—	—	—	Auction
26-Sep-00	BOT	6 months	30-Mar-01	182	29-Sep-00	Auction
26-Sep-00	CTZ	18 months	—	—	—	Auction
11-Oct-00	BOT	3 months	15-Jan-01	91	16-Oct-00	Auction
11-Oct-00	BOT	12 months	15-Oct-01	364	16-Oct-00	Auction
11-Oct-00	CTZ	24 months	—	—	—	Auction
26-Oct-00	BOT	6 months	30-Apr-01	181	31-Oct-00	Auction
26-Oct-00	CTZ	18 months	—	—	—	Auction
10-Nov-00	BOT	3 months	15-Feb-01	92	15-Nov-00	Auction
10-Nov-00	BOT	12 months	15-Nov-01	365	15-Nov-00	Auction

(Continued)

Auction	Instrument	Term	Matures	Days	Issue	Format
10-Nov-00	CTZ	24 months	—	—	—	Auction
27-Nov-00	BOT	6 months	31-May-01	182	30-Nov-00	Auction
27-Nov-00	CTZ	18 months	—	—	—	Auction
12-Dec-00	BOT	3 months	15-Mar-01	90	15-Dec-00	Auction
12-Dec-00	BOT	12 months	14-Dec-01	364	15-Dec-00	Auction
12-Dec-00	CTZ	24 months	—	—	—	Auction
22-Dec-00	BOT	6 months	29-Jun-01	182	29-Dec-00	Auction
22-Dec-00	CTZ	18 months	—	—	—	Auction

Source: Italian Treasury

Outcome of BOT Issues in 2000

Auction	Instrument	Term	Target	Matures	Days	Settles	Issue	Sold	Bids	Bid/cover	Stop rate
11-Jan-00	BOT	3 months	4000	14-Apr-00	92	13-Jan-00	Auction	4000	15 400	3.9	3.270
11-Jan-00	BOT	12 months	7000	15-Jan-01	367	14-Jan-00	Auction	7000	19 730	2.8	3.890
26-Jan-00	BOT	6 months	6250	31-Jul-00	182	31-Jan-00	Auction	6250	16 637	2.7	3.550
10-Feb-00	BOT	3 months	3250	15-May-00	90	15-Feb-00	Auction	3250	6 360	2.0	3.350
10-Feb-00	BOT	12 months	7000	15-Feb-01	366	15-Feb-00	Auction	7000	20 060	2.9	4.010
24-Feb-00	BOT	6 months	5250	31-Aug-00	184	29-Feb-00	Auction	5250	15 190	2.9	3.780
10-Mar-00	BOT	3 months	2000	15-Jun-00	92	15-Mar-00	Auction	2000	3 591	1.8	3.550
10-Mar-00	BOT	12 months	5500	15-Mar-01	365	15-Mar-00	Auction	5500	12 496	2.3	4.220
28-Mar-00	BOT	6 months	5000	29-Sep-00	182	31-Mar-00	Auction	5000	20 316	4.1	3.990
11-Apr-00	BOT	3 months	4000	14-Jul-00	91	14-Apr-00	Auction	4000	8 757	2.2	3.837
11-Apr-00	BOT	12 months	7000	17-Apr-01	368	14-Apr-00	Auction	7000	17 417	2.5	4.212
20-Apr-00	BOT	6 months	6000	31-Oct-00	186	28-Apr-00	Auction	6000	20 985	3.5	4.170
10-May-00	BOT	3 months	3500	15-Aug-00	92	15-May-00	Auction	3500	8 522	2.4	4.260
10-May-00	BOT	12 months	6000	15-May-01	365	15-May-00	Auction	6000	16 714	2.8	4.670
26-May-00	BOT	6 months	4000	30-Nov-00	183	31-May-00	Auction	4000	15 915	4.0	4.560
12-Jun-00	BOT	12 months	5250	15-Jun-01	365	15-Jun-00	Auction	5250	18 332	3.5	4.940

Source: Bloomberg, Reuters, Italian Treasury and authors

Outcome of CTZ Issues in 2000

Auction	Instrument	Term	Target	Matures	Days	Settles	Issue	Sold	Bids	Bid/cover	Stop rate
11-Jan-00	CTZ	24 months	1500	15-Oct-01	640	14-Jan-00	Auction	1500	5350	3.6	4.260
26-Jan-00	CTZ	18 months	2000	30-Mar-01	424	31-Jan-00	Auction	2000	7920	4.0	3.950
10-Feb-00	CTZ	24 months	1750	15-Oct-01	608	15-Feb-00	Auction	1750	6190	3.5	4.380
24-Feb-00	CTZ	18 months	2500	31-Aug-01	549	29-Feb-00	Auction	2500	9400	3.8	4.350
10-Mar-00	CTZ	24 months	2500	15-Mar-02	729	16-Mar-00	Auction	2500	6202	2.5	4.630
28-Mar-00	CTZ	18 months	2000	31-Aug-01	518	31-Mar-00	Auction	2000	5833	2.9	4.390
11-Apr-00	CTZ	24 months	2000	15-Mar-02	700	14-Apr-00	Auction	2000	7004	3.5	4.500
20-Apr-00	CTZ	18 months	2000	31-Aug-01	490	28-Apr-00	Auction	2000	4895	2.4	4.440
10-May-00	CTZ	24 months	1500	15-Mar-02	669	15-May-00	Auction	1500	5046	3.4	4.880
26-May-00	CTZ	18 months	2000	30-Nov-01	548	31-May-00	Auction	2000	3835	1.9	4.940
12-Jun-00	CTZ	24 months	1000	15-Mar-02	638	15-Jun-00	Auction	1000	3132	3.1	5.070

Source: Bloomberg, Reuters, Italian Treasury and authors

Outcome of CCT Issues in 2000

Auction	Instrument	Coupon	Term	Target	Settles	Matures	Issue	Sold	Total Bids	Bid/sold	Stop r.	Stop pr.
28-Jan-00	CCT	Variable	7 years	2000	01-Feb-00	01-Dec-06	Auction	2000	4640	2.32	3.420	100.690
28-Feb-00	CCT	Variable	7 years	2000	01-Mar-00	01-Dec-06	Auction	2000	5650	2.83	3.880	100.780
30-Mar-00	CCT	Variable	7 years	1500	04-Apr-00	01-Dec-06	Auction	1500	4419	2.95	4.180	100.790
27-Apr-00	CCT	Variable	7 years	1250	02-May-00	01-Dec-06	Auction	1250	4225	3.38	4.300	100.750
30-May-00	CCT	Variable	7 years	1000	02-Jun-00	01-Dec-06	Auction	1000	2496	2.50	4.710	100.770

Source: Bloomberg, Reuters, Italian Treasury and authors

Outcome of BTP Issues in 2000

Auction	Instrument	Coupon	Term	Target	Settles	Matures	Issue	Sold	Total Bids	Bid/sold	Stop r.	Stop pr.
03-Jan-00	BTP	3.75%	3 years	1500	05-Jan-00	01-Sep-02	Auction	1500	3075	2.05	4.660	97.850
03-Jan-00	BTP	4.75%	5 years	3000	05-Jan-00	01-Jul-05	Auction	3000	5028	1.68	5.250	97.950
14-Jan-00	BTP	3.75%	3 years	2000	18-Jan-00	01-Sep-02	Auction	2000	4850	2.43	4.570	—
14-Jan-00	BTP	4.75%	5 years	2500	18-Jan-00	01-Jul-05	Auction	2500	5560	2.22	5.220	—
14-Jan-00	BTP	5.25%	30 years	1500	18-Jan-00	01-Nov-29	Auction	1500	1990	1.33	6.290	—
28-Jan-00	BTP	4.25%	10 years	1750	01-Feb-00	01-Nov-09	Auction	1750	3410	1.95	5.810	89.050
31-Jan-00	BTP	4.50%	3 years	3000	02-Feb-00	15-Jan-03	Auction	3000	5490	1.83	4.850	99.200
31-Jan-00	BTP	4.75%	5 years	1750	02-Feb-00	01-Jul-05	Auction	1750	2750	1.57	5.380	97.400
11-Feb-00	BTP	4.50%	3 years	2000	15-Feb-00	15-Jan-03	Auction	2000	3266	1.63	4.940	98.970
11-Feb-00	BTP	4.75%	5 years	1750	15-Feb-00	01-Jul-05	Auction	1750	3193	1.82	5.440	97.150
11-Feb-00	BTP	5.25%	30 years	1500	15-Feb-00	01-Nov-29	Auction	1500	2936	1.96	6.200	88.250
28-Feb-00	BTP	4.25%	10 years	2000	01-Mar-00	01-Nov-09	Auction	2000	3990	1.995	5.680	89.950
29-Feb-00	BTP	4.50%	3 years	1750	02-Mar-00	15-Jan-03	Auction	1750	4678	2.67	4.830	99.250
29-Feb-00	BTP	4.75%	5 years	1000	02-Mar-00	01-Jul-05	Auction	1000	2997	3.00	5.280	97.840
15-Mar-00	BTP	4.50%	3 years	1500	17-Mar-00	15-Jan-03	Auction	1500	3186	2.12	4.820	99.290
15-Mar-00	BTP	4.75%	5 years	1250	17-Mar-00	01-Jul-05	Auction	1250	2406	1.92	5.200	98.200
15-Mar-00	BTP	6.00%	30 years	3000	17-Mar-00	01-May-31	Auction	3000	7376	2.46	5.910	102.400
30-Mar-00	BTP	5.50%	10 years	3500	04-Apr-00	01-Nov-10	Auction	3500	6800	1.94	5.490	100.650
31-Mar-00	BTP	4.50%	3 years	1500	05-Apr-00	15-Jan-03	Auction	1500	3665	2.44	4.720	99.540
31-Mar-00	BTP	4.75%	5 years	1250	05-Apr-00	01-Jul-05	Auction	1250	2612	2.09	5.080	98.740
14-Apr-00	BTP	4.75%	3 years	3000	19-Apr-00	15-Apr-03	Auction	3000	5547	1.85	4.780	100.080
14-Apr-00	BTP	4.75%	5 years	1250	19-Apr-00	01-Jul-05	Auction	1250	2256	1.80	5.080	98.766
14-Apr-00	BTP	6.00%	30 years	2250	19-Apr-00	01-May-31	Auction	2250	3272	1.45	5.770	104.500
27-Apr-00	BTP	5.50%	10 years	2000	02-May-00	01-Nov-10	Auction	2000	4250	2.13	5.52	100.410
28-Apr-00	BTP	4.75%	3 years	2500	03-May-00	15-Apr-03	Auction	2500	4361	1.74	4.960	99.590
28-Apr-00	BTP	4.75%	5 years	1500	03-May-00	01-Jul-05	Auction	1500	3003	2.00	5.21	98.210
11-May-00	BTP	4.75%	3 years	2000	16-May-00	15-Apr-03	Auction	2000	3748	1.87	5.130	99.140
11-May-00	BTP	4.75%	5 years	1750	16-May-00	01-Jul-05	Auction	1750	2514	1.44	5.370	97.540
11-May-00	BTP	6.00%	30 years	1750	16-May-00	01-May-31	Auction	1750	2313	1.32	5.950	101.900
30-May-00	BTP	5.50%	10 years	1000	02-Jun-00	01-Nov-10	Auction	1000	2666	2.67	5.470	100.750
31-May-00	BTP	4.75%	3 years	1500	02-Jun-00	15-Apr-03	Auction	1500	3412	2.27	5.250	98.860
31-May-00	BTP	4.75%	5 years	750	02-Jun-00	01-Jul-05	Auction	750	1719	2.29	5.330	97.710
14-Jun-00	BTP	5.00%	3 years	2000	16-Jun-00	15-Jun-03	Auction	2000	3267	1.63	5.120	99.820
14-Jun-00	BTP	4.75%	5 years	750	16-Jun-00	01-Jul-05	Auction	750	1547	2.06	5.240	98.130
14-Jun-00	BTP	6.00%	30 years	750	16-Jun-00	01-May-31	Auction	750	886	1.18	5.880	102.800

Source: Bloomberg, Reuters, Italian Treasury and authors

10
The Portuguese Government Bond Market

10.1 INTRODUCTION

The Portuguese public debt market has undergone far-reaching changes over the last 20 years, affecting its organisational structures as much as the composition of its debt. Much, however, remains to be done. In its favour, the country has one of the lowest public debt/GDP ratios in Europe, targeted to decline further to 53% in 2002 under the Republic of Portugal Stability Programme. The Portuguese government also envisages a reduction in the public deficit from 2% at end-1999 to 0.8% in 2002.

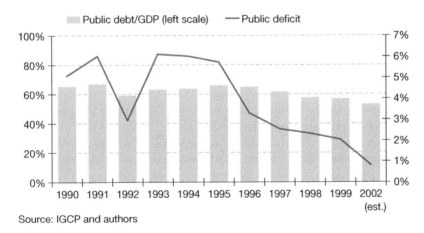

Source: IGCP and authors

Figure 10.1 Portuguese public deficit and public debt/GDP (Eurostat)

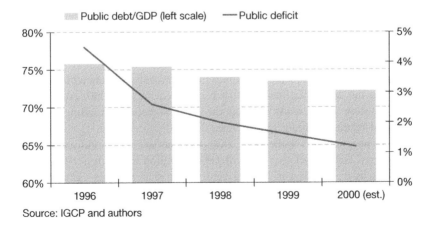

Source: IGCP and authors

Figure 10.2 Euro-zone public deficit and public debt/GDP

The Portuguese Treasury (*Instituto do Gestão do Crédito Público*, IGCP), created in December 1996, is responsible for managing Portugal's central government debt and executing its financing programme, in accordance with the Public Debt Law and the guidelines set by the government.

Increased competition from sovereign issuers in the euro zone, where market liquidity is the key to success, has had two major consequences for Portugal:

- Elimination of exchange risk and integration within an area of monetary stability has delivered an overall reduction in the yield spread between Portuguese debt and that of the other euro-zone countries.
- Paradoxically, Portugal's lower borrowing requirement (evident in its smaller issuance) has actually pushed up its relative financing costs, contrary to the experience of other countries.

In a bid to obtain acceptable financing terms despite market narrowness, the IGCP has developed a strategy based on the following guidelines:

- Utilise the euro as the main funding currency and the euro zone as the domestic market for Portuguese public debt (80% of 1999 issuance was in euros, and 75% of the remaining 20% was swapped into euros).
- Concentrate issuance on domestic debt instruments (OTs or bonds) with standard maturities (5 and 10 years).
- Achieve high outstanding balances for benchmark OTs in order to raise their liquidity without incurring excessive future refinancing risks.
- Work together with a group of market makers (OEVTs) with proven capacity for distributing government debt instruments within the euro zone. All such market-making entities have undertaken to develop the Portuguese public debt market through ongoing collaboration with the Treasury in distribution of its securities, whether issued at auction or by syndication (66% of total issuance is via auction among OEVTs and auction participants or OMPs).
- Identify and take advantage of market niches or segments providing low-cost funding opportunities (a 1 billion dollar Eurobond issue was conducted in September 1999 and immediately swapped into euros).
- Increase the average maturity and duration of debt.
- Smooth out the public debt maturities curve by an appropriate distribution of maturity dates.

Further to this same aim of boosting Portuguese debt tradeability, an electronic secondary market based on the MTS platform was to be created during 2000. An existing electronic auction system had already slashed the interval between bidding deadlines and announcement of results to under five minutes.

The financing programme for the year 2000, with an issuance requirement amounting to 10 billion euros, centred on two lines of OTs (5 billion euros in a 10-year bond and 2.5 billion euros in a new 5-year line), 1 billion euros in Savings Certificates (geared to the retail investor), and 1.5 billion euros to leverage funding opportunities in other segments or foreign currencies. Finally, the Treasury planned an exchange programme to replace insufficiently liquid OTs with 'on-the-run' lines, in order to consolidate the outstanding balance structure and improve market liquidity.

Table 10.1 Composition of Portuguese public debt

Euro-denominated debt	31-May-00
Tradeable debt	45 613
BT Treasury Bills	0
ECP	10
OT Fixed-rate Treasury Bonds	34 394
OTRV Variable-rate Treasury Bonds	4 394
Eurobonds	2 649
MTN	664
Global bonds	1 665
Others	1 836
Non-tradeable debt	15 270
Savings Certificates	13 095
CEDIC	68
Others	2 107
Total (1)	60 883

Foreign-currency debt	31-May-00
Tradeable debt	3 833
ECP	170
Eurobonds	693
MTN	1 645
Global bonds	1 081
Others	244
Non-tradeable debt	278
Total (2)	4 111

Total debt (1) + (2)	64 994

Millions of euros
Source: IGCP and authors

10.2 ASSETS ISSUED BY THE PORTUGUESE TREASURY

The Portuguese Treasury, IGCP, issues a wide range of securities, including Treasury bills (BT), fixed-rate (OT) and floating-rate (OTRV) bonds in the domestic market, and Eurobonds, ECP, EMTNs and global bonds in international markets. The focus here is on OTs (bonds) and BTs (bills), in view of their benchmark roles in money and capital markets.

10.2.1 *Obrigaçoes do Tesouro* (OTs)

Portuguese Treasury fixed-rate bonds are tradeable instruments with medium- (3 and 5 year) and long-term (10 and 15 year) maturities. They pay a fixed annual or semiannual interest rate, depending on the year of issue (a semiannual coupon prior to 1994, whereas later issues pay an annual coupon) and the principal is redeemable at nominal value upon maturity.

Accrued interest is calculated in gross terms from the date of the last payment until the date of settlement. Prior to the euro, interest rates in the secondary market were calculated on a 30/360 basis. For bonds issued as of 1999, the basis switched to Current/Current, applied also to all bonds redenominated in euros. In the latter case, the new basis came into effect from the first coupon payment in 1999 onwards.

10.2.2 Obrigaçoes do Tesouro a Rendimiento Variable (OTRVs)

The financial markets crisis of 1994 conspired with the uncertain outlook for interest rates to discourage investment in fixed-rate instruments. In response, the Portuguese Treasury resumed its floating-rate issues in 1995, indexed to the 3-month LISBOR, with 5- and 6-year maturities and payment of a semiannual coupon. The basis for price quotation and calculation of interest was set at 30/360.

Issues of this asset group were discontinued in 1997, leaving the outstanding balance as shown below:

Reference	Interest payments	Outstanding
OTRV 1995–2001	Jan–July	1339.80
OTRV 1996–2002	Jan–July	1307.83
OTRV 1996–2003	Feb–Aug	1180.05
OTRV 1997–2004	Jan–July	509.64
Total	—	**4397.33**

Millions of euros

10.2.3 Bilhetes do Tesouro (BTs)

BTs, or Treasury bills, are tradeable instruments issued at a discount with maturities of 91, 182 and 364 days. The principal is reimbursable at nominal value upon maturity, and securities are registered in the Book-Entry System of the Bank of Portugal's Central Depository. BTs are usually placed by auction, although syndication is also an option. The Bank of Portugal is in charge of conducting auctions on the Treasury's behalf. The market convention for calculation of prices and yields is a Current/360 basis.

Treasury bills have ceased to be an instrument of monetary policy and are used merely as a Treasury funding instrument. Consequently, their outstanding balance has dwindled over recent years to just 1.5% approximately of total debt in issue.

The formula for BT prices is as follows:

$$P = \frac{N}{1 + R \times \dfrac{d}{360 \times 100}}$$

where

P = price
N = nominal or reimbursement value
d = exact number of days between value date and date of redemption
R = average interest rate of Treasury bills*, expressed in percentage points and multiples of 1/16

---

* The average interest rate for Treasury bills with a specific maturity is equal to the semiannual nominal interest rate, equivalent to the effective annual average rate, weighted by the amount of the last 12 primary-market issues at the same maturity. The Bank of Portugal calculates this average rate.

10.3   OVERVIEW OF THE PORTUGUESE PUBLIC DEBT MARKET

The redenomination into euros of Portuguese public debt extends to 94% of volumes in issue. A certain amount of foreign-currency debt remains in the form of ECP, Eurobonds and MTNs. The majority (75%) of instruments issued are tradeable on secondary markets. The composition of tradeable debt, in euros and foreign currencies, is shown in Figure 10.3.

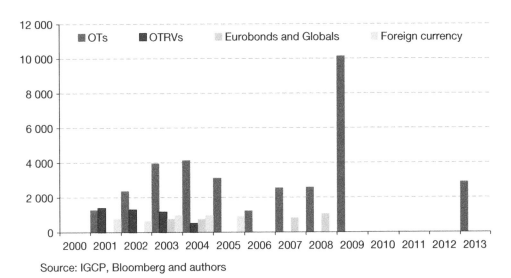

Source: IGCP, Bloomberg and authors

Figure 10.3   Portuguese public debt maturities as of August 2000 (in millions of euros)

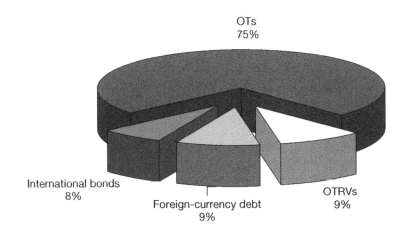

Source: IGCP, Bloomberg and authors

Figure 10.4   Tradeable Portuguese public debt as of August 2000

Fixed- and floating-rate OTs account for 55.4% of total debt in issue. Savings Certificates geared to the individual investor represent a significant 20% of the total outstanding. The remaining balance comprises several issues of ECP, MTNs, Eurobonds and global bonds denominated in euros and other currencies.

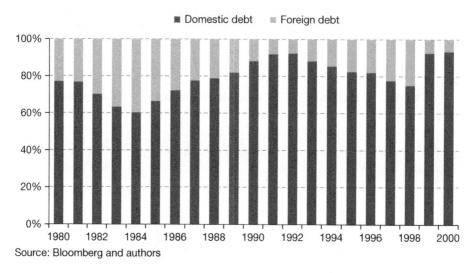

Source: Bloomberg and authors

Figure 10.5   Portuguese domestic and foreign debt 1980–2000

10.4   THE PRIMARY MARKET

Three procedures are used for securities issuance:

- *Competitive auction*: Treasury bills (BTs) and bonds (OTs and OTRVs) are usually issued in competitive auctions with a second-round system, conducted by the Bank of Portugal and the IGCP respectively.
- *Syndication*: the first tranche of each new OT line (roughly 1.5 billion euros) is usually placed with a syndicate of Specialist Primary Dealers (OEVTs), as a means of shoring up liquidity and ensuring an appropriate distribution of securities in the euro setting. As a rule, a consortium of financial institutions syndicates one or more tranches of OTs or, in some cases, the complete series.
- *Subscription*: debt securities may also be placed by limited subscription offers, used by the IGCP for new OT issues tailored to specific OEVTs or auction participants (OMPs).

The rest of this section deals solely with the auction format, in view of its preponderant role in primary-market issuance.

10.4.1   Competitive Auctions

Competitive auctions of bonds are held monthly; those of Treasury bills are held at irregular intervals, depending on the Treasury's funding needs. The dates of OT auctions are published in an annual calendar, supplemented by a quarterly calendar setting out the references and the amounts to be issued.

A new 10-year OT auction is usually held on the second Wednesday of each month, whereas auctions for 5- and 15-year OTs, if held, take place on the fourth Thursday, in accordance with the quarterly calendar. In 1999, 15-year OTs were auctioned on the fourth Thursday of February and March, and 5-year OTs every fourth Thursday from April onwards.

The auction is announced three working days $(T - 3)$ before the tender or allocation date in the case of OTs, and two working days $(T - 2)$ before in the case of BTs. The announcement includes the following information:

- auction date
- line(s) and nominal amount(s) of the OTs or BTs to be issued (this amount can be increased up to an additional 30% at auction)
- settlement or payment date and date from which interest accrues
- identification code of the security to be issued
- process and channel for bid presentation
- any other pertinent information.

Table 10.2 Announcement of OT 3.625% issue, August 2004

Issue announcement date	17/6/99
ISIN code	PTOTEDOE 0002
Target amount (guide)	250 million euros
Auction date	23/6/99
Payment date	28/6/99
Date interest begins to accrue	22/3/99
Accrued interest at payment date	0.97328767% (98 days)
First coupon payment	19/8/99

Source: authors

Table 10.3 Example of announcement of BT issue

Issue announcement date	22/3/99
ISIN code	PTBT99052500
Nominal amount to be issued	150 million euros
Maturity	60 days
Auction date	24/3/99
Payment date	26/3/99
Date of maturity	25/5/99

Source: authors

10.4.2 Competitive OT and OTRV Auctions

Competitive OT auctions consist of two rounds: a first, competitive tranche and a second, non-competitive round open only to OEVTs.

First round or competitive tranche:

- *Auction participants*: OEVTs, OMPs, Portuguese banks and Portuguese branches of foreign banks.
- *Presentation of competitive bids*: from the announcement date $(T - 3)$ until 9.30 local time on the auction day $(T - 0)$. Each participant may make a maximum of five bids

with an overall value which may in no case exceed the ceiling amount set for the competitive stage.

- *Bid format*: each bid must specify the nominal bond amount to be subscribed and the interest rate sought, in the case of fixed-rate or zero-coupon bonds. In the case of variable-interest bonds, in addition to the amount requested, bids must state their chosen price as a percentage of nominal value. Both figures must be expressed to three decimal places.
- *Minimum denomination*: 1 000 000 euros and multiples of the same.
- *Auction resolution*: (i) for fixed-rate or zero-coupon OTs, bids are sorted in ascending order by interest rate. The IGCP then proceeds to accept all bids entered at the maximum (marginal) rate or higher; (ii) for OTRVs, bids are sorted in descending order of price, those with a price equal to or above the minimum (marginal) price as defined by the IGCP being allotted. If necessary, bids may be allotted on a pro rata basis at the marginal rate or price, in minimum lots of 1000 euros.
- *Publication of first-round results*: the outcome of the competitive stage of each auction is announced before 10.15 local time on the IGCP pages of the usual screens. In addition, prior to 10.30 local time, individual results are announced to each subscribing institution, specifying the amounts allotted at minimum, average and maximum rates or prices.
- *Payment/value date*: three working days after auction date (T + 3) by payment on delivery in the IGCP's account at the Bank of Portugal.

Second round or non-competitive tranche:

- *Second-round issuance amount*: one-third of the auction offering is reserved for distribution to market makers at the lowest placement price or highest interest rate, i.e. at the stop-out price or rate resulting from the first, competitive round.

Table 10.4   Example of 5-, 10- and 15-year OT issues

	OT 3.625% July 2004	OT 3.95% July 2009	OT 5.45% Sep 2013
Competitive tranche or first round:			
Auction date	26/05/99	09/06/99	24/03/99
Settlement date	31/05/99	15/06/99	29/03/99
Guide amount	250 m euros	250 m euros	250 m euros
Bids	685 m euros	474 m euros	688 m euros
Allocation	250 m euros	250 m euros	250 m euros
Minimum rate	3.420%	4.554%	4.556%
Average rate	3.464416%	4.569056%	4.580252%
Marginal rate	3.471%	4.579%	4.589%
Average price	100.76%	95.0870%	109,0340%
Stop-out price	100.7291%	95.0108%	108.93730%
Bids at marginal rate	170 m euros	20 m euros	30 m euros
Pro rata basis	35.882%	45%	20%
Non-competitive tranche or second round:			
Non-competitive allocation	35.5 m euros	36.4 m euros	3.1 m euros

Source: authors

- *Second-round participants*: exclusively OEVTs authorised by the Public Credit Board (*Junta do Crédito Público*).
- *Presentation of non-competitive bids*: from immediately after publication of competitive results up to 11.00 local time on the day the round is held, each market maker (OEVT) must communicate the nominal amount to be subscribed. This amount may not exceed the subscription limit notified one working day before the auction date, as determined in proportion to the percentages obtained in the first round of the last three OT auctions.
- *Payment/value date*: on T + 3, by delivery against payment in the IGCP's account at the Bank of Portugal.

10.4.3 Competitive BT Auctions

- *Auction participants*: OEVTs, OMPs, Portuguese banks and Portuguese branches of foreign banks.
- *Presentation of competitive bids*: from the announcement date $(T - 2)$ up to 9.30 local time on the auction day (T − 0). Each participant may make a maximum of five bids, but the overall amount may in no case exceed the ceiling announced for the competitive phase of the auction.
- *Bid format*: each bid must specify the nominal amount of securities to be subscribed and the interest rate sought. Both figures should be stated to three decimal places.
- *Minimum denomination*: 1 000 000 euros and multiples of the same.
- *Auction resolution*: the Bank of Portugal is in charge of allocating Treasury bill auctions. Bids are sorted in ascending order of interest rate, and all those with rates equal to or below the maximum (marginal) rate determined by the Bank are accepted. If necessary, bids made at the marginal rate are allotted on a pro rata basis in minimum lots of 1000 euros.
- *Auction results*: posted before 10.15 local time on the Bank of Portugal pages on the usual screens. The Bank also notifies each subscriber of the nominal and discounted value of allotted bills, the weighted average auction price and the total amount allotted.
- *Payment/value date*: T + 3, by delivery against payment in the IGCP's account at the Bank of Portugal.
- *Payment/value date*: two working days after the auction date (T + 2). The amount discounted is deposited in the Treasury's account at the Bank of Portugal and the subscriber's account at the Bank of Portugal is credited with the amount corresponding to the bills acquired.

Table 10.5 Example of 3-month BT issue

Auction date	17/3/99
Payment/value date	19/3/99
Date of maturity	18/6/99
Maturity (days)	91
Amount to be issued (guide)	150 million euros
Bid volume	60 million euros
Amount allotted	50 million euros
Average interest rate at auction	2.950%
Marginal rate at auction	2.950%
Minimum rate	2.950%
Pro rata at marginal rate	100%

Source: authors

10.5   THE SECONDARY MARKET

OTs, in their fixed-rate variant particularly, are the securities most heavily traded on secondary markets and accordingly the most liquid. Two trading segments co-exist, and will do so until completion of the trading environment reform begun at end-1999:

1.   The retail or continuous market on the Lisbon Stock Exchange (LSE). This is an electronic on-screen trading market and its activity is waning (1.5% of total turnover in 1999).
2.   The electronic Special Market for Block Trading (MEOG), or wholesale market, managed by the Lisbon Stock Exchange. This is the most important secondary market in which banks, as well as brokers and dealers, are allowed to operate directly without intermediaries. Transaction costs are appreciably lower, since banks can match transactions directly with their clients, by-passing the commissions charged by the stock market and broker–dealers. Agents participating in the MEOG pay a regular commission of 175 million escudos to the Lisbon Stock Exchange.

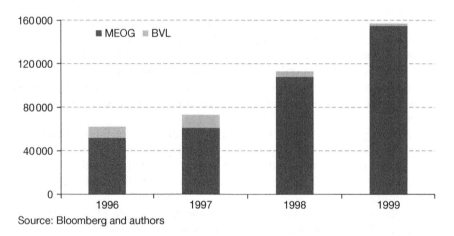

Source: Bloomberg and authors

Figure 10.6   Turnover in Portuguese Treasury securities (in millions of euros)

The trading environment restructuring project (1999–2000) is a root-and-branch programme aimed at producing a secondary market in keeping with the more competitive framework brought by the euro. The IGCP, in close collaboration with the OEVTs (the largest participants in the Portuguese public debt market), plans to create the following secondary-market structure:

• A designated retail segment on the Oporto and Lisbon Exchanges for small-volume transactions. Corporation members will be the participants in this market segment.
• A second over-the-counter (OTC) trading segment for financial intermediaries and their clients, privileging maximum operating flexibility in trading and settlement (without heavy commissions).
• A third segment for block trading (mainly among market makers) which will seek to centralise wholesale operations by offering the best, most efficient trading conditions.

This third segment, called MEDIP (the Portuguese acronym for Special Public Debt Market), will be governed by the Investment Services Directive and operate under the MTS electronic platform. It was due to reopen officially in 2000 as MTS Portugal, along the lines of the other MTS systems functioning in the euro zone. As a regulated market, its access conditions, operating rules and code of conduct will be non-discriminatory and subject to approval by the National Securities Market Commission (CNVM).

Trading on this market will be similar to that conducted on a 'blind' market, i.e. total counterparty anonymity and 'firm' prices quoted on screens. Furthermore, as on other euro-zone national MTS platforms, the market will be divided between market makers and market takers. The makers, whose primary privilege is their price-setting function, must quote such prices for pre-set operations over a specific time period and under certain spread and minimum-volume conditions.

Finally, shares in MEDIP and the Portuguese MTS are to be divided between the OEVTs or market makers, the IGCP and MTS Italia SpA, the trading system supplier.

10.5.1   The Futures Market

Future contracts on 10-year OTs have been traded since June 1996 on the Oporto Futures and Options Exchange. Their principal features are summarised below:

- *Underlying asset*: a notional bond with an annual 6.5% coupon and a nominal value of 100 000 euros.
- *Expiry*: in the months of March, June, September and December.
- *Expiry date*: the third Wednesday of the month the instrument matures; the last day of trading is the next-to-last working day before maturity date.
- *Delivery date*: the underlying asset is delivered four working days after the last trading day.
- *Price format*: the price of the futures contract is expressed as a percentage of the nominal price.
- *Tick size*: 0.01% (one basis point).
- *Tick value*: 10 euros.
- *Guide price fluctuation level*: ±140 ticks.
- *Trading hours*: 8.30 to 16.30 local time.
- *Settlement price at session end*: weighted average price by volume of the last 12 transactions.
- *Initial margin*: simple position: 3000 euros; spread: 2500 euros.
- *Commission levels*: trading: 2.75 euros; settlement: 4.5 euros; roll-over (per transaction): 2.25 euros.
- *Settlement at maturity*: physical delivery of Portuguese government bonds (OTs) with a minimum residual life of 6.5 years and a maximum of 11 years on the date of delivery.
- *OT 10 pages*: Reuters: 0#BDPOT, Datastream: PGB, Bloomberg: PQA Comdty.

The OT 10 market makers are:

Banco Mello Investimentos
Banco Espírito Santo
Banco Português do Atlântico
Banco Português de Investimento

Banco Totta & Açores
Caixa Geral de Depósitos

10.5.2 The Repo Market

Repo trading in Portugal is negligible in comparison with that of any other Euro-11 country. The market is therefore short on liquidity and trading volumes are very small. Transactions are settled via two alternative systems:

- *Through the money market*: in this case, repos are settled in the Central Securities Depository (CVM) (e.g. operations settled together with cash delivery).
- *Through the derivatives market*: in this case, settlement is via the Oporto Futures and Options Exchange (e.g. repo transactions settled together with future delivery of the security). This market has developed an automatic repo operation trading system (*Arts*).

10.5.3 The Strips Market

Treasury securities cannot be stripped at present.

10.6   CLEARING AND SETTLEMENT

Domestic clearance and settlement of public debt operations are performed almost exclusively through the Central Securities Depository (CVM), the Securities Market Commission and by the Bank of Portugal on a book-entry basis. Both the CVM and TRADIS—the on-line or continuous market-confirmation system—belong to INTERBOLSA, which in turn owns the governing corporations of the Lisbon Stock Exchange and the Oporto Futures and Options Exchange. OT operations carried out on the continuous market and the wholesale market (MEOG) are settled on the third working day post-trade (T + 3).

International settlement of OT operations is via CEDEL and EUROCLEAR, and the value date is the same as for domestic operations, i.e. T + 3.

10.7   TAXATION

The immediate return of the 20% withholding tax on non-resident coupon payments (with exceptions mentioned at the end of this section) came into force in June 1994 for all OTs except those issued prior to 1992. Non-residents and exempt residents may thus acquire securities free of withholding tax on the interest paid or received.

In order to establish non-residence, candidates must authorise their securities depository to furnish the Portuguese supervisory authorities with a document accrediting them as non-resident for tax purposes, as well as the investor's residence certificate. The depository institution, in turn, must be authorised to provide the Public Credit Board (JCP) and Portuguese tax authorities with full information regarding the transactions carried out by the investors.

Non-residents owning a permanent establishment in Portugal to which income may be imputed cannot benefit from this exemption and are automatically liable for withholding tax. Non-residents in Portugal with residence in a country or territory whose tax treatment is clearly more favourable than Portugal's (e.g. tax havens) are likewise subject to withholding tax.

10.8   SPECIALIST PRIMARY DEALERS (OEVTs) AND AUCTION PARTICIPANTS (OMPs)

The IGCP grants Specialist Primary Dealer (OEVT) status to certain financial institutions, in order to ensure public debt market liquidity. OEVT appointments are made at the end of each year and are renewable annually.

10.8.1   Specialist Primary Dealers (OEVTs)

The current OEVTs in the Portuguese public debt market are:

Caixa Geral de Depósitos
Banque Nationale de Paris (BNP)
Banco Chemical Finance
Commerzbank
Banco Português do Atlântico
ABN AMRO
Banco Português de Investimentos
Merrill Lynch
Banco Espírito Santo
Deutsche Bank
BSCH
Salomon Smith Barney
Société Générale

The principal rights of OEVTs are as follows:

- Exclusive access to OT auction second rounds
- advising the IGCP on matters of mutual interest
- preferential access to syndicated issues and other forms of public debt placement, such as limited subscription offerings.

Their obligations are:

- to participate actively in auctions, presenting bids in accordance with normal market conditions
- to maintain a bond subscription quota no lower than 3% of the amounts placed in the last six auctions
- to participate actively in the secondary market in public debt, to ensure the liquidity of securities and their wide distribution
- to quote bid and ask prices open to any market participant continuously between 8.30 and 16.30 local time under the following conditions:

(a)   The following references are mandatory:

OT 8.75% March 2001	OT 5.25% October 2005
OT 5.75% March 2001	OT 9.5% February 2006
OT 4.8125% April 2003	OT 5.375% June 2008
OT 10.625% June 2003	OT 5.85% May 2010
OT 11.875% February 2005	OT 5.45% September 2013

(b) New issues of more than 500 million euros are also mandatory.
(c) Securities maturing in under one year are automatically excluded from the above list.
(d) Quotations should be grouped in lots, with a nominal value equivalent to 5 million euros for lines issued from 1998 onwards, and only 2.5 million euros for lines issued earlier.
(e) The bid/ask spread must not exceed 5 bp for OTs with maturities of five years or less and 10 bp for OTs with maturities between 5 and 15 years.

- to maintain a permanently updated page with access to previous quotes
- to offer the IGCP all such information as it may require regarding their status as market makers.

10.8.2 Auction Participants (OMPs)

The IGCP grants OMP status to financial institutions with a proven capacity to invest regularly in Portuguese public debt, and to contribute to the liquidity of instruments by placing or trading them on international, European or domestic markets. OMP status is awarded at the end of each year and renewable annually.

The Current OMPs in the Portuguese public debt market are:

BBVA
Banco Nacional de Crédito Imobiliario
Barclays Bank
Caja de Crédito Agricola Mutuo
Crédit Agricole Indosuez
Montepio Geral
Nomura International PLC
Rabobank International
Bayerische Landesbank
Crédit Suisse First Boston
Tokyo Mitsubishi International

The principal rights of OMPs are as follows:

- access to the first round of OT auctions
- the opportunity to acquire OEVT status on meeting activity requirements in the primary and secondary markets in public debt.

Their obligations are:

- to subscribe bonds for a total of six consecutive auctions
- to adhere to all rules adopted by the IGCP.

ANNEXE: THE PORTUGUESE PUBLIC DEBT MARKET

Outcome of OT Issues in 2000

Auction	Instrument	Coupon	Term	Target	Settles	Matures	Format	Sold	Total Bids	Bid/sold	Stop rate	Average rate
11-Jan-00	OT	5.85%	10 years	2500	20-Jan-00	20-May-10	Syndicate	2500	2500	1.00	*Bund* + 34 bp	—
09-Feb-00	OT	5.85%	10 years	400	14-Feb-00	20-May-10	Auction	443	1484	3.71	5.787	5.776
08-Mar-00	OT	5.85%	10 years	600	13-Mar-00	20-May-10	Auction	620	2022	3.26	5.720	5.712
14-Mar-00	OT	5.25%	5 years	1500	20-Mar-00	14-Oct-05	Syndicate	1500	1500	1.00	*Bobl* + 15 bp	—
12-Apr-00	OT	5.85%	10 years	500	17-Apr-00	20-May-10	Auction	500	1430	2.86	5.502	5.489
10-May-00	OT	5.25%	5 years	500	15-May-00	14-Oct-05	Auction	500	1070	2.14	5.454	5.445
14-Jun-00	OT	5.85%	10 years	500	19-Jun-00	20-May-10	Auction	500	1423	2.85	5.542	5.536
12-July-00	OT	5.85%	10 years	500	17-July-00	20-May-10	Auction	515	2582	5.01	5.592	5.587

Millions of euros
Source: Bloomberg, Reuters and authors

Bibliography

SPAIN

BANCO de España: http://www.bde.es
_____(2000): *Boletín de la Central de Anotaciones.*
_____(1999): *Boletín de la Central de Anotaciones.*
_____(1999): *Informe anual.*
_____(1998): *Informe anual.*
MANZANO, Daniel and VALERO, Francisco José (1996): *Guía del sistema financiero español.* 2nd ed. Escuela de Finanzas Aplicadas, Madrid.
_____(2000): *Guía del sistema financiero español en el nuevo contexto europeo.* 3rd ed. Escuela de Finanzas Aplicadas, Madrid.
TESORO Público español: http://www.mineco.es/tesoro
_____(2000): *Boletín mensual.* Parte 2, Mercados de Deuda del Estado.
_____(1999): *Boletín mensual*: Parte 2, Mercados de Deuda del Estado.
_____(1999): *Memoria anual.*
_____(1998): *Memoria anual.*

GERMANY

DEUTSCHE Bundesbank: http://www.bundesbank.de
_____(2000): *Monthly report.*
_____(2000): *Press releases.*
_____(1999): *Annual report.*
_____(1999): *Monthly report.*
_____(1999): *Press releases.*
_____(1998): *Annual report.*
_____(1998): *Press releases.*
_____(1998): *The market for German Federal securities.* 2nd ed.
EUREX Deutschland (formerly Deutsche Terminbörse): http://www.eurexchange.com

AUSTRIA

BUNDESMINISTERIUM der Finanzen: http://www.bundesfinanzministerium.de
ÖSTERREICHISCHE *Bundesfinanzierungsagentur* (OeBFA or Austrian Federal Financing Agency): http://www.oebfa.co.at

ÖSTERREICHISCHE Kontrollbank (2000): *The Austrian Bond Market.*
ÖSTERREICHISCHE Nationalbank: http://www.oenb.co.at
_____(2000): *Cross border sales and purchases of Austrian Government Bonds.*
_____(1999): *Cross border sales and purchases of Austrian Government Bonds.*
ÖSTERREICHISCHE Nationalbank and Financial Markets Austria Services (2000): *The Austrian Financial Markets: a survey of Austria's Capital Markets.*

BELGIUM

BELGIAN Securities Regulation Fund (Fonds des Rentes): http://www.fondsdesrentes.be /rk/fonds.htm
DEBT Agency of the Treasury of the Kingdom of Belgium: http://www.treasury.fgov.be /interdette/EN/Debtpre/Einstit.htm
_____(1999): *The Belgian Government Debt Market after EMU*, presentation to Spanish investors, Madrid and Barcelona, December.
NATIONAL Bank of Belgium (2000): *Belgian Prime News.* Numbers 7–9.
_____(1999): *Belgian Prime News.* Numbers 3–6.
_____(1999): *Annual report.*
_____(1998): *Annual report.*
_____(1997): *Annual report.*
TREASURY of the Kingdom of Belgium (2000): *Linear Bonds (OLOs).* January.
_____(2000): *Treasury Certificates.* January.
_____(1999): *Annual report.*
_____(1998): *Annual report.*
_____(1998): *The financial products of the Belgian Treasury: a summary of financial instruments.*

FINLAND

BANK of Finland (2000): *Finnish Bond Issues 1999.*
_____(1999): *Annual report.*
_____(1998): *Annual report.*
FINNISH Central Securities Depository: http://www.apk.fi
FINNISH State Treasury: http://www.valtiokonttori.fi/
_____(2000): *Finnish Treasury monthly bulletin.* January–October.
_____(1999): *Finnish Treasury monthly bulletin.* January–December.
HELSINKI Securities and Derivatives Exchange (HEX): http://www.hex.fi/eng

FRANCE

BANQUE de France (2000): *Bulletin de la Banque de France.*
_____(1999): *Bulletin de la Banque de France.*
_____(1999): *Annual report.*
_____(1998): *Annual report.*
FRANCE Trésor: http://www.francetresor.gouv.fr
_____(2000): *1999/2000 Annual report.*
_____(2000): *1999 Annual review.*
_____(2000): *France Trésor monthly bulletin.* January–October.

_____(2000): *Technical data-sheets.*

_____(1999): *1998/1999 Annual report.*

_____(1999): *1998 Annual review.*

_____(1999): *France Trésor monthly bulletin.* August–December.

_____(1999): *Technical data-sheets.*

MINISTERE de l'Economie des Finances et de l'Industrie (1999): *Euro-bulletin—French Government Securities.* January–August.

NETHERLANDS

DUTCH National Bank (2000): *Quarterly bulletin.* September.

_____(2000): *Statistical bulletin.* September.

_____(1999): *Annual report and Statistical annex.*

_____(1999): *Quarterly bulletin.* September and December.

_____(1999): *Statistical bulletin.* September and December.

_____(1998): *Annual report and Statistical annex.*

DUTCH State Treasury Agency: http://www.dutchstate.nl

MINISTRY of Finance of the Netherlands (2000): *Dutch Government Securities.*

_____(2000): *Quarterly review.* Numbers 1–4.

_____(1999): *Dutch Government Securities.*

_____(1999): *Quarterly review.* Numbers 1–4.

_____(1998): *Dutch Government Securities.*

IRELAND

NATIONAL Treasury Management Agency: http://www.ntma.ie

_____(1999): *Highlights and Results.*

_____(1999): *Report and Financial Statements for the year ended 31st December.*

_____(1998): *Report and Financial Statements for the year ended 31st December.*

_____(1997): *Report and Financial Statements for the year ended 31st December.*

ITALY

MINISTERO del Tesoro, del Bilancio e della Programmazione Economica, Dipartimento del Tesoro: http://www.dgt.tesoro.it

_____(2000): *Bollettino Trimestrale.* January–September.

_____(2000): *The Italian Treasury Securities Market.*

_____(1999): *Bollettino Trimestrale.* January–December.

_____(1999): *Strategic guidelines for the management of the Public Debt 2000–2001.*

_____(1998): *Guide to the Government Bond Market.*

PORTUGAL

BANCO de Portugal: http://www.bportugal.pt

DIRECÇAO Geral do Orçamento: http://www.dgo.pt

INSTITUTO de Gestão do Crédito Público: http://www.igcp.pt

_____(2000): *Dívida Pública: boletim mensal.* January–October.

_____(1999): *Dívida Pública: boletim mensal.* June–December.

INSTITUTO Nacional de Estadística (INE): http://www.ine.pt/index.asp

Index

Printed and bound by CPI Group (UK) Ltd, Croydon, CR0 4YY

23/04/2025

14660954-0001